AF490712

HOW THE SOUTH TURNED RED

FROM A DEMOCRATIC PAST TO A REPUBLICAN PRESENT

Jim Heath

4

ISBN: 9798990481107

Printed in the United States of America

5

DEDICATION

Thank you to my parents, Rol and Doris Heath, for always encouraging my passion for presidential history, politics, and broadcast journalism.

Although the path feels lonelier without them by my side, I am continually guided by their profound love and enduring hope for liberty and justice for all people everywhere.

FOREWORD

By Hon. Charles D. Steele

In "How the South Turned Red: From a Democratic Past to a Republican Present," Jim Heath masterfully explores the significant political shifts in the American South. As someone deeply versed in the law and having observed the GOP's evolution firsthand over decades, I find Heath's account of the party's metamorphosis both compelling and unsettling. Once heralded for its commitment to a strong Union and civil rights, the Republican Party, as depicted by Heath, has changed so dramatically that it is scarcely recognizable from its origins.

Leveraging his extensive background as a news anchor and political reporter in South Carolina, Heath meticulously charts the region's transformation from a Democratic stronghold into a Republican bastion. His analysis is enriched by thorough historical research, personal interviews, and decades of journalistic insight, showcasing his profound connection with the political milieu.

The narrative commences with Abraham Lincoln's presidency, highlighting his determination to end slavery and preserve the Union, and progresses to a pivotal moment in 1964 when Strom Thurmond's defection to the Republican Party marked a wider regional realignment centered around states' rights. Through Heath's perspective, we traverse critical periods including Reconstruction, the New Deal, and the Civil Rights Movement, spanning the administrations of FDR to LBJ. Heath also assesses the roles of figures like segregationist George Wallace, Richard Nixon's Southern Strategy, the historical significance of Barack Obama's presidency, and Donald Trump's admiration for Andrew Jackson.

"How the South Turned Red" delivers a thorough examination of the strategic decisions and ideological shifts that have fundamentally altered Southern politics. This book is vital for anyone eager to deeply comprehend these significant changes and their extensive impact on American electoral dynamics and national policy discussions.

Integrating detailed historical analysis with personal interviews and his extensive journalistic experience, Jim Heath astutely explores the correlations between cultural, economic, and ideological changes and national political strategies that have pushed the South towards the Republican brand. This book does more than recount events; it aims to elucidate the broader implications of these shifts, providing a comprehensive understanding of American political dynamics.

Jim Heath's narrative is both intriguing and instructive, tracing the evolution of the Republican Party from its inception by Abraham Lincoln to its contemporary alignment with historical figures like Andrew Jackson. This book offers a captivating and insightful examination of American political transformations, serving as an essential resource for anyone seeking to understand the complex dynamics that have shaped the political landscape.

- Charles D. Steele

About the Author of the Foreword:

Hon. Charles D. Steele is a former judge of the Van Wert County Court of Common Pleas. He holds a B.S. in American Studies, an M.S. in American History, and a J.D. from Ohio Northern University. A distinguished veteran of the United States Marine Corps, Steele's military service includes commendations including the Purple Heart and the Legion of Merit. His unique perspective on American history, leadership and governance enriches the themes discussed in this book.

FROM THE AUTHOR

My passion for presidential history was ignited at the tender age of three, sparked by a set of presidential figurines from the Marx Toy Company that my Grandma Coralie Heath shared with me. Before I could even recite the alphabet, I was already naming the presidents—a story my mom loved to recount.

This work delves into one of the most profound transformations I've witnessed over the years: the role reversal between the major U.S. political parties. The narrative traces the Democrats from their beginnings with Andrew Jackson and his populist, state's rights coalition, to the Republicans' origins as the party of Abraham Lincoln, celebrated as the first Civil Rights president. This exploration details how and why these parties have exchanged ideological places. Over the last decade, I have deeply engaged myself in this transformation, exploring presidential library archives, analyzing newspaper and media sources dating back to the 1800s, and revisiting my own interviews from more recent campaigns. I've scrutinized specific details from the congressional record concerning bills and proposed legislation, supported by insights from historians like Doris Kearns Goodwin, who have extensively documented these subjects. My goal is to create a narrative that is both engaging and accessible, appealing to everyone from seasoned political aficionados to casual readers intrigued by the dramatic shift of the South from blue to solid red.

Throughout my journalism career, I spent considerable time living and reporting in the South. I am profoundly grateful to the people of South Carolina and beyond for sharing their insights into their political views, cultural heritage, and the ongoing impact of race on their communities. With this enriched background, I strive to provide a thorough yet digestible exploration of how the South turned red, offering a vivid and insightful look into one of the most profound political shifts in recent history.

In the text, I decided to **bold** the names of major figures as they are introduced to help keep the narrative flowing smoothly. Each is bolded just once, but I thought this would aid in storytelling. If you find yourself pondering by the end of this book whether you are "Team Jackson" or "Team Lincoln," that's good. It's intriguing to consider whether these historical giants would recognize the current political landscape. Lincoln, in particular, might find it surreal to see the South—once a region he fought to unify and emancipate—now serving as the Republican Party's stronghold.

From those early days playing with presidential figurines to writing this book, my enthusiasm for the figures who have shaped our national story remains unwavering. I invite you to join me on this fascinating journey through American political history.

Enjoy the read!

Jim Heath

ACKNOWLEDGEMENTS

This book owes its depth and richness to a multitude of sources and the generous contributions of numerous individuals and institutions. My deepest gratitude is extended to:

The **Library of Congress** for its unparalleled repositories of historical documents and public records that have been indispensable in the research for this book, including the papers of President Theodore Roosevelt.

The **National Archives** for preserving our nation's history and making it accessible, providing invaluable resources that have greatly informed the narratives within these pages.

I am profoundly grateful to the following **Presidential Libraries** and related institutions that have provided specialized resources, each contributing significantly to the chapters dedicated to their respective Presidents:

- **The Andrew Jackson Hermitage**
- **The Abraham Lincoln Presidential Library and Museum**
- **Andrew Johnson Papers Online**
- **The Ulysses S. Grant Presidential Library**
- **Rutherford B. Hayes Presidential Library and Museum**
- **Woodrow Wilson Presidential Library and Museum**
- **Warren G. Harding Presidential Center**
- **Calvin Coolidge Presidential Library and Museum**
- **Herbert Hoover Presidential Library and Museum**
- **Franklin D. Roosevelt Presidential Library and Museum**
- **Harry S. Truman Presidential Library and Museum**
- **Eisenhower Presidential Library**
- **John F. Kennedy Presidential Library and Museum**
- **LBJ Presidential Library**

- **Richard Nixon Presidential Library and Museum**
- **Jimmy Carter Library and Museum**
- **Ronald Reagan Presidential Library and Museum**
- **George Bush Presidential Library and Museum**
- **William J. Clinton Presidential Library and Museum**
- **George W. Bush Presidential Library and Museum**

Special thanks are also due to those who provided personal interviews during my career, enriching this book with their unique insights and expertise:

- **President Barack Obama**
- **Secretary of State Hillary Clinton**
- **Senator Mitt Romney**
- **Reverend Jesse Jackson**
- **The late Senator Barry Goldwater**
- **The late Senator John McCain**
- **The late Senator Fred Thompson**
- **Historian Doris Kearns Goodwin**

My research was further enhanced by the archives of leading publications and institutions, which have meticulously documented American political life over the decades:

- **King Library and Archives**
- **Civil Rights Digital Library**
- **Strom Thurmond Collection - Clemson University**
- **Alabama Department of Archives and History**
- **The University of Southern Mississippi**

Special appreciation goes to my sister and brother-in-law, **Marianne and Don Noel**. Their insightful and ongoing questions about the subject matter have greatly enriched this narrative, adding depth and clarity to the story.

The Visual Story of Blue to Red

1860 Election Results - Democrats Win South

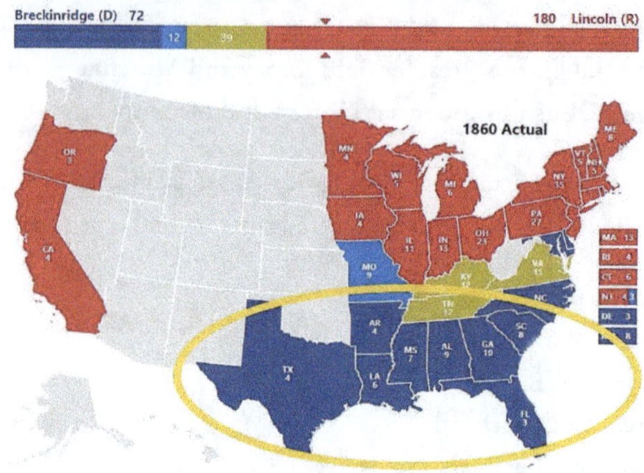

2016 Election Results - Republicans Win South

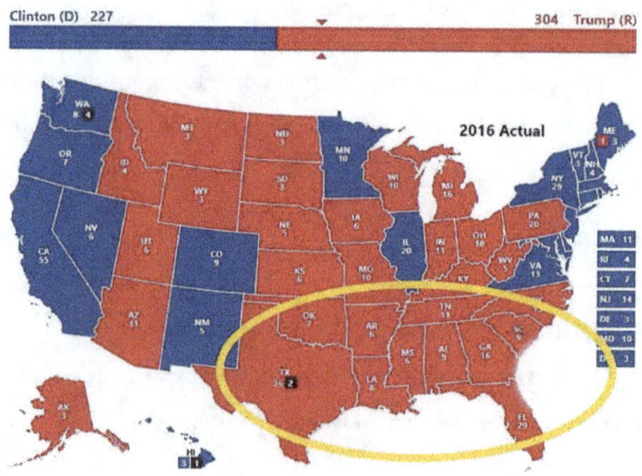

A Declaration by the Representatives of the UNITED STATES OF AMERICA, in General Congress assembled.

When in the course of human events it becomes necessary for ~~one~~ a people to ~~dissolve the political bands which have connected them with another, and to~~ assume among the powers of the earth the ~~equal &~~ separate and equal station to which the laws of nature & of nature's god entitle them, a decent respect to the opinions of mankind requires that they should declare the causes which impel them to the ~~change~~ separation.

We hold these truths to be ~~sacred & undeniable~~ self evident, that all men are created equal ~~& independent~~; that ~~from that equal creation they derive~~ they are endowed by their creator with ~~rights~~ inherent & inalienable ~~rights~~; among ~~which~~ these are the preservation of life, & liberty, & the pursuit of happiness; that to secure these ~~ends~~, governments are instituted among men, deriving their just powers from the consent of the governed; that whenever any form of government ~~shall~~ becomes destructive of these ends, it is the right of the people to alter or to abolish it, & to institute new government, laying it's foundation on such principles & organising it's powers in such form, as to them shall seem most likely to effect their safety & happiness. prudence indeed will dictate that governments long established should not be changed for light & transient causes: and accordingly all experience hath shewn that mankind are more disposed to suffer while evils are sufferable, than to right themselves by abolishing the forms to which they are accustomed. but when a long train of abuses & usurpations [begun at a distinguished period & pursuing invariably the same object, evinces a design to ~~subject~~ reduce them ~~to arbitrary power~~, it is their right, it is their duty, to throw off such ~~government~~ & to provide new guards for their future security. such has been the patient sufferance of these colonies; & such is now the necessity which constrains them to ~~expunge~~ their former systems of government. the history of ~~his~~ present ~~king of Great Britain~~ is a history of ~~unremitting~~ injuries and usurpations [among which ~~appears no solitary fact~~ to contradict the uniform tenor of the rest ~~but all have~~] in direct object the establishment of an absolute tyranny over these states. to prove this, let facts be submitted to a candid world [for the truth of which we pledge a faith yet unsullied by falsehood]

"He has waged cruel war against human nature itself, violating its most sacred rights of life & liberty in the persons of a distant people who never offended him, captivating & carrying them into slavery in another hemisphere, or to incur miserable death in their transportation thither. This piratical warfare, the opprobrium of infidel powers, is the warfare of the Christian king of Great Britain. Determined to keep open a market where MEN should be bought & sold, he has prostituted his negative for suppressing every legislative attempt to prohibit or to restrain this execrable commerce: and that this assemblage of horrors might want no fact of distinguished die, he is now exciting those very people to rise in arms among us, and to purchase that liberty of which he has deprived them, by murdering the people upon whom he also obtruded them: thus paying off former crimes committed against the liberties of one people, with crimes which he urges them to commit against the lives of another."

-From Thomas Jefferson's original draft of the Declaration of Independence, dated June 28, 1776, which included this strong condemnation of King George III for perpetuating the slave trade

Preface

The transformation of Southern Democrats into a Republican stronghold represents a pivotal chapter in the complex narrative of American politics. Over the past century, this shift has dramatically reshaped the political landscape of the South, influencing the broader spectrum of national politics and contributing to increasing polarization.

In many Southern states, the transition has been stark, with Republican dominance among white voters in presidential elections often reaching ratios as high as nine to one—a dramatic shift from the once "Solid South" that reliably delivered overwhelming Democratic majorities. For instance, there was a time when South Carolina consistently delivered more than 95 percent of its votes to Democratic candidates, even those defeated nationally.

To fully grasp the magnitude of this transformation, it is essential to revisit the origins of the United States. The story begins with **Thomas Jefferson**, a Southerner who penned the Declaration of Independence. In its early drafts, written in June 1776, Jefferson included a passage criticizing **King George III** for imposing the slave trade on the colonies: "He has waged cruel war against human nature itself, violating its most sacred rights of life and liberty in the persons of a distant people who never offended him." This language made it clear that the new country was appalled by the enslavement of human beings and sought to establish a nation where all men were created equal.

However, this passage faced fierce opposition from delegates of Southern colonies where slavery was integral to their economic systems. As June turned into July, tensions ran high at Independence Hall, and Southern delegates threatened to withdraw their support. The fragile unity of the colonies hung in the balance.

Jefferson, initially resolute in his stance, faced immense pressure. One could imagine the private discussions, with voices like **John Adams** of Massachusetts and **Benjamin Franklin** of Pennsylvania, both adamantly opposed to slavery, pleading with Jefferson. They argued passionately about the greater good, warning that the dream of independence could be shattered if unanimity was not achieved. The vision of a free and united nation, they contended, must come first.

Reluctantly, Jefferson conceded, knowing the crack in the foundation of liberty would be costly for the new nation in the years ahead. His notes recorded, "The clause reprobating the enslaving the inhabitants of Africa, was struck out in complaisance to South Carolina and Georgia, who had never attempted to restrain the importation of slaves, and who on the contrary still wished to continue it." Consequently, the anti-slavery passage was removed, securing the necessary unanimous consent for the Declaration, which was adopted on July 4, 1776.

The Revolutionary War, led by General **George Washington**, united the colonies against a common enemy but did little to resolve the entrenched issues related to the institution of bonded labor. After achieving independence and ratifying the Constitution, the young nation faced the challenge of addressing the status of those held in bondage within its borders.

By the time Washington, unanimously elected president, began his second term in 1793, the United States was still grappling with deep-seated tensions around this issue. It was during this period that the first Fugitive Slave Act was enacted, designed to enforce the constitutional right of slaveholders to recover those who had escaped. The law authorized local governments to seize and return these individuals to their owners and imposed penalties on those who aided their escape. However, it lacked strong enforcement mechanisms, leading to resistance and varying compliance across the states.

Washington's stance on this contentious issue provides significant insight into the complexities of the era. Although he was a slaveholder, Washington was the only Founding Father who freed his slaves upon his death, a decision that underscored his evolving views on the moral contradictions of his time.

It is widely believed and supported by historical and genetic evidence that Jefferson had a relationship with **Sally Hemings**, one of his slaves, and fathered several of her children. This relationship and its implications on Jefferson's legacy continue to be a topic of considerable interest and debate in understanding the complexities of his life and the broader context of the forced labor system in early America. Over the first six decades of the United States, twelve presidents from Washington to Ulysses S. Grant either owned slaves while in office or had owned them previously.

Washington notably declined a third term as president, underscoring his commitment to avoiding a monarchical structure, which was a central opposition in the American Revolution. In his poignant farewell address, Washington famously warned against the dangers of political parties, expressing his fear that they could lead to factionalism and potentially undermine the republic. Despite his cautionary words, political divisions quickly deepened. His Vice President, Adams, and Secretary of State, Jefferson, emerged as leaders of the newly-formed Federalist and Democratic-Republican parties, respectively, each championing diverging visions for America's future.

This divergence marked the beginning of the country's long-standing two-party system, reflecting the complexities of governance that Washington had hoped to avoid. This political schism paved the way for the rise of **Andrew Jackson** and the consolidation of the Democratic Party, which initially garnered substantial support from the Southern states due to its strong stance on states' rights and agrarian interests. With this development, the era of fierce partisanship had begun, marking a definitive shift in the dynamics of American political life.

This shift highlighted the enduring conflict over slavery and states' rights, issues that would continue to shape and challenge the nation's fabric for centuries to come.

New Democrats

The 1828 election is often celebrated as a transformative moment in U.S. history, marking the beginning of modern political campaigning and the establishment of a more structured party system. This pivotal change was triggered by the controversial 1824 election, where no candidate secured a majority of electoral votes, leading to a decision by the House of Representatives.

Senator Andrew Jackson, who led with 99 electoral votes, was bypassed in favor of Secretary of State **John Quincy Adams**, who had only 84 votes. This outcome came after Speaker **Henry Clay**, the candidate with the fewest votes, threw his support behind Adams. Jackson's supporters vociferously condemned this maneuver as the "corrupt bargain," especially after Clay was appointed Secretary of State by Adams. Feeling profoundly betrayed, Jackson labeled the election "rigged" and vehemently denounced Clay, stating, 'the Judas of the West has closed the contract and will receive 30 pieces of silver." Subsequently, Jackson resigned his Senate seat and vowed to challenge Adams in the next election.

Throughout the four years leading up to the 1828 election, a sense of grievance became central to Jackson's narrative. He used his belief that he had been cheated out of the presidency to rally his base, positioning his campaign as a fight against corruption and elitism in Washington. This narrative resonated deeply with many voters and significantly influenced the style and intensity of the campaign. His supporters broke away from the traditional Democratic-Republican Party to form the Democratic Party, promoting Jackson as a populist champion. Jackson's campaign effectively employed grassroots strategies to engage a broad swath of voters, sharply contrasting with the elitist tendencies that had previously dominated political interactions.

The campaign was notably acrimonious. Jackson's supporters depicted Adams as an out-of-touch aristocrat, pointing to his purchase of a billiard

table for the White House as evidence of his elitism. Conversely, Adams' supporters cast Jackson as self-indulgent and irresponsible, highlighting his indulgence in horse racing, gambling, and cockfighting. Amid this fervent campaigning, a new form of entertainment emerged in the South—a minstrel show featuring a character named 'Jim Crow,' who performed in blackface, perpetuating derogatory stereotypes of African Americans. This act gained popularity and spurred the growth of similar performances.

Jackson's overwhelming victory in his rematch with Adams culminated in the 1829 inauguration, a landmark event in American political culture. It was the first time a president was elected by directly appealing to the general electorate, sidelining traditional political elites. The inauguration was a vibrant affair that openly welcomed the public into the White House, a stark departure from previous ceremonies.

However, the celebration quickly spiraled into chaos. Throngs of attendees swarmed the venue, knocking over furniture, spilling drinks, and breaking fine china. The excitement peaked when Jackson, besieged by well-wishers, was forced against a wall. His aides had to help him escape through a window to avoid the crush. To disperse the crowd, servants placed tubs of alcoholic punch on the White House lawn, which eventually cleared the building but not before significant damage had occurred.

Margaret Smith, a notable Washington socialite, captured the essence of the event in her writings. She described it as "the People's day, and the People's President and the People would rule." This vivid depiction underscored not only the populist underpinnings of Jackson's ascendancy but also his profound connection with the American public. The chaotic jubilation at the White House that day highlighted a pivotal transformation: the engagement of a broader segment of society in the political process, a legacy that would deeply influence the character of the presidency and American politics in general.

The period known as Jacksonian Democracy marked a transformative era in American political life, characterized by an emphasis on a lean, frugal government and minimal state interference. Jackson and his Democratic Party advocated against excessive government spending and corporate privileges, especially opposing bank charters and other incorporations, which they believed disproportionately favored the elite over the average worker.

Jackson, often referred to as 'Old Hickory,' symbolized the rise of the "era of the common man" in American politics. However, this era was fraught with profound contradictions. While advocating for the expansion of white male suffrage, Jackson's policies simultaneously curtailed the rights of free people of color and women, who remained disenfranchised. Under his influence, several states saw a rollback in voting rights and citizenship for free Black individuals, significantly restricting their participation in the political process.

The Missouri Compromise of 1820 was a critical legislative measure aimed at maintaining the balance of power between free and slave states. It emerged from Missouri's request to join the Union as a slave state, which threatened to disrupt the existing balance of political power between the North and the South. To resolve this, the compromise allowed Missouri to enter as a slave state while Maine was admitted as a free state, keeping the Senate balanced. Additionally, it established the 36°30' latitude as a boundary north of which slavery was prohibited in the Louisiana Territory, except for Missouri. This compromise managed to temporarily quell the sectional tensions but did not eradicate the underlying issues between the North and South, setting the stage for future conflicts.

One such conflict arose during Jackson's presidency in the Nullification Crisis of 1832. South Carolina, driven by economic grievances over federal tariffs enacted in 1828 and 1832, which were perceived as unfavorable to Southern agricultural interests, adopted the radical theory of 'nullification.' This theory proposed that states had the authority to nullify any federal law deemed unconstitutional. The crisis represented a significant escalation in the debate over states' rights versus federal authority, themes initially broached during the Missouri Compromise era.

The Nullification Crisis was further intensified by the personal and political rift between Jackson and his Vice President, **John C. Calhoun**. Calhoun was a staunch supporter of nullification and states' rights, which placed him in direct opposition to Jackson's views on federal authority. Their disagreement culminated in Calhoun resigning his vice presidency to represent South Carolina in the Senate, marking a dramatic split in U.S. political leadership.

Jackson responded to the crisis with a firm hand, signaling his willingness to preserve the Union at all costs. He pushed through Congress the 'Force Bill,' which authorized the use of military force against states that resisted federal laws. Meanwhile, he supported efforts led by Henry Clay to defuse the situation with a compromise tariff, which proposed a gradual reduction in the tariffs that had so aggrieved the Southern states.

Ultimately, the combination of Jackson's resolute stance and the legislative concessions made through the compromise tariff led South Carolina to back down. In March 1833, the state repealed its ordinance of nullification, thus defusing the immediate crisis. This resolution underscored Jackson's deep convictions about the indissolubility of the Union and set a precedent for federal authority over state legislation.

As a staunch anti-abolitionist and slave owner, Jackson's tenure was marked by entrenched racial inequalities. An inventory from January 1829, just before he assumed office, detailed the names, ages, and familial relationships of ninety-five enslaved individuals at his Tennessee plantation, The Hermitage. Upon moving to the White House, he brought several enslaved people with him, and records from the 1830 census indicate fourteen enslaved individuals in the presidential household—a number believed to have increased throughout his presidency.

Jackson's administration was marked by policies that starkly contrasted with the humanitarian and reform movements emerging at the time, demonstrating an overtly anti-egalitarian stance. A particularly infamous example was the Indian Removal Act of 1830, which mandated the forced displacement of thousands of Native Americans. This policy led to the tragic

Trail of Tears, involving the relocation of several Native American nations—including the Cherokee, Muscogee (Creek), Seminole, Chickasaw, and Choctaw—from their ancestral lands in the Southeastern United States to areas west of the Mississippi River.

The Trail of Tears was a catastrophic event in American history, with a

devastating death toll. Approximately 4,000 of the roughly 16,000 Cherokees who embarked on the journey in 1838 and 1839 perished due to disease, exposure, and starvation. When accounting for all affected tribes, the total number of deaths is often estimated to be in the thousands.

Chief **John Ross** of the Cherokee Nation poignantly described the profound sorrow and injustice experienced by his people in a letter to the U.S. Congress: "Our hearts are sickened, our utterance is gone, and we are enveloped with mental darkness; we go forth sorrowful, knowing that wrong has been done." The Trail of Tears stands as a grave human rights atrocity, emblematic of Jackson's presidency. Driven by a racially motivated agenda to clear Native lands for white settlers, this policy led to the devastating displacement and deaths of thousands of Native Americans. This tragic event remains a somber reminder of the historical injustices faced by Indigenous peoples in the United States.

Despite his vocal opposition to the 'elitists' in Washington, Jackson simultaneously entrenched another controversial practice—rewarding his political supporters with government jobs, which he dubbed as 'reform.' This approach was robustly defended by Jackson supporter Senator **William**

Marcy of New York, who famously declared, 'To the victor belongs the spoils of the enemy.' This era not only highlighted the contradictions in Jackson's policies but also solidified the Democratic Party's dominance in the South. Here, the party vigorously defended the interests of slaveholders and advocated for the expansion of slavery into new territories. These policies led to significant legislative and judicial developments, profoundly shaping the political landscape and having a lasting impact on the nation's trajectory.

While Jacksonian Democracy expanded democratic participation for certain segments of the population, notably poor white men, it also deeply entrenched systemic inequalities and injustices. This duality underscores the complex and often troubling legacy of Jackson's presidency, which continues to resonate in American history.

Historian Jon Meacham, in his book *American Lion: Andrew Jackson in the White House*, captures the dichotomy of Jackson's character and policies. Meacham writes, "He was the most contradictory of men: A champion of extending freedom and democracy to even the poorest of whites, Jackson was an unrepentant slaveholder. A sentimental man who rescued an Indian orphan on a battlefield to raise in his home, Jackson was responsible for the removal of Indian tribes from their ancestral lands. An enemy of Eastern financial elites and a relentless opponent of the Bank of the United States, which he believed to be a bastion of corruption, Jackson also promised to die, if necessary, to preserve the power and prestige of the central government. Like us and our America, Jackson and his America achieved great things while committing grievous sins."

Amistad

> THE AMISTAD. We learn that the committee in behalf of the Africans taken in the Amistad, have engaged the services of the Hon John Quincy Adams, as senior council, and that he will make the closing argument in the Supreme Court of the United States· at Washington, next January.

After losing the election to Jackson in 1828, John Quincy Adams made a remarkable return to public service by being elected to the U.S. House of Representatives in 1830—the only president to serve in Congress after his presidency. Like his father, John Adams, the nation's second president, John Quincy ardently believed that slavery was morally reprehensible. He dedicated his post-presidential career to advocating for universal freedom, significantly influencing the early abolition movement.

Among his most significant contributions to the abolitionist cause was his role in the 1841 Supreme Court case, *United States v. The Amistad*. Adams was an ideal representative for the Mende Africans before the Supreme Court, due to his extensive governmental experience, prior engagements at the Supreme Court, his involvement in international treaty negotiations, and his profound opposition to slavery.

The *La Amistad* case revolved around a group of Mende individuals who were kidnapped in Africa and illegally sold into slavery in Cuba, in violation of international treaties that prohibited the transatlantic slave trade. The Africans were placed aboard the Spanish ship *La Amistad* for transport to plantations on the island. However, under the leadership of **Sengbe Pieh**, also known as Joseph Cinqué, they revolted at sea, seizing control of the ship. They killed the captain and the cook but spared two Spaniards who falsely promised to navigate them back to Africa. Instead, these navigators misled the Africans and steered the ship northward, where it was eventually intercepted by the U.S. Navy near Long Island, New York.

Once in the United States, the Africans were imprisoned and charged with mutiny and murder, sparking a legal battle that reached the Supreme Court. For 8 ½ hours, the 74-year-old Adams passionately and eloquently defended the Africans' right to freedom on both legal and moral grounds. He cited treaties that prohibited the slave trade and referenced the Declaration of Independence, drawing parallels between the Africans' struggle and the American fight for independence.

The Supreme Court, moved by his arguments, ruled in favor of the Africans' right to freedom, establishing a significant legal precedent for universal human rights. However, the decision also underscored the exceptional nature of the *Amistad* case, indicating that, generally, enslaved individuals did not have the right to rebel or escape their bondage according to U.S. law at the time.

In November 1841, in recognition of his efforts, the Mende Africans presented Adams with a Bible as a token of their gratitude. An accompanying letter expressed their deep appreciation: "The Mendi People give you thanks for all your kindness to them. They will never forget your defense of their rights before the Great Court at Washington. They feel that they owe to you, in a large measure, their deliverance from the Spaniards, and from Slavery or Death. They will pray for you, Mr. Adams, as long as they live."

Adams harbored a vision of a world devoid of slavery and war, a sentiment he often articulated with poignant eloquence: "Roll, years of promise, rapidly roll round, till not a slave shall on this earth be found." He believed fervently that the United States had a pivotal role in leading the global effort to eradicate slavery. By leveraging its international influence, promoting ethical business practices, and enhancing prosecutions against human trafficking, the

U.S. could advance Adams's legacy and strive towards realizing his prophetic vision of universal freedom.

In stark contrast to Adams, Jackson pursued a legacy deeply intertwined with the institution of slavery. After leaving office in 1837, Jackson retired to The Hermitage but remained a significant political figure. He continued to wield influence by mentoring his successor, Martin Van Buren, during the onset of the Panic of 1837. This severe economic depression, marked by widespread bank failures, unemployment, and a downturn in economic activity, struck early in Van Buren's presidency and had a profound impact on the institution of slavery.

As the economy faltered, the demand for labor, especially in agriculture and manufacturing sectors where enslaved individuals were heavily employed, significantly declined. This economic downturn led to a noticeable drop in slave prices in certain areas. Importantly, the financial crisis also fueled a rise in anti-slavery sentiments in the North. The worsening economic conditions led many to question both the morality and the economic viability of slavery, contributing to the growth of abolitionist movements.

Meanwhile, Jackson's management of his plantation at The Hermitage vividly illustrated the entrenchment of slavery in the Southern economy. His cotton plantation relied heavily on the labor of enslaved individuals. Over his lifetime, Jackson owned hundreds of slaves, with 161 still under his ownership at the time of his death, marking him as one of the most prominent slaveholders of his era.

Nation Divided Over Slavery

"Americans are so enamored of equality that they would rather be equal in slavery than unequal in freedom." This profound statement is one of many from **Alexis de Tocqueville** in his seminal work, 'Democracy in America.' During his travels across the United States in 1831, the French nobleman and author meticulously documented his observations, offering a nuanced analysis of American society. His writings praised the generosity and entrepreneurial spirit of Americans, and he boldly predicted that the United States would surpass European powers to become a leading global force.

While Tocqueville was optimistic about the prospects for resolving slavery peacefully, historical events soon demonstrated the complexity of these issues. Between 1845 and 1850, a series of pivotal developments sharply escalated tensions within the United States, edging the nation closer to civil war. The annexation of Texas in 1845 as a slave state significantly heightened the conflict between pro-slavery and anti-slavery factions by expanding the territory where slavery was legally recognized. This situation was further exacerbated by the outcome of the Mexican-American War in 1848, which concluded with the Treaty of Guadalupe Hidalgo and resulted in substantial territorial gains for the United States. The question of whether slavery would be permitted in these new territories became a central and contentious debate.

In response to these territorial expansions, **David Wilmot**, a Democratic congressman from Pennsylvania, introduced the Wilmot Proviso, which proposed banning slavery in any territory acquired from Mexico. The proviso repeatedly passed the House of Representatives, where Northern states wielded greater influence due to their larger populations, but consistently failed in the Senate, where the balance of power was more evenly distributed between free and slave states. Although the Wilmot Proviso never became law, it played a crucial role in the national debate over slavery, highlighting deep sectional divisions that threatened the unity of the nation.

The controversy over slavery in new territories continued to intensify, especially with the onset of the California Gold Rush in 1849. This event triggered a massive influx of settlers to California, rapidly accelerating its push for statehood. The sudden population boom raised urgent questions about whether California would enter the Union as a free or slave state, further inflaming the ongoing national debate and moving the country closer to the brink of conflict.

The culmination of these tensions led to the Compromise of 1850, signed by Democrat President **Millard Fillmore**. This series of legislative measures aimed at quelling the brewing conflict included admitting California as a free state, a victory for anti-slavery forces. However, it also allowed the territories of New Mexico and Utah to decide on slavery through popular sovereignty, meaning the settlers in those territories would vote on the issue.

A critical component of the Compromise was the Fugitive Slave Act of 1850, designed to appease Southern states amid growing sectional tensions. Far more stringent and controversial than the earlier 1793 law, this Act created a network of federal commissioners empowered to enforce the law and oversee cases involving fugitive enslaved people. Commissioners were given financial incentives to rule in favor of slaveholders. Alleged fugitives were denied the right to a jury trial and could not testify on their own behalf, with commissioners having the authority to decide the fate of the accused based solely on the testimony of the claimant, who merely needed to assert ownership.

The Act imposed severe penalties, including fines and imprisonment, on anyone who aided a fugitive enslaved person or obstructed their capture. This included providing food, shelter, or any form of assistance. Law enforcement officials and citizens in free states were required to assist in the capture and return of fugitive enslaved people, effectively nationalizing the issue and forcing free states to participate in the institution of slavery.

The Act heightened tensions between the North and South, galvanizing abolitionist sentiment in the North where many were outraged by the requirement to enforce slavery laws and the denial of due process for accused fugitives. The law spurred the activities of the Underground Railroad, a network of secret routes and safe houses used by African-American slaves to escape into free states and Canada with the aid of abolitionists and allies.

Despite its name, the Underground Railroad was not a literal railroad but rather a series of coordinated actions through which fugitive slaves were passed from one "station" to another. Conductors, who were abolitionists both black  and white, provided shelter, food, guidance, and sometimes transportation to help escapees move from place to place under cover of night.

One of the most famous conductors was **Harriet Tubman**. Born into slavery, Tubman endured severe hardships, including physical violence that caused lifelong health problems. In 1849, she escaped to Philadelphia, but rather than live in peace, she repeatedly risked her life by returning to the South to lead her family and other slaves to freedom via the Underground Railroad. Tubman is estimated to have made 13 missions to rescue approximately 70 enslaved people. Known as "Moses" for never losing a passenger, she used a variety of tactics to evade capture and guide others to safety.

During the Civil War, Tubman served the Union Army as a cook, nurse, and spy. In 1863, she became the first woman to lead an armed assault during the Civil War. The Combahee River Raid in South Carolina resulted in the liberation of more than 700 slaves. Tubman's legacy as a figure of indomitable spirit and commitment to justice is celebrated, and there has been a proposal to place her image on the U.S. $20 bill, replacing Andrew Jackson.

Notable cases under the Fugitive Slave Act, such as the capture of **Anthony Burns** in Boston in 1854, drew significant public attention and outrage. Burns was an African-American born into slavery in Virginia in 1834. His life took a significant turn when he escaped from slavery in 1854, making his way to Boston, Massachusetts. However, his freedom was short-lived; he was captured under the Fugitive Slave Act, which mandated the return of escaped slaves to their owners even if they had reached free states. Burns' capture and trial in Boston marked a defining moment in the fight against slavery. His arrest under the Fugitive Slave Act led to fervent protests and riots throughout the city, turning his plight into a rallying cry that intensified the abolitionist movement's efforts.

Among those who stepped forward to defend Burns were notable individuals like **Richard Henry Dana Jr.**, an esteemed author known for his compelling sea narrative, *Two Years Before the Mast*. Alongside him was the Reverend **Leonard Grimes**, a respected African American minister and a pivotal figure in the abolitionist movement. Their participation highlighted the widespread resistance to the enforcement of the Fugitive Slave Act. Despite a spirited defense and public outcry, Burns was eventually returned to Virginia following a highly publicized and controversial trial.

This incident not only exposed the North's complicity in the institution of slavery through the enforcement of the Fugitive Slave Act but also fueled further abolitionist sentiment in the region. Burns' case is often remembered as a pivotal moment that highlighted the moral and legal contradictions of slavery in America. His story does have a somewhat redemptive conclusion. Sympathizers eventually raised enough money to purchase his freedom from slavery. After his release, Burns moved to Canada, where he lived until his death in 1862.

Overall, the Compromise of 1850 can be seen as a pragmatic short-term solution, much like putting a band-aid on a large wound. It staved off immediate disunion but failed to address the fundamental issues dividing the nation, contributing significantly to the growing sectional tensions that would eventually lead to the Civil War.

Uncle Tom's Cabin

"Uncle Tom's Cabin," written by **Harriet Beecher Stowe** and published in

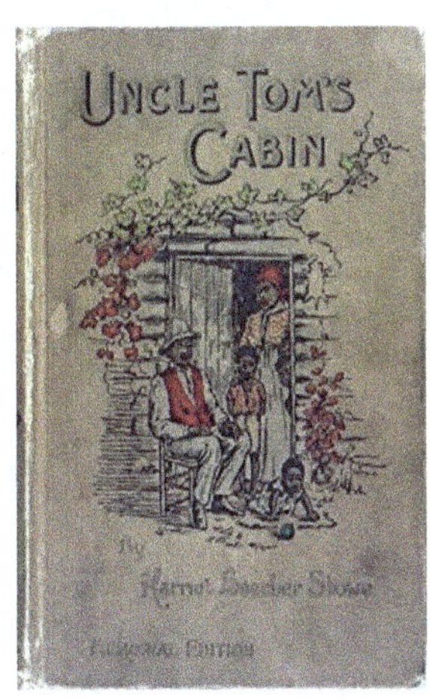

1852, profoundly impacted the discourse on slavery in the United States. The novel provides a powerful critique of slavery, vividly depicting the brutal conditions and emotional suffering endured by African Americans who were enslaved. Through the lives of its characters, especially the kind and noble Uncle Tom—a middle-aged black man who faces severe cruelty from various masters—the book explores the moral conflicts and legal intricacies surrounding slavery.

Central themes of "Uncle Tom's Cabin" include the moral conflict over slavery, Christian redemption, and the harsh realities of the institution. Stowe's narrative highlights not only the physical abuse suffered by enslaved individuals but also the widespread destruction of families through the slave trade. Additionally, her portrayal of female characters, both African American and white, emphasizes the gendered aspects of slavery and the specific vulnerabilities faced by women in this oppressive system.

The impact of 'Uncle Tom's Cabin' was profound and far-reaching. It became the best-selling novel of the 19th century and the second most purchased book after the Bible. Stowe's work is credited with humanizing the suffering of enslaved individuals and galvanizing Northern opposition to slavery, aligning public sentiment with the policies that Abraham Lincoln would later implement during his presidency. During the Civil War, Lincoln reportedly remarked to Stowe at the White House, 'So this is the little lady who started this great war,' highlighting the widespread belief in the novel's substantial influence on American history.

"Uncle Tom's Cabin" also prompted a surge of anti-slavery literature and was adapted into numerous plays and films, further embedding its messages into American culture. However, over the years, the novel has faced criticism for its use of racial stereotypes and the patronizing portrayal of its African American characters, particularly Uncle Tom, who is sometimes viewed as overly submissive. Despite these criticisms, the book remains a pivotal work in American literature and an essential component of anti-slavery activism.

Dreadful Decision

Nearly two decades after Andrew Jackson left office, the political landscape was dramatically reshaped by the Democrats' support for the Kansas-Nebraska Act of 1854, introduced by Senator **Stephen A. Douglas** of Illinois. This legislation allowed territories to decide for themselves whether to permit slavery, effectively nullifying the Missouri Compromise that had previously banned slavery in certain new territories. This policy shift deepened the national divide over slavery and triggered violent conflicts, most notably in Kansas.

The period, famously dubbed "Bleeding Kansas," was characterized by severe clashes between pro-slavery and anti-slavery factions, symbolizing the intense struggle over whether Kansas would enter the Union as a free or slave state. These conflicts highlighted the dangerous consequences of the act and underscored the volatile nature of America's sectional tensions, setting the stage for a broader national crisis.

In the 1856 presidential election, the Democratic platform explicitly supported the expansion of slavery, aligning with contentious Southern interests during a decade marked by intense national discord. This platform endorsed the principle of "popular sovereignty" as established by the Kansas-Nebraska Act, appealing to Southern voters concerned about the potential for new territories to be admitted as free states. The platform also emphasized the protection of states' rights, asserting that the federal government should not intervene in slavery decisions within the territories. Moreover, it took a strong stance against anti-slavery agitation, viewing it as a threat to the union's stability and advocating opposition to preserve national harmony.

James Buchanan, who had been a perennial candidate in previous elections, leveraged this platform to secure the presidency, despite not winning the popular vote. He is often cited as one of the most ineffectual presidents in American history. His presidency was marred by a series of failed policies and a notable inability to steer the nation away from the escalating crisis that would ultimately lead to the Civil War. Under his leadership, the Democratic Party's support for slavery and states' rights fueled the political conflicts of the era, highlighting deep divisions within the United States that were intensifying on the brink of civil conflict.

In 1857, the predominantly pro-slavery Supreme Court, appointed mainly by Democratic presidents, issued the Dred Scott decision, one of the most criticized rulings in American judicial history. This ruling emerged from the case of **Dred Scott**, an enslaved African American man who had resided in regions where slavery was outlawed under the Missouri Compromise and sought legal affirmation of his freedom. The court declared that African Americans, whether enslaved or free, were not recognized as American citizens and thus lacked the legal standing to file lawsuits in federal courts.

This not only effectively denied Dred Scott his freedom but also underscored the status of African Americans as non-citizens, excluded from constitutional protections.

Chief Justice **Roger B. Taney** authored the decision, arguing that Congress lacked the authority to ban slavery in the territories, a stance that invalidated the Missouri Compromise. He contended that restricting slavery violated the Fifth Amendment, which protects against property seizure without due process—with enslaved individuals considered property legally at that time. By ruling that the federal government could not restrict slavery in the territories, the decision shifted control over the expansion of slavery to the states and territories, framing it as a matter of states' rights. This ideological shift suggested that decisions about the legality and spread of slavery were best left to local jurisdictions, intensifying the regional tensions that ultimately divided the nation.

The case was fraught with personal drama and legal oddities, including multiple retrials and changes in the respondent's name due to clerical errors. The human element of Dred Scott's struggle, alongside his wife Harriet and their daughters, added a poignant layer to the legal proceedings. The ruling galvanized the abolitionist movement, intensifying efforts to support fugitive slaves and deepening divisions that would eventually lead to the Civil War. The decision was substantially supported by Democrats, who found in it a convenient alignment with their interests. Advocating for states' rights allowed them to sidestep the morally reprehensible goal of the ruling—to perpetuate the enslavement of human beings—while supporting the Southern slave-holding aristocracy and maintaining their political influence in regions where slavery was economically and culturally entrenched.

This decision remains a pivotal example of how Supreme Court rulings can reflect societal prejudices and exacerbate national divisions, serving as a cautionary tale about the judicial system's potential impact on justice and constitutional rights. It also highlights how such rulings can influence political landscapes, contributing directly to the fragmentation of political parties and the rise of anti-slavery platforms that led to significant historical shifts.

As Buchanan left the White House in 1861, he remarked to incoming president **Abraham Lincoln**, "If you are as happy in entering the presidency as I am in leaving it, then you are a very happy man." Buchanan's lack of decisive action and failure to address the escalating tensions between the North and South are viewed as major shortcomings, which not only led to increased instability but also pushed the country closer to the brink of war. In my view, these failures distinctly rank him as the worst president in our nation's history.

Birth Of Republican Party

The Republican Party was officially organized in Ripon, Wisconsin, in 1854, formed by anti-slavery activists, ex-Free Soilers, and disaffected Whigs who were united in their opposition to the spread of slavery. This alignment positioned the Republican Party as the original civil rights party during a pivotal era in American history. The party quickly rose to prominence, driven by a commitment to halt the inhumane practice of slavery and to promote greater rights for African Americans.

Unlike the Democrats, the Republicans strongly opposed the Kansas-Nebraska Act, with the party's platform built primarily around this opposition. Abolitionists, who played a critical role in shaping the early Republican Party, were activists dedicated to the immediate end of slavery. Their strong moral and religious convictions ensured that the issue of slavery remained central to the Republican agenda.

The party articulated its ideals clearly in its platform, stating on June 18, 1856: "We hold it to be a self-evident truth, that all men are endowed with the inalienable right to life, liberty, and the pursuit of happiness, and that the primary object and ulterior design of our Federal Government were to secure these rights to all persons under its exclusive jurisdiction...we deny the authority of Congress, of a Territorial Legislation, of any individual, or association of individuals, to give legal existence to Slavery in any Territory of the United States, while the present Constitution shall be maintained."

Horace Greeley, the founder of the *New York Tribune*, was a crucial figure in American journalism and politics. His newspaper served as a key platform for promoting the emerging Republican Party's ideals, especially its opposition to slavery and the states' rights doctrine that upheld it. Greeley used the Tribune to influence public opinion and shape the political landscape, advocating for progressive reforms and the abolition of slavery.

Frederick Douglass, an escaped slave from Maryland, became a leading voice in the abolitionist movement. By the 1850s, he had emerged as a prominent African American abolitionist, orator, and writer, renowned for his powerful speeches and compelling writings that called for the abolition of slavery and equal rights for all races. His autobiography, "Narrative of the Life of Frederick Douglass, an American Slave," published in 1845, played a significant role in promoting the abolitionist cause.

Douglass furthered his influence by founding the abolitionist newspaper "North Star" in 1847, emphasizing the need for political action against slavery. His involvement extended beyond abolition to include supporting women's rights and Irish home rule. Through extensive speaking tours in the U.S. and internationally, Douglass used his formidable oratory skills and personal experiences to advocate against slavery and racial injustice, shaping the national dialogue on these critical issues.

Initially skeptical of the Republican Party's dedication to racial equality, Douglass, along with other abolitionist leaders, eventually supported the party, swayed by its firm stance against the spread of slavery. This alliance between the Republican Party and abolitionist principles not only solidified the party's role as a major political entity but also positioned it at the forefront of the movement for civil rights in America. The party's foundational opposition to the Kansas-Nebraska Act, combined with the moral imperatives championed by abolitionists, catalyzed significant shifts in the political and social landscape of the nation.

The birth of the Republican Party occurred during a time of rising nativist attitudes, evidenced by the formation of the Know-Nothing Party. This party vehemently opposed immigrant groups, fearing they would dilute what was perceived as the "American" identity and compete for jobs with native-born citizens. While the Republican Party's primary aim was to prevent the expansion of slavery into new territories and states, it also harbored factions concerned about the effects of immigration. These concerns were largely economic and cultural, distinct from the xenophobic or racially motivated undercurrents typical of groups like the Know-Nothings.

The Republicans adopted a more measured approach to immigration, focusing on its potential impact on American workers and cultural norms. This stance helped forge the early identity of the Republican Party as it tackled these intricate social issues, all while striving to curb the spread of slavery.

The Democratic Party's stance on immigration during this time period was complex and varied regionally, but it often aligned with nativist sentiments, particularly among its members in the Northern states. David Goldfield, author of The Gifted Generation: When Government Was Good, explains, "The Republican Party was strictly a sectional party, meaning that it just did not exist in the South. The South couldn't care less about immigration. But it did care about preserving slavery."

John C. Frémont, known as "The Pathfinder," was the first Republican presidential nominee in 1856. His life, marked by adventure, political ambition, and significant historical impact, remains a fascinating chapter in America's tumultuous 19th century. Born in Savannah, Georgia, in 1813, Frémont became renowned for his exploration of the American West in the 1840s. His vivid reports and maps not only guided settlers through treacherous landscapes but also fueled the American imagination and westward expansion.

Transitioning seamlessly from exploration to politics, Frémont served as one of California's first U.S. Senators in 1850. His foray into presidential politics came in 1856 when he was nominated by the newly formed Republican Party. Unlike Andrew Jackson, the first Democratic presidential candidate who won the presidency and reshaped American politics, Frémont was unsuccessful in his bid for the White House.

After the Civil War, Frémont's career experienced both highs and lows, including a stint as Governor of Arizona Territory. His later years were marked by various business ventures, not all successful, but his life story remains a fascinating chapter in the saga of America's tumultuous 19th century.

Throughout the late 1850s, as the national debate over slavery and states' rights intensified, the Republican Party firmly opposed the expansion of slavery, viewing it as morally wrong and contrary to the principles of freedom and equality. This stance established the Republicans as the civil rights party of the era, particularly in defense of African Americans' rights.

In contrast, the Democratic Party, especially its Southern factions, defended and sought to preserve slavery, arguing that it was vital to the Southern economy and way of life. Many Democrats saw attempts to restrict or abolish slavery as an infringement on states' rights. The stark contrast between the two parties' platforms—Republicans opposed to slavery and Democrats defending it—set the stage for the profound political and social conflicts that would eventually culminate in the Civil War.

Lincoln of Illinois

Abraham Lincoln, born on February 12, 1809, in a log cabin in Hardin County, Kentucky, had a childhood marked by hardship and scant education. His family moved to Indiana when he was seven, a frontier region where his formative years were spent performing physical labor and intermittently attending sparse, itinerant schools. Despite these challenges, Lincoln was an avid reader and largely self-educated.

In 1830, his family moved again, this time to Illinois, where Lincoln eventually struck out on his own. He worked a variety of jobs including splitting rails for fences, working on a flatboat, and general store clerking, all while continuing to educate himself by reading voraciously. His interest in law was piqued early on, and he began his legal studies independently, borrowing books from lawyers and teaching himself.

Lincoln's political career began in the early 1830s. He served four successive terms in the Illinois State Legislature as a member of the Whig Party starting in 1834, and he was admitted to the bar in 1836, beginning his practice as a lawyer in Springfield, Illinois. His reputation as a skilled attorney and orator grew as he traveled the circuit of courts in Illinois.

Lincoln served a single term in the U.S. House of Representatives from 1847 to 1849, during which he vocally opposed the Mexican-American War and supported **Zachary Taylor**, the Whig candidate, for president. After his term, Lincoln returned to Springfield to resume his law practice, becoming increasingly disenchanted with politics, largely due to the contentious issue of slavery, which he opposed. His views on slavery and racism were shaped by a complex interplay of moral, political, and personal influences, evolving significantly over his lifetime. Though Lincoln often referenced the Bible in his speeches, he was not a traditional Christian, and his moral framework was not strictly guided by religious doctrine. Instead, his ethical convictions were deeply rooted in a personal sense of justice and equality, as well as the principles outlined in the Declaration of Independence, asserting that all men are created equal.

Lincoln's personal experiences also played a significant role in shaping his views. Having grown up in Kentucky and Indiana, he witnessed the realities of slavery firsthand, which left a lasting impact on him. Moreover, his interactions with African Americans, both through his legal practice and in his personal life, further informed his understanding of the human cost of slavery. This deepened his opposition to the expansion of slavery in the territories, rekindling his political interests as the nation grappled with the Kansas-Nebraska Act. Lincoln joined the newly formed Republican Party, and actively engaged in political debates, articulating his views on governance and slavery by stating, "I have no prejudice against the Southern people; I surely will not blame them for not doing what I should not know how to do myself." He further emphasized the principles of democratic governance by adding, "No man is good enough to govern another man without that other's consent."

In a letter to his close friend Joshua F. Speed dated August 24, 1855, Lincoln expressed, "In 1841 you and I had together a tedious low-water trip, on a Steam Boat from Louisville to St. Louis. You may remember, as I well do, that from Louisville to the mouth of the Ohio there were, on board, ten or a dozen slaves, shackled together with irons. That sight was a continual torment to me; and I see something like it every time I touch the Ohio, or any other slave-border. It is hardly fair to you to assume that I have no interest in a thing

which has, and continually exercises, the power of making me miserable."
This early expression showcases his personal moral opposition to the
institution, even though he was cautious about how to address it politically.

In 1858, Abraham Lincoln's campaign against Stephen A. Douglas for a U.S.
Senate seat included a series of seven debates that would become historic.
Despite Douglas winning the election, these debates significantly boosted
Lincoln's national profile. The detailed discussions on critical issues,
particularly slavery and states' rights, showcased Lincoln's articulate and
compelling rhetorical abilities. This exposure was instrumental in launching
him onto the national stage, setting the groundwork for his successful
presidential campaign just two years later.

The primary theme of the debates was slavery, particularly its expansion into
the new territories. Douglas defended the doctrine of popular sovereignty,
which held that the residents of a territory should decide for themselves
whether to allow slavery, a principle he had championed in the
Kansas-Nebraska Act. This stance was intended to appeal to voters who
favored local control over federal intervention.

In contrast, Lincoln argued that slavery was a moral, social, and political
wrong. He believed that the government should prevent the spread of slavery
into new territories and thus contain its existence until it could gradually be
abolished. Douglas accused Lincoln of supporting racial equality, which
Lincoln clarified by stating he did not believe in political and social equality
between races, but he did believe that all men, regardless of color, should have
the same rights to liberty and the fruits of their labor as guaranteed by the
Declaration of Independence.

The extensive coverage of the debates in newspapers helped to spread
Lincoln's ideas on slavery and his reputation as a compelling political thinker
and speaker, setting him up as a significant figure in the Republican Party and

a contender for the presidency in 1860. These debates remain famous as a classic confrontation over the values and future direction of the United States.

During this campaign, Lincoln delivered his now-famous "House Divided" speech, asserting, "A house divided against itself cannot stand. I believe this government cannot endure, permanently half slave and half free. I do not expect the Union to be dissolved—I do not expect the house to fall—but I do expect it will cease to be divided. It will become all one thing or all the other."

In the climactic Lincoln-Douglas debate, Lincoln articulated that the issues debated were not merely contemporary concerns but represented a much larger, enduring conflict between individual rights and the divine right of kings. He stated, "That is the real issue. That is the issue that will continue in this country when these poor tongues of Judge Douglas and myself shall be silent. It is the eternal struggle between these two principles—right and wrong—throughout the world. They are the two principles that have stood face to face from the beginning of time, and will ever continue to struggle. The one is the common right of humanity and the other the divine right of kings. It is the same principle in whatever shape it develops itself. It is the same spirit that says, 'You work and toil and earn bread, and I'll eat it.' No matter in what shape it comes, whether from the mouth of a king who seeks to bestride the people of his own nation and live by the fruit of their labor, or from one race of men as an apology for enslaving another race, it is the same tyrannical principle."

These statements crystallized the core conflict of the era and underscored the unsustainable nature of a nation divided on such a fundamental issue. Though he lost the Senate race, Lincoln's articulate stand on moral and political principles served as a rallying cry for those opposed to the spread of slavery, further deepening the ideological divides between the North and the South.

In an April 6, 1859 letter to Henry L. Pierce, Lincoln articulated a more hardened stance against slavery, emphasizing a fundamental principle of moral justice. He wrote: "This is a world of compensations; and he who would be no slave, must consent to have no slave. Those who deny freedom to others, deserve it not for themselves; and, under a just God, cannot long retain it." This statement reflected Lincoln's deepening conviction that slavery was not only a moral wrong but also inherently contradictory to the values of freedom and equality.

Lincoln's reputation as a moderate within the burgeoning anti-slavery movement was instrumental in securing his Republican nomination for the presidency in 1860. His campaign platform, which opposed the expansion of slavery yet promised not to interfere with the institution where it already existed, appealed to a broad spectrum of Northern voters.

However, the dynamics of his position underwent a significant transformation shortly after his election, a change catalyzed by the secession of Southern states.

Sowing of the Wind

Understanding the integral role of slavery in Southern society is crucial. Since the first African-Americans arrived in 1619, slavery formed the foundation of Southern prosperity, particularly on plantations. The notion of 'civilizing' Africans was often touted as a noble service, with slaves viewed paternalistically as children or extended family members.

However, this guise masked severe abuses. Some masters interpreted the adage 'spare the rod and spoil the child' to extremes, subjecting slaves to barbaric punishments such as being rolled down hills in barrels lined with nails or having salt and pepper rubbed into their lash-inflicted wounds and blisters, followed by allowing a cat to claw at the sores until they bled. Further, the sexual exploitation of enslaved women by white men was rampant, with many being forced to submit. Healthy men were often rented out to other plantations.

Rations were minimal, only enough to sustain slaves through grueling 80-hour workweeks in the fields. Children often ate from troughs to simplify meal cleanups. The investment in feeding the labor force was minimal compared to the capital spent on machinery, reflecting the stark contrast in how the North and South approached labor. While the North advanced with labor-saving technologies and new innovations, the South's prosperity depended on extracting more labor from slaves.

Southern society was increasingly tense, sitting atop a powder keg of potential rebellion. Slaveholders comprised only 25% of the population; the rest were either enslaved or poor whites, many of whom resented the planters' control over regional politics. Beneath the surface, even those who defended the system recognized its unsustainable nature. As Southern intellectual George Fitzhugh noted, a prevailing set of ideas about governance and control would eventually dominate. He predicted that slavery would either be abolished globally or reinstated universally.

The powder keg finally exploded with the actions of **John Brown**, an

abolitionist who fervently believed in using armed insurrection to overthrow the institution of slavery in the United States. In Kansas Territory, Brown and his followers were involved in a series of confrontations between anti-slavery and pro-slavery settlers. In an act of vengeance for the sacking of the free-soil town of Lawrence, Brown and his men killed five pro-slavery settlers in what became known as the Pottawatomie Massacre.

In October 1859, he led a raid on the federal armory at Harpers Ferry, Virginia (now West Virginia). With 21 followers, Brown aimed to seize weapons from the armory and incite a widespread slave rebellion throughout the South. The raid, however, was unsuccessful. Local militia and U.S. Marines, led by Colonel **Robert E. Lee**, quickly overwhelmed Brown and his men. Ten of Brown's followers were killed, and Brown himself was captured. During his trial, when asked about his motives, Brown consistently answered that he wanted to free the slaves and believed that God had given him this mission.

After a swift verdict, Brown was convicted, and on December 2, 1859, he was hanged four blocks from the courthouse in Charleston, West Virginia. Found guilty of treason, murder, and conspiring with slaves to incite an insurrection, Brown faced his fate with a note predicting more bloodshed. The note read,

"I, John Brown, am now quite certain that the crimes of this guilty land will never be purged away but with blood. I had, as I now think, flattered myself that without very much bloodshed it might be done."

Brown's raid on Harpers Ferry is often cited as a catalyst for the Civil War, as it heightened the conflict between the North and South. Despite being called insane by some, Brown received praise during his trial from prominent thinkers such as **Henry David Thoreau**, who compared him to "the best of those who stood at Concord, Lexington, and Bunker Hill." Poet **Henry Wadsworth Longfellow** also honored Brown, writing that his execution would be the "sowing of the wind to reap the whirlwind, which will soon come."

Civil War

Abraham Lincoln's election in November 1860, achieved without securing any electoral votes from Southern states, sharply emphasized the deep national divide regarding slavery. Lincoln triumphed over Southern Democrat **John C. Breckinridge**, Democrat Stephen A. Douglas, and Constitutional Union candidate **John Bell**. This clear regional division highlighted the escalating tensions and foreshadowed the impending secession of Southern states, heralding the onset of the Civil War. Consequently, Lincoln's presidency commenced amidst a grave threat of national disunion.

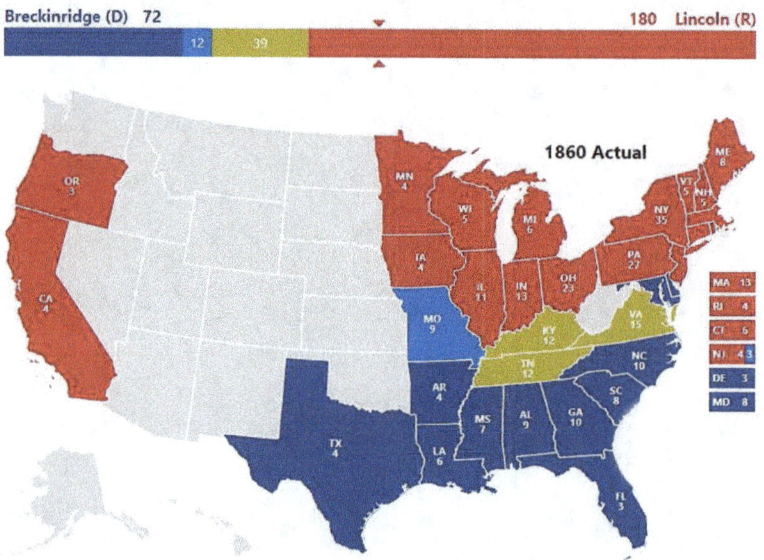

As Springfield, Illinois, reveled in Lincoln's victory, Charleston, South Carolina, stood in stark contrast, having not cast a single vote for him. South Carolina swiftly called for a secession convention, setting off a chain reaction across the Southern states. Within three months, seven states had seceded from the Union.

Local sentiment, captured by the *Charleston Mercury*, proclaimed, "The tea has been thrown overboard, the revolution of 1860 has been initiated." Shortly thereafter, South Carolina's U.S. Senators resigned, and on December 20, 1860, the state legislature unanimously passed an ordinance dissolving its union with the other states.

This wave of secession led to similar actions in Mississippi, Florida, Alabama, Georgia, Louisiana, and Texas, all of which left the Union by February 1. On February 4, delegates from these states, excluding Texas, convened in Montgomery, Alabama, to form the Confederate States of America.

They elected **Jefferson Davis** as their president. Davis held views that supported the institution of slavery and the idea of white supremacy. These beliefs were integral to the ideology of the Confederacy, which was established explicitly to preserve and protect the institution of slavery.

Davis defended the immoral practice both as a U.S. Senator and as President of the Confederacy, arguing that it was beneficial both for enslaved Africans and the American economy. He believed in the racial superiority of whites and viewed the enslavement of Black people as justified and natural.

On the brink of secession, Davis delivered a stark defense of slavery, stating, "I say that the lower race of human beings that constitute the substratum of what is termed the slave population of the South, elevates every white man in our community ... It is the presence of a lower caste, those lower by their mental and physical organization, controlled by the higher intellect of the white man, that gives this superiority to the white laborer. Menial services are not there performed by the white man. We have none of our brethren sunk to the degradation of being menials. That belongs to the lower race—the descendants of Ham."

This speech encapsulates the deeply ingrained racial prejudices and justifications for slavery that were prevalent among many Southern leaders at the time. With these declarations, the stage was set. The South had drawn its line in the sand; now it was Lincoln's turn to respond.

After his inauguration in April 1861, by which time several states had already seceded, Lincoln was confronted with the bombardment of Fort Sumter in South Carolina. The very next day, he cautiously refrained from declaring it a 'war,' choosing instead to describe it as a state of 'insurrection.' This was strategic, as acknowledging a civil war might have implied recognizing the Confederacy as a legitimate, sovereign entity, potentially leading to international recognition and support for it. Lincoln responded by calling for 75,000 volunteers to serve for three months, signaling his resolute effort to preserve the Union at all costs.

As the conflict escalated, Lincoln's rhetoric shifted accordingly. The Union government's actions, such as blockading Southern ports and calling for additional troops, led to the term 'civil war' becoming more prevalent in government communications and public discourse. The initial volunteer call after Fort Sumter received an overwhelmingly enthusiastic response, with many more men volunteering than were needed. This surge of patriotic fervor was evident in the large rallies, fervent speeches, and extensive newspaper support that characterized the early days of the conflict.

During these turbulent months, Lincoln faced significant challenges to the Union's stability, including a rebellion across several Southern states and the threat of Confederate sympathizers and spies within Union territory. In response, he controversially suspended the writ of habeas corpus, a fundamental civil liberty that protects against unlawful detention. This suspension allowed military authorities to arrest and detain individuals suspected of aiding the Confederacy or engaging in activities detrimental to the Union war effort without immediate recourse to civilian courts. This drastic measure, which Lincoln deemed necessary under the circumstances, sparked widespread debate and legal challenges regarding its constitutionality.

Critics argued that Lincoln had exceeded his presidential powers and violated individual rights. Nevertheless, Lincoln defended his decision as crucial for the survival of the Union, contending that the rebellion posed a direct threat to the government and justified extraordinary measures.

The Civil War catalyzed profound economic transformations in the United States, propelling it from a predominantly agrarian economy in the South to a Northern-led industrial society. This shift marked a significant change, as the conflict accelerated industrialization in the North, sparking advancements in manufacturing, transportation, and technology.

In the midst of these national turmoils, Lincoln faced personal tragedy in 1862 with the death of his eleven-year-old son Willie, who succumbed to typhoid fever likely contracted from the contaminated White House water supply. His intense mourning period seemed to deepen his reflections on life and death, as evidenced by a haunting dream he shared shortly after. In the dream, he wandered through the quiet rooms of the White House until he came upon a funeral in the East Room. Upon asking who had died, he was told it was the president, who had been assassinated.

This dream, often cited as an example of Lincoln's melancholic disposition and contemplation of mortality, highlights how the immense pressures of leading the nation during the Civil War and enduring personal tragedies profoundly impacted him.

On January 1, 1863, Lincoln issued the Emancipation Proclamation, a landmark decree that significantly redefined the goals of the Civil War. It asserted that the conflict was not solely about states' rights but also fundamentally about abolishing slavery. The proclamation declared that all slaves in the Confederate states currently in rebellion against the Union 'are, and henceforward shall be free.' This critical declaration shifted the war's focus to include a clear moral imperative—the destruction of slavery—which in turn, allowed the Union to recruit African American soldiers and bolstered the North's moral and political position both domestically and internationally. By undermining the labor foundation of the Confederacy, the proclamation also strategically weakened the Southern war effort.

Jefferson Davis reacted sharply to Lincoln's decree, condemning it as 'the most execrable measure recorded in the history of guilty man,' and viewing it as an attempt to incite slave insurrections. The brutal reality of this policy shift was reflected in the treatment of African American soldiers by Confederate troops, who often executed black prisoners of war, as seen in massacres at locations like Fort Pillow, Tennessee. While Lincoln championed rights for all Americans, Davis decreed the re-enslavement of 'all free Negroes in the Southern Confederacy,' highlighting the stark and brutal opposition to the Union's evolving moral stance.

Although the Emancipation Proclamation did not immediately free all slaves, it fundamentally transformed the nature of the Civil War and laid the groundwork for the eventual abolition of slavery, framing the Union's war effort as a fight for human liberty. This starkly contrasted with the Confederate leadership, which continued to advocate for and enforce a system based on racial subjugation.

Gettysburg Address

On November 19, 1863, Lincoln delivered one of the most iconic speeches in American history—the Gettysburg Address—following the Union's pivotal victory at Gettysburg, which had effectively repelled General Robert E. Lee's invasion of the North. This speech was given during the dedication ceremony for the national cemetery at the Gettysburg battlefield, a site now marked by the sacrifices of those who fought there.

Lincoln's brief yet profound address connected the immense sacrifices at Gettysburg to the foundational ideals of the Declaration of Independence. Here is the full text of the address:

"Four score and seven years ago our fathers brought forth on this continent, a new nation, conceived in Liberty, and dedicated to the proposition that all men are created equal.

Now we are engaged in a great civil war, testing whether that nation, or any nation so conceived and so dedicated, can long endure. We are met on a great battlefield of that war. We have come to dedicate a portion of that field, as a final resting place for those who here gave their lives that that nation might live. It is altogether fitting and proper that we should do this.

But, in a larger sense, we can not dedicate—we can not consecrate—we can not hallow—this ground. The brave men, living and dead, who struggled here, have consecrated it, far above our poor power to add or detract. The world will little note, nor long remember what we say here, but it can never forget what they did here.

It is for us the living, rather, to be dedicated here to the unfinished work which they who fought here have thus far so nobly advanced. It is rather for us to be here dedicated to the great task remaining before us—that from these honored dead we take increased devotion to that cause for which they gave the last full measure of devotion—that we here highly resolve that these dead shall not have died in vain—that this nation, under God, shall have a new birth of freedom—and that government of the people, by the people, for the people, shall not perish from the earth."

The ideals articulated by Lincoln at Gettysburg later resonated through the Reconstruction Amendments—the Thirteenth, Fourteenth, and Fifteenth Amendments—which abolished slavery, anchored the commitment to freedom and equality from the Declaration of Independence into the Constitution, and sought to eradicate racial discrimination in voting. These amendments were designed to realize Lincoln's vision of "a new birth of freedom," thus profoundly shaping the trajectory of American democracy.

As the Civil War progressed, support in the North became increasingly complex and divided. The prolonged conflict, mounting casualties, and economic strain severely tested Northern morale. The introduction of the draft in 1863 and the Emancipation Proclamation, which linked the war effort to the abolition of slavery, further polarized public opinion. Opposition was particularly strong among groups like the "Copperheads," Peace Democrats who advocated for immediate peace negotiations with the Confederacy. The extensive toll of the war on resources and the high casualty rates fueled a growing weariness among the general populace.

Against this backdrop of division and fatigue, Lincoln faced a challenging reelection campaign in 1864. His opponent was **George B. McClellan**, a former Union general whom Lincoln had previously dismissed. Running as the Democratic nominee, McClellan's platform, which advocated for peace negotiations, resonated with many voters exhausted by the ongoing conflict.

However, Lincoln's prospects for reelection were significantly bolstered by key Union military victories in late 1864, notably General **William Sherman**'s capture of Atlanta. Strategically crucial to the Confederacy as a major railroad center and manufacturing base for war supplies, Atlanta's capture was a major objective of Sherman's Atlanta Campaign, which began in the spring of 1864.

The campaign involved a series of battles across northern Georgia, with Sherman's forces advancing from the northwest through tactical maneuvers rather than direct assaults, eventually leading to significant Union victories.

These victories revitalized Northern morale and reinforced Lincoln's standing, demonstrating the potential for a successful conclusion to the war. This shift in the war's momentum helped to diminish the appeal of McClellan's peace platform, ultimately securing Lincoln's reelection. This victory not only affirmed public support for Lincoln's leadership but also underscored a renewed commitment to his policies of preserving the Union and ending slavery.

Lincoln's second inaugural address, delivered on March 4, 1865, stands out in American history for its tone of reconciliation and healing. With the Civil War nearing its conclusion, Lincoln opted for a tone of conciliation and unity rather than triumph. His speech was remarkably brief but deeply resonant, emphasizing national forgiveness and renewal.

In his address, Lincoln famously stated, "With malice toward none, with charity for all, with firmness in the right as God gives us to see the right, let us strive on to finish the work we are in, to bind up the nation's wounds." These words encapsulated his vision for the Reconstruction era, focusing not on victory or vengeance but on healing the divided nation and restoring the Southern states to the Union without bitterness.

The speech also reflected on the causes of the war and the immense suffering it had caused, suggesting that the war was divine punishment for the sin of slavery. Lincoln implored the nation to proceed with "malice toward none" and "charity for all" to recover from the war's devastation and to work together towards a lasting peace.

The defeat of Major General **George E. Pickett**'s Confederate forces at the Battle of Five Forks on April 1, 1865, was a pivotal moment that allowed

Union forces to cut off the South Side Railroad west of Petersburg, Virginia, the following day. This victory was crucial, setting the stage for the fall of Petersburg. Shortly after this battle, Lincoln visited the site, where the harsh realities of war deeply moved him. Observing the aftermath, Lincoln expressed his mixed feelings about the victory to Lieutenant General **Ulysses S. Grant**, lamenting, "I fear this victory has cost too much."

In the days following, against the advice of his security detail who feared for his safety amidst the unstable conditions, Lincoln made a significant visit to Richmond, which had just been abandoned by the Confederate government and suffered extensive  damage due to a massive fire. Accompanied by his young son Tad and a cadre of anxious soldiers, Lincoln walked from the wharf to key sites including the Virginia Statehouse and the Confederate White House.

During his tour, Lincoln was warmly greeted by jubilant African Americans who celebrated their impending freedom, the preservation of the Union, and the end of the war. This poignant moment was captured in an illustration by artist **Lambert Hollis**, who documented the president's reception among the crowds.

A week after Lincoln's visit to Richmond, the Civil War reached its conclusion with Lee's surrender to Grant at Appomattox Court House. By that time, Lee's forces were critically depleted, suffering from widespread desertion and failed resupply efforts. Despite a last-ditch assault to change the course of the war, Lee's efforts were unsuccessful.

The surrender proceedings began with an awkward exchange of small talk before a somber Lee steered the conversation toward the terms of surrender. Known for his clear and concise writing style, Grant quickly drafted the terms, focusing solely on military issues. At Lee's request, Grant allowed Confederate soldiers to retain their personal horses, crucial for their return to farming, and arranged for the distribution of food rations to the starving Southern troops. As Lee departed on his horse, Traveller, Union soldiers spontaneously erupted into cheers, marking the end of America's most devastating conflict.

Lee's role in promoting peace after the Civil War was pivotal in aiding national reunification. Historian Douglas Southall Freeman remarked that for Confederates, emulating Lee in peace was as patriotic as following him in war, saying, "More than any other American, Lee kept the tragedy of the war from being a continuing national calamity." Even his critics, like Civil War-era author and historian Elizabeth Brown Pryor, acknowledged his post-war contributions. Pryor noted that Lee reached his pinnacle of greatness through his "enlightened decisions to foster peace and rebuild the South in the early aftermath of the war." His dignified surrender and early calls for reconciliation not only preserved dignity but also set a standard for an army and a nation overwhelmed by defeat and destruction.

The Civil War, which spanned over four years, claimed the lives of approximately 640,000 soldiers from both the U.S. and Confederate forces—more than two percent of the combined population of the U.S. and Confederate states at the time. In the Confederate states alone, 30 percent of military-aged white men perished. The pervasive trauma of the war touched nearly every home, leaving a lasting impact on the American social and cultural landscape.

Presidential historian Doris Kearns Goodwin elaborated on this during an interview I conducted with her at the Ohio Statehouse in Columbus—the very place where Lincoln had learned in 1861 that he had been officially chosen by the electors to be president. Goodwin explained, "If Lincoln had allowed the South to go, then the framers' whole experiment would have been undone. The idea that ordinary people can govern themselves—that's what the framers counted on. This was an era of monarchs and dictators, and the idea that you could just let people govern themselves seemed very strange and it's what's so great about America. Lincoln made it possible, and he knew that's what he was fighting for. Lincoln saves the Union, wins the war, and ends slavery forever."

It is important to acknowledge that in recent years, as we have increasingly scrutinized our nation's leaders, we have sometimes found, perhaps shockingly, that they were not without flaws Lincoln, widely celebrated for his role in abolishing slavery, did make statements during his career that could be considered racist by today's standards. For example, during the Lincoln-Douglas debates in 1858, he stated, "I am not, nor ever have been, in favor of bringing about in any way the social and political equality of the white and black races." While such comments are startling today, they were not uncommon among even the more progressive individuals of his time.

The mid-19th century was an era deeply entrenched in racial prejudices and societal norms that explicitly institutionalized racism. Lincoln, navigating this complex landscape, adopted pragmatic approaches that, while reflective of his time, sometimes clash with modern ideals of equality.

However, Lincoln's presidency witnessed a significant evolution in his views on slavery and racial equality. Influenced by his interactions with African American leaders, his reflections on the legal and moral dimensions of slavery, and the shifting sentiments of the Northern public, Lincoln's stance underwent a profound transformation.

This shift was exemplified by the Emancipation Proclamation, declaring the freedom of all slaves in the rebellious states, and his staunch support for the Thirteenth Amendment, which permanently abolished slavery across the United States. These actions marked a pivotal realignment of the Civil War's aims, marrying the Union's military goals with the moral imperative of abolition.

Lincoln's evolving perspective on racial issues also garnered respect from prominent African American figures, including Frederick Douglass, who met with Lincoln on multiple occasions. Douglass, initially a critic, came to view Lincoln with great respect and nuanced understanding, particularly noting Lincoln's genuine concern for the welfare of Black Americans. Douglass described Lincoln as devoid of the common racial prejudices of his time, noting after one White House meeting in 1864, "I was never more quickly or more completely put at ease in the presence of a great man than in that of Abraham Lincoln."

After Lincoln's death, Douglass famously referred to him as "the black man's president," highlighting him as "emphatically the colored man's President: the first to show any respect to their rights as men." This recognition underscores the complexity of Lincoln's legacy as one intertwined with the striving towards greater equality.

"You have to look at leaders in the context of their times," Kearns Goodwin explained during our interview. "Consider that in the North, in states like Illinois and Ohio, there were Black Laws that prohibited African Americans from sitting on juries or having any kind of equal rights. So, it's important to judge Lincoln on how he grew and evolved, not simply on what he said back in the 1850s. What I find most interesting in Lincoln is this self-confidence, ability to think for yourself, coupled with open mindedness and willingness to listen to criticism. Lincoln rises to the occasion."

The legacy of Abraham Lincoln, the first Republican president, is both nuanced and multifaceted. Shaped by the complex societal norms of his era, Lincoln held certain beliefs influenced by the prevailing attitudes of the 19th century. However, his decisive actions during the Civil War reveal a profound commitment to transformative change. His steadfast determination to confront and challenge the deeply entrenched racism of his time has left a lasting impact on the nation's history. Undoubtedly, Lincoln stands as the first, and arguably the most significant, Civil Rights president in American history.

The Southern Successor

Just days before his assassination, President Abraham Lincoln publicly advocated for extending voting rights to African Americans. This pivotal stance, articulated in one of his last public addresses on April 11, 1865, proposed granting the franchise to certain groups, notably those who had served in the Union Army during the Civil War. Lincoln's support for black suffrage marked a significant evolution in his views on civil rights and was the first time a sitting U.S. president had explicitly endorsed voting rights for African Americans. This was particularly momentous given the contentious atmosphere following the Civil War and the complex Reconstruction processes underway in the Southern states.

Tragically, this progressive stance contributed to the motives of **John Wilkes Booth**, who became enraged upon hearing Lincoln's speech. Booth, present in the audience, declared, 'That means nigger citizenship. Now, by God, I'll put him through.' On April 14, 1865, while the Lincolns attended a comedy at Ford's Theatre, Booth entered the presidential box and fatally shot Lincoln in the back of the head. As Lincoln slumped in his chair, Booth leaped from the balcony onto the stage, proclaiming, 'Sic semper tyrannis! The South is avenged,' before fleeing.

Booth, whose diaries and letters revealed he viewed Lincoln and the Union government as tyrannical and harbored a deep-seated allegiance to Confederate ideologies, remained at large for twelve days. After being located in a Virginia barn and refusing to surrender, the barn was set on fire. Booth was subsequently shot by a Union soldier. Mortally wounded and dragged from the barn, Booth died a few hours later.

Lincoln's death profoundly shocked and grieved the country. At the moment of his passing, Secretary of War **Edwin Stanton**, once a political rival turned key cabinet member in Lincoln's 'team of rivals,' solemnly declared, 'Now he belongs to the ages.' Lincoln had believed that surrounding himself with intelligent, albeit occasionally disagreeing, men was preferable to leaving them as adversaries. This approach highlighted his strategic and inclusive leadership style. Many Americans, who had viewed Lincoln as the leader who guided the nation through its most perilous period, were plunged into despair by his sudden assassination. Public expressions of mourning were widespread and intense. Buildings and homes were draped in black bunting, and people wore black armbands as signs of their grief. Lincoln's funeral procession from Washington, D.C., to his final resting place in Springfield, Illinois, drew large crowds of mourners along the route, reflecting the deep respect and affection held for him. The nation's mourning reflected not only sorrow over the loss of a beloved leader but also anxiety about the future of a nation still fractured by war and now facing reconstruction without Lincoln's guidance. His assassination tragically cut short the potential for a more progressive and extensive post-war Reconstruction effort under his leadership.

In June 1865, amidst the national period of mourning, a profound event unfolded in Galveston, Texas. Major General **Gordon Granger**, leading a group of Union soldiers, made a historic announcement that marked the official end of the Civil War and the emancipation of all enslaved people in the region. This announcement came two and a half years after Lincoln's Emancipation Proclamation, which had officially outlawed slavery in the Confederate states effective January 1, 1863. Due to slow and inconsistent enforcement, especially in remote areas like Texas, many were still enslaved until Granger's declaration. Delivered via General Order Number 3, the announcement stated: 'The people of Texas are informed that, in accordance with a proclamation from the Executive of the United States, all slaves are free.' This momentous day, combining the words June and nineteenth, became known as Juneteenth, and is also referred to as Emancipation Day or Juneteenth Independence Day. It was officially designated as a federal holiday in 2021.

After the surrender of General Robert E. Lee and the assassination of Lincoln by a Confederate sympathizer, newly inaugurated President **Andrew Johnson** swiftly acted against the rebel leader, Jefferson Davis. Johnson issued a substantial reward of $100,000—equivalent to about $1.8 million today—for the capture of Davis as he attempted to flee southward. Weeks later, Union troops located the former Confederate leader in Georgia. In a hasty attempt to evade capture, Davis threw on his wife's waterproof cloak or shawl, which led to some initial confusion among the soldiers who mistook him for a woman. Capitalizing on this mix-up, Northern cartoonists, in the tense aftermath of the bloody war, gleefully depicted him in women's dresses, fueling public ridicule.

Davis was subsequently captured and taken to Fort Monroe near Norfolk, where he was shackled and confined to a small, guarded room. A federal court in Washington indicted him for treason, accusing him of conspiring to 'stir, move, and excite rebellion, insurrection, and war' against the United States. This indictment aligned with the Union's view of Davis as a traitor, who had led the Southern states in seceding from the Union. His leadership was widely criticized, even within his own military, Congress, and among the public, as the Confederacy crumbled under his presidency.

The trial of the 57-year-old Davis was set to be held in Richmond, the former Confederate capital. However, the proceedings were marred by significant delays and debates over how to handle the case. Some officials feared that convicting Davis might reopen the wounds of the Civil War. Moreover, an acquittal could potentially legitimize the Confederate rebellion. The complex legal and political issues led to Davis remaining in prison for two years under worsening health conditions. Eventually, his bail was set at the substantial sum of $100,000.

Davis was released in May 1867, thanks to efforts from influential supporters and Northerners who believed that a trial would only deepen national divisions. Following his release, Davis remained defiant and unrepentant. In a notable 1884 speech to the Mississippi Legislature, he declared, 'It has been said that I should apply to the United States for a pardon. But repentance must precede the right of pardon, and I have not repented... If it were all to do over again, I would again do just as I did in 1861.' Davis later settled in Mississippi, where he wrote his memoirs, defending the Southern cause and his role in the war.

Davis continued to be a controversial figure, embodying the Lost Cause ideology for many in the South until his death on December 6, 1889, in New Orleans. The delays in his trial ultimately prevented him from facing justice, leaving his legal status and the legitimacy of his actions a topic of historical debate and contention. Reflecting on Davis's legacy, Senator Henry Wilson remarked, 'Jefferson Davis will go down to posterity with the stigma of having been the head of a great band of robbers and murderers, who for four years desolated the fairest portion of this country.'

Although Lincoln witnessed the passage of the 13th Amendment by Congress and actively supported and influenced its approval, he did not live to see its ratification process completed, leaving a pivotal moment in American history without his guiding presence.

The 13th Amendment, which abolished slavery, was indeed a cornerstone of what would become a series of measures aimed at rebuilding and redefining American society after the Civil War. These measures, known as the Reconstruction Amendments, include the 13th, 14th, and 15th

Amendments. Each played a crucial role in shaping the legal framework for civil rights in the United States:

1. **13th Amendment (1865)**: This amendment abolished slavery and involuntary servitude, except as punishment for a crime. It was a monumental step in ending the institution of slavery, which had deeply divided the country.

2. **14th Amendment (1868)**: This amendment addresses several aspects of citizenship and the rights of citizens. The most significant sections assert that all persons born or naturalized in the United States are American citizens, including former slaves, and are guaranteed equal protection of the laws. It also includes provisions about the due process clause, which ensures fair treatment through the normal judicial system, and it addresses post-Civil War issues related to the former Confederate states.

3. **15th Amendment (1870)**: This amendment prohibits the government from denying a citizen the right to vote based on that citizen's "race, color, or previous condition of servitude." It was aimed at enabling the newly freed slaves and other non-white citizens to participate in the electoral process, although many states implemented laws that effectively circumvented this amendment and disenfranchised many African Americans until the Civil Rights Movement of the 1960s.

Following the war, the former Confederate states were compelled to draft new constitutions and were only readmitted to the Union after ratifying the 14th Amendment. The 15th Amendment, meanwhile, empowered over half a million Black men in the South during the 1870s, although women would not achieve national voting rights until 1920. These new voters predominantly supported the Republican Party, the party of Lincoln, whom they revered as the Great Emancipator. While Republicans secured various significant offices, including governorships and Senate seats in Southern states, white candidates continued to win a substantial majority of state and local offices throughout the South. This period was marked by significant electoral participation from these new Black voters, yet the overall political landscape remained dominated by white officials.

Hannibal Hamlin, who served as Abraham Lincoln's Vice President from 1861 to 1865, experienced mixed feelings about being replaced on the ticket for Lincoln's second term. While he understood the strategic political reasoning behind this decision, it undoubtedly came with personal disappointment. However, Hamlin remained a dedicated supporter of the Union cause. In 1864, as the Civil War continued, Lincoln selected Andrew Johnson, the Democratic Military Governor of Tennessee, as his new vice-presidential candidate. This choice was strategically aimed at bolstering his re-election prospects by promoting national unity and inclusiveness.

Johnson, who supported the Northern war effort, played a key role in Lincoln's strategy to forge a coalition that included both War Democrats and moderate Republicans. This was particularly critical in border states and Northern areas with significant Democratic populations. At a time when Lincoln's popularity was suffering due to the ongoing war and its heavy casualties, this diverse alliance was crucial.

Lincoln's choice of Johnson highlighted his pragmatic approach to governance, seeking to unify a divided country through a symbolic cross-party partnership. The inclusion of a Southern Democrat like Johnson also balanced the ticket, combining Lincoln's progressive policies with Johnson's more moderate stances. This strategic blend aimed to appeal to a wide range of voters, easing concerns about the nation's post-war direction.

Following Lincoln's assassination, Johnson assumed the presidency and took charge of Reconstruction. His approach to rebuilding the post-Civil War South significantly diverged from Lincoln's vision, leading to profound conflicts with Congress that altered the course of recovery. Lincoln had proposed a lenient plan for Reconstruction, known as the "10 percent plan," which allowed for the reintegration of Southern states into the Union once 10 percent of their 1860 election voters swore an oath of allegiance to the Union and agreed to abide by emancipation. His primary aim was reconciliation, intending to heal the nation swiftly and without punitive measures.

While Johnson also favored leniency towards the South during Reconstruction, he allowed Southern states considerable freedom in re-establishing their governments. This leniency sparked controversy, as Johnson's conservative stance on Reconstruction—deeply rooted in his views on race and states' rights—contrasted sharply with the Radical Republicans in Congress. The Radical Republicans advocated for strict policies to dismantle the old Southern order and pushed for civil and voting rights for freed slaves. Key figures among the Radical Republicans were Senator **Charles Sumner** of Massachusetts and Representative **Thaddeus Stevens** of Pennsylvania. Both were vocal supporters of abolition and instrumental in the passage of the Reconstruction Amendments. Stevens also played a crucial role in establishing the Freedmen's Bureau to help former slaves transition to freedom.

One of the most infamous episodes of political violence in American history occurred on May 22, 1856, when Sumner was brutally attacked by Representative **Preston Brooks** of South Carolina in the United States Senate chamber. This shocking conflict arose from a speech Sumner delivered two days earlier, titled 'The Crime Against Kansas,' in which he fiercely criticized the spread of slavery into Kansas and insulted several pro-slavery senators, including **Andrew Butler** of South Carolina. Feeling that Sumner's remarks had dishonored his family and the South, Brooks, a pro-slavery advocate and a relative of Butler, retaliated by striking Sumner repeatedly with a heavy gutta-percha cane while the senator was seated at his desk in the

Senate chamber. Trapped under the bolted-down desk, Sumner struggled to free himself and was left bleeding and unconscious. Brooks continued his assault until his cane broke.

The brutality of the attack left Sumner with traumatic brain injuries that necessitated years of recovery. He was absent from the Senate for much of this time but retained his seat. After resigning his seat, Brooks was overwhelmingly re-elected in a special election by his constituents in South Carolina, who largely viewed his act as a justifiable defense of Southern honor. This incident dramatically escalated tensions between the North and South and is often cited as a prelude to the American Civil War.

Johnson's approach to Reconstruction became particularly apparent when he reversed General William Sherman's Special Field Orders No. 15. Initially, this order had allocated approximately 400,000 acres of land along the coasts of South Carolina, Georgia, and Florida to be distributed as homesteads to African American families. Each family was to receive up to 40 acres of confiscated Confederate land. Moreover, the Army planned to allocate unneeded mules to these families, aiding their efforts to establish self-sustaining farms. However, Johnson rescinded these orders, thereby returning the land to its former Confederate owners. This reversal effectively nullified the promise of "forty acres and a mule," a profound blow to the freed slaves who hoped for security and a self-sustaining future. The failure to fulfill this promise left many without the necessary resources to support their newfound freedom, significantly hampering their transition to independent lives.

Furthermore, Johnson vetoed several key Reconstruction bills, including the Civil Rights Bill of 1866 and the second Freedmen's Bureau Bill. These bills were essential for defining and supporting the transition of African Americans from slavery to freedom and often included measures for land redistribution. Despite their significance, Johnson's vetoes were overridden by Congress, highlighting the deep divisions between his administration and the legislative branch on Reconstruction.

Johnson's lenient approach also facilitated the emergence of "Black Codes," laws passed by Southern states to restrict African Americans' freedoms and ensure a labor force similar to that of slavery. This lax enforcement in protecting civil rights led to significant tensions between Johnson and the Radical Republicans, who sought a transformative approach to Reconstruction. During his "Swing Around the Circle" speaking tour in 1866, Johnson infamously stated, "This is a country for white men, and by God, as long as I am President, it shall be a government for white men." This tour was an attempt by Johnson to gain public support for his lenient Reconstruction policies and his stance against the more radical measures proposed by Congress, which included broader rights for freed slaves.

The tour proved to be politically disastrous for Johnson. His speeches often included confrontational rhetoric, and he sometimes engaged in verbal altercations with hecklers. His inflammatory remarks, such as the one about the government being for white men, only served to alienate him further from the Radical Republicans and many in the Northern public who were sympathetic to the cause of civil rights for freedmen.

Johnson's presidency was characterized by these tensions and his frequent clashes with a Congress dominated by the Radical Republicans. These conflicts culminated in his impeachment, primarily over his alleged violation of the Tenure of Office Act by firing Secretary of War Edwin Stanton, a key Radical Republican ally. The broader disputes over Reconstruction policies further fueled the impeachment efforts. Johnson narrowly avoided removal from office, as the Senate vote fell just one short of the necessary two-thirds majority for conviction.

His tenure was further marred by personal issues, including allegations of alcoholism, which damaged his public image and undermined his effectiveness. Johnson left office under a cloud of disgrace, marking his presidency as a pivotal yet turbulent period in American political history.

Elizabeth R. Varon, a professor of American history at the University of Virginia, offers a critical perspective on Johnson's presidency. She notes that as the first president after the Civil War, "Johnson did more to extend the period of national strife than he did to heal the wounds of war."

In the aftermath, the Democratic Party solidified its opposition to the Republican-led Reconstruction efforts, gradually regaining its stronghold over the South. This resurgence was characterized by the emergence of "yellow dog Democrats"—voters so loyal to the Democratic Party that they would rather vote for a mutt than a candidate from Lincoln's party, underscoring the deep-seated resistance to the Republican agenda in the region. David Goldfield, an expert on this period, explains, "The Democratic Party came to be more than a political party in the South—it came to be a defender of a way of life. And that way of life was the restoration as much as possible of white supremacy. The Confederate statues you see all around were primarily erected by Democrats."

AIn the tense environment of Reconstruction, several prominent white Southerners notably supported civil rights, despite prevailing racial prejudices. **James Longstreet**, a leading Confederate general during the Civil War and a trusted lieutenant to Lee, notably joined the Republican Party after the war. His support for Reconstruction policies and civil rights for African Americans alienated him from many former Confederates, leading to backlash from the Southern white community who considered him a traitor for his collaboration with the Louisiana Reconstruction government and his command of African American troops.

George Washington Cable, born in New Orleans in 1844, emerged as a prominent author and journalist. He became famous for his vivid depictions of Southern life, particularly Creole culture and racial complexities, in works such as "Old Creole Days" and "The Grandissimes: A Story of Creole Life." Cable was also a vocal critic of racism and segregation, using his literary talents to advocate for social justice and making him a significant figure in American literature and social commentary.

William Mahone, another former Confederate general, distinguished himself as a strategic leader during the Civil War. After the war, he served as a U.S. Senator from Virginia and led the Readjuster Party, advocating for civil rights and the political inclusion of African Americans. His efforts helped to reduce racial tensions and improve conditions for African Americans during a critical period in American history.

Despite their significant roles during the Reconstruction era, both Sumner and Stevens began to fade from the forefront of American politics after their unsuccessful attempt to remove Johnson from office. Both faced increasing opposition and challenges within their own party, and from the changing priorities of the nation.

Reconstruction Regrets

The initial optimism that Republicans had for Ulysses S. Grant, revered as a Civil War hero expected to invigorate Southern Reconstruction, quickly faded. His presidency soon became overshadowed by the severe economic crisis of 1873, known as the Panic of 1873, which spiraled into a prolonged depression affecting both the United States and Europe. Characterized by collapsing property values, failing railroads, and widespread agricultural distress, this economic downturn diverted Northern Republicans' focus and resources from critical issues like racial equality and integration, leading to a gradual decline in their commitment to Reconstruction.

Grant entered the White House with considerable reluctance, as politics held little appeal for him. He had previously voted for Democrats in both 1856 and 1860 and only aligned with Republican values during Lincoln's reelection, influenced by his experiences as a military officer. As the last former slaveholder to be elected president, Grant's military role forced him to consider African Americans both as human beings and soldiers. Although he did not fully transcend the racism of his era, he assumed responsibility for all who served under him, regardless of race. Like Abraham Lincoln, Grant believed in extending governmental responsibility to veterans, and he saw denying civil rights and citizenship to those who had fought as contrary to his sense of duty. However, Grant also harbored some of Andrew Johnson's sympathies for the Southern whites, influenced by his friendships with many Southern officers from the old army, his marriage to a Southerner related to Confederate General James Longstreet, and his avoidance of pre-war sectional debates.

This background helps explain why Grant's approach to Reconstruction was marked by inconsistencies. While he assertively deployed federal troops to South Carolina to uphold the civil rights of African Americans, his efforts were less vigorous in other Southern states like Louisiana, where challenges to

Reconstruction persisted. He advocated for legislation which allowed him to suspend the writ of habeas corpus and impose martial law in areas where local officials failed to protect citizens' rights. His administration took decisive action against the Ku Klux Klan—a secret society committed to maintaining white dominance—by deploying federal troops and leveraging the newly established Justice Department to combat this domestic terrorism.

Reconstruction state governments, controlled by a mix of carpetbaggers (northern whites with varying motives), scalawags (Southern whites who supported Reconstruction), and former slaves, varied in integrity. Critics often described these governments as carnivals of corruption. Enforcement of Reconstruction laws waned over time as northerners grew weary of the ongoing resistance by Southern whites to any attempts at controlling state governments and subjugating the black population. This frustration led to efforts to achieve these ends by other means, suggesting that any condemnation of the Grant administration for abandoning Reconstruction reflects a broader national failure.

As the war years receded, Southern whites eventually regained control over the South. During this period, white Southern Democrats, initially marginalized during Reconstruction, spent over a decade strategically planning to regain their former influence. Their primary aim was to end Reconstruction and reassert control over the region's social and political landscape.

Early in his presidency, Grant invited his former Confederate counterpart, Robert E. Lee, to the White House. This meeting was as stiff as their previous encounter at Appomattox four years earlier. **Adam Badeau**, who served under Grant and was close to him, described how the conversation awkwardly turned to the topic of railroads. Grant attempted to lighten the mood, jokingly remarking to Lee, "You and I, General, have had more to do with destroying railroads than building them." However, Lee did not respond with a smile or engage with the humor, and the meeting concluded after just 15 minutes.

The context of their military and post-war interactions was further complicated by significant actions taken by the Union. Notably, the area around Lee's Arlington House was transformed into a military cemetery, now known as Arlington National Cemetery. This strategic decision effectively prevented the Lee family from reclaiming the property. Additionally, in 1863, the government established Freedman's Village on the same property, a community designed to support self-emancipated African Americans.

Despite his defeat and the significant loss of his pre-war status, Lee is often credited with supporting reconciliation. However, he spent his post-war years under the shadow of potential treason charges and did not actively support Reconstruction efforts. Publicly, he continued to express beliefs aligned with white paternalism and supremacy. Lee passed away in 1870, leaving a legacy that remains steeply controversial. Reflecting on this, **Ty Seidule**, a retired U.S. Army brigadier general and author, critically assessed Lee's military and post-war contributions, noting, "No one has lost more completely in American history than Robert E. Lee. There is no general that has been more crushed, more defeated, at the strategic, tactical, operational level. How much genius does it take to lose absolutely and completely?" This statement highlights the intense and ongoing debates about Lee's role and impact, both as a military leader and in the broader context of American history.

Throughout his presidency, Grant remained committed to national unity. By mid-1870, all former Confederate states had complied with the necessary conditions for readmission to the Union. In 1872, he signed the Amnesty Act, restoring voting rights and eligibility to hold office to nearly all former Confederates. Grant also strongly supported the 15th Amendment, which guaranteed voting rights to all male citizens, irrespective of race, color, or previous condition of servitude.

In addition, Grant took a markedly different approach to Native American relations than his predecessors, notably diverging from Andrew Jackson's

 policies such as the Trail of Tears. He condemned policies aimed at Native American extinction and advocated for a more humane approach. Grant supported extending full citizenship to Native Americans, a goal that was eventually realized in 1924. This policy shift represented a significant change in the U.S. government's approach to Native American affairs and

underscored Grant's broader commitment to reform and justice for marginalized communities.

In an intriguing historical twist, Grant faced a challenge from Horace Greeley in the 1872 presidential election. Greeley was the candidate for both the Democratic Party and the Liberal Republican Party, the latter formed by Republicans dissatisfied with Grant's handling of Reconstruction and corruption allegations. Despite his long-standing ties to the Republican Party, Greeley accepted the nomination from the Liberal Republicans and received endorsement from the Democrats, who saw a chance to unseat Grant by backing a candidate appealing to both reform-minded Republicans and Democrats. Despite this coalition, Greeley was unsuccessful, and Grant secured a decisive victory for a second term.

Although Grant remained relatively clean and sober during his presidency, his administration was tarnished by accusations of bribery involving high-ranking officials, including his Attorney General and Secretary of War. The Whiskey Ring scandal implicated his private secretary in defrauding the government of tax revenues. Financial manipulators **Jim Fisk** and **Jay Gould** tricked Grant into inadvertently aiding their scheme to corner the gold market, leading to the Black Friday financial crisis. Moreover, Grant's own brother, Orvil, was involved in a kickback scheme that led the military to overpay for supplies. These scandals significantly eroded public trust, overshadowing many of his achievements.

Known for his leadership during the Civil War, Grant found the complex political landscape of post-war America challenging to navigate. His presidential leadership, though well-intentioned, was not as effective as his military command, reflecting the difficulties he faced in reconciling the diverse and often conflicting demands of a nation in transition. The presidents who succeeded him similarly struggled to effectively address these challenges, marking a period of continued turbulence and uncertainty in American leadership during the critical years following the war.

Rutherfraud

The 1876 election, marking the end of Grant's presidency, unfolded amid significant controversy. **Samuel Tilden**, the Democratic nominee from New York, clearly surpassed Ohio Representative **Rutherford B. Hayes**, the Republican candidate, in the popular vote. Yet, allegations of electoral fraud, election violence, and the disenfranchisement of predominantly Republican Black voters clouded the results. After the initial count, Tilden had secured 184 electoral votes—just one shy of victory—while Hayes had 165, with 20 votes from Florida, Louisiana, South Carolina, and Oregon remaining unresolved due to disputes.

Southern Democrats, eager to regain political control and curtail the Reconstruction efforts that had empowered Black populations, resorted to violent intimidation. Paramilitary groups like the Red Shirts and the White League, composed predominantly of white Southern Democrats, played instrumental roles. The Red Shirts, active mainly in Mississippi, South Carolina, and North Carolina, were known for their distinctive red shirts, which they wore as a uniform at rallies and acts of violence, serving both as a symbol of their allegiance and an intimidation tactic. Their primary objective was to restore Democratic control of the South by disrupting Republican meetings, intimidating or physically preventing Blacks from voting, and using violence to influence elections. They were particularly influential during the 1876 presidential election.

Meanwhile, the White League, founded in 1874 and primarily active in Louisiana, was more organized and militant than the Red Shirts. They openly declared themselves as the "military arm of the Democratic Party" and were responsible for acts of large-scale violence aimed at reversing the political gains made by Blacks and Republicans. Notable incidents involving the White League include the Colfax Massacre of 1873, where they killed over 100 African American men, and the Battle of Liberty Place in 1874, where they fought against the racially integrated New Orleans police and state militia to challenge the Reconstruction government.

To address the constitutional crisis, Congress established the Electoral Commission, predominantly composed of Republicans. A pivotal meeting at the Wormley Hotel in Washington, D.C., led by Congressman **James Garfield** of Ohio—who would later become president—resulted in the Compromise of 1877. This agreement included promises by Southern Democrats to cooperate with Hayes's policy initiatives and awarded all twenty disputed electoral votes to Hayes in exchange for the withdrawal of the last federal troops from the South. This compromise earned Hayes the derisive nickname "Rutherfraud," as many viewed his presidency as illegitimately secured at the expense of Black civil rights.

Tilden, a millionaire lawyer serving his first term as Governor of New York, gained national fame for his role in dismantling the corrupt Tweed political ring of Tammany Hall. Despite having legitimate complaints about election fraud, Tilden conceded defeat graciously, stating, "I can retire to public life with the consciousness that I shall receive from posterity the credit of having been the instrument of averting civil war."

Thomas Nast, a formidable political cartoonist, was celebrated for his sharp depictions of the corruption of Tammany Hall, the Civil War, and the Reconstruction era, as well as his steadfast anti-slavery and anti-segregation stances. His incisive critiques of political events and figures significantly influenced public opinion and political discourse. In one of his most evocative pieces, "A Truce - Not a Compromise, but a Chance for High-toned Gentlemen to Retire Gracefully from Their Very Civil Declarations of War," Nast vividly captured the essence of the Compromise of 1877.

Published in *Harper's Weekly* at the time, this illustration portrays the end of the Reconstruction era not as a genuine compromise but as a mere cessation of hostilities, allowing leaders from both the South and the North to step back from their confrontational stances. Nast depicted these "high-toned gentlemen" — politicians from both sides — as retiring "gracefully" from their public disputes. His critical tone suggests a lack of honor in how these politicians navigated the crisis, particularly in their abandonment of the promises of Reconstruction and the rights of freed slaves. Nast used visual elements like weary expressions and tired postures to communicate the moral compromise and exhaustion of the situation.

Today, Nast's cartoons serve as a potent reminder of how satire and visual commentary can challenge political corruption and advocate for social justice. His work continues to spark discussions about the importance of integrity and transparency in public affairs, illustrating the power of art to provoke thought and prompt societal reflection. Moreover, Nast is renowned for significantly shaping the modern image of Santa Claus. He skillfully combined elements from earlier traditions and introduced unique touches, which helped cement Santa's image in the public consciousness as the cheerful and benevolent figure known worldwide today.

The Compromise, largely orchestrated by Democrats, allowed them to continue supporting the Southern slave-holding aristocracy and maintain their political influence while ostensibly stepping back from direct conflict. Almost immediately after Hayes was inaugurated and federal troops were withdrawn, Southern Democratic leaders reneged on their promises. This led directly to the resurgence of white supremacist groups and the establishment of laws that effectively disenfranchised African Americans. The failure of Southern Democrats to uphold their promises had long-lasting effects, marking the beginning of a prolonged period of systemic racial segregation and inequality that persisted until the civil rights movements of the mid-20th century.

Before his presidency, Hayes was celebrated as a staunch defender of the Union and an advocate for civil rights. However, his support for the Compromise of 1877 marked a significant departure from these principles as he prioritized political expediency over long-term ethical commitments. Hayes believed his administration would better serve African Americans than his opponent's, yet this decision led to complex and morally ambiguous choices that have marked his political legacy. While he invited African American leaders to the White House and publicly supported African American causes—actions that held symbolic importance—they did not lead to substantial policy shifts. Ultimately, despite his intentions, the compromise ended Reconstruction and significantly rolled back civil rights protections, casting a long shadow over the advancements his presidency might have otherwise supported.

During these tumultuous political times, **Lucy Webb Hayes**, often affectionately called "Lemonade Lucy," brought her own set of values and influences to the White House. As the first First Lady to hold a college degree, having graduated from Wesleyan Female College in Cincinnati, Ohio, in 1850, Lucy was deeply religious and a staunch advocate for education and veterans' welfare. Her decision not to serve alcoholic beverages at White House functions, reflecting her support for the temperance movement, was both praised and criticized, underscoring her commitment to personal conviction that paralleled her husband's more controversial political compromises. Her tenure as First Lady from 1877 to 1881, marked by warm hospitality and social graces, earned her much admiration despite the controversy over her temperance stance.

Historians like William Gillette, in his book "Retreat from Reconstruction, 1869–1879," suggest that the end of Reconstruction could have been handled with more finesse. Emory University historian Dan T. Carter highlights that Hayes's decision to remove the troops was made under limited political options and a lack of broad support, leading to a controversial decision to "knuckle under to terrorism."

Yearning to Breathe Free

The United States has long been celebrated as a nation of immigrants—a melting pot where men and women from diverse backgrounds have sought refuge and opportunity. Historically, many of these immigrants fled religious or political persecution, war, or intolerable socioeconomic conditions in their home countries, each wave contributing uniquely to the fabric of American society.

For decades, America welcomed these new arrivals with open arms, allowing them to integrate into the country's economic and political life. Immigrants built new lives, enriching their adopted country with their diverse cultures and aspirations. However, over time, the initially wide-open doors began to close, and the narrative around immigration shifted. The nation saw growing concerns about the challenges posed by new immigrants, leading to restrictive policies that sought to control who could enter.

The unveiling of the Statue of Liberty on October 28, 1886, at New York Harbor was a historic event. Officially titled "Liberty Enlightening the World," this imposing figure stands 305 feet tall, a monumental gift from France symbolizing the shared values of freedom and democracy cherished by both nations.

As the day of the unveiling approached, the statue's sculptor, **Frédéric Auguste Bartholdi**, watched over the bustling harbor, teeming with hundreds of vessels each carrying passengers eager to witness this significant moment. However, the project faced considerable financial challenges, especially concerning the funding required for its substantial pedestal. When it became apparent that the French funds were insufficient, **Joseph Pulitzer**, a Hungarian immigrant and the publisher of the "New York World," took a proactive approach to resolve the crisis.

Pulitzer launched a fervent fundraising campaign, appealing directly to the American public. His call resonated not just with the affluent but especially with the poor, the middle class, and thousands of schoolchildren who contributed their spare change—pennies, dimes, and quarters. Pulitzer's passionate pleas emphasized the communal nature of the effort. "We must raise the money!" he declared in his newspaper. "The World is the people's paper, and now it appeals to the people to come forward and raise the money... Let us not wait for the millionaires to give this money. It is not a gift from the millionaires of France to the millionaires of America, but a gift of the whole people of France to the whole people of America." This grassroots campaign successfully amassed over $350,000, an impressive sum for that era, ensuring that the pedestal could be completed and the statue fully assembled.

The Statue of Liberty has evolved into a global symbol of human rights, frequently referenced in discussions and movements advocating for freedom and justice worldwide. Constructed from copper and designed to endure the harsh conditions of New York Harbor, the statue not only represents resilience and endurance but also reflects the lasting nature of the principles it upholds. As such, the Statue of Liberty transcends its role as a physical monument to become a profound emblem of universal ideals that resonate around the world.

During this time, inspired by the sight of Jewish immigrants arriving in America and fleeing pogroms in Russia, poet **Emma Lazarus** wrote "The New Colossus." Her famous lines, "Give me your tired, your poor, Your huddled masses yearning to breathe free," later inscribed on the statue's pedestal, forever linked the Statue of Liberty with the ideals of refuge and welcome.

Nearby, Ellis Island opened on January 1, 1892, as the nation's premier federal immigration station, serving as the gateway for millions seeking new opportunities in the United States. This facility was pivotal in the history of American immigration, especially in 1891, the year before it opened, when the U.S. witnessed a significant influx of approximately 430,000 immigrants.

During this period, substantial immigration from Germany, Italy, and Ireland led to significant social and political upheavals, primarily in the northern states. German immigrants faced notable prejudices; while Catholic Germans experienced religious discrimination, Germans in general were often perceived as insular and resistant to assimilation into American society. This perception stemmed from their continued use of the German language and adherence to cultural traditions, setting them apart from mainstream American culture.

Italian immigrants grappled with both racial prejudices and cultural barriers. The largest wave of Italian immigration to the United States began in the 1880s and peaked between 1900 and 1914, driven by economic hardship, overpopulation, and natural disasters. These immigrants often faced considerable discrimination due to their predominantly Catholic faith in a primarily Protestant country, as well as linguistic and cultural differences. Those from Southern Italy encountered even harsher treatment, often stereotyped and mistreated because of their darker complexions—a reflection of the broader racial prejudices prevalent in the U.S. at the time. This discrimination was evident in segregation in housing and employment, and extended to acts of violence and racial slurs, mirroring the struggles endured by Black Americans.

Similarly, Irish immigrants were predominantly Catholic, fueling fears among Protestants that they were more loyal to the Pope than to American democratic principles. Popular culture and media often portrayed the Irish as unruly, intemperate, and prone to violence, further marginalizing them within society. Economically, Irish immigrants typically found themselves in the lowest-paid and most hazardous jobs, stirring resentment among American workers who viewed them as threats to their employment opportunities. The Irish were often accused of depressing wages and worsening living conditions by accepting lower pay and enduring poor working conditions.

In 1886, Seattle became the epicenter of a severe outbreak of anti-Chinese violence, part of a broader wave of racial hostility that swept through the American West Coast during the late 19th century. This incident was marked by violent mobs storming through parts of the city, destroying property, and forcibly expelling around 200 Chinese residents. The mob loaded these individuals onto ships bound for San Francisco, effectively purging them from the city following the rioting. This violent reaction was fueled by economic tensions, as Chinese immigrants were often willing to work for lower wages than other workers. This willingness made them targets for resentment during economic downturns, as they were perceived as undercutting the wages of other laborers.

The situation in Seattle was not an isolated event but a manifestation of widespread anti-Chinese sentiment prevalent across the Pacific Northwest and other parts of the United States during this period. The anti-Chinese riots in Seattle and similar events in other cities highlighted the harsh realities of racial prejudice and the struggles of Chinese immigrants in America. These incidents led to increased public and legislative actions aimed at restricting Chinese immigration and rights, culminating in laws like the Chinese Exclusion Act of 1882. This legislation not only limited immigration but also set a precedent for future immigration restrictions based on race and nationality.

Reflecting on these historical challenges, **Thomas Paine**'s vision of the United States as "an asylum for the persecuted lovers of civil and religious liberty" seems at odds with the reality many immigrants faced. The treatment of newcomers often contradicted the warm welcome Paine had envisioned, as reflected in the struggles they endured, poignantly captured in his words from 'The American Crisis': "These are the times that try men's souls."

Between the dedication of the Statue of Liberty in 1886 and its centennial rededication in 1986, approximately 25 to 35 million immigrants arrived in the United States. This figure underscores the significant changes in U.S. immigration policy—from the massive influx during the late 19th and early 20th centuries to restrictive measures in the mid-20th century, eventually giving way to more liberalized laws. These shifts highlight the evolving American attitudes toward immigrants and the diverse origins of those seeking a new home in the U.S., as Ellis Island emerged as a powerful yet complex symbol of America's welcoming spirit.

Forgotten Chances

Between the presidencies of Rutherford B. Hayes and Herbert Hoover, progress in civil rights was notably slow and marred by setbacks, affecting African Americans and other minorities deeply. During this period, **Grover Cleveland**, a Democrat, navigated a significant personal scandal in his first presidential campaign in 1884. He was accused by Maria Halpin of fathering her child and allegedly orchestrating the child's placement in an orphanage and her commitment to a mental asylum. Cleveland never explicitly denied paternity but claimed he was assuming responsibility perhaps to shield the reputations of his married friends who might have been involved.

The Republican opposition capitalized on this scandal with the taunt, "Ma, Ma, where's my Pa?" Despite the potential damage, Cleveland's approach to the allegations helped him retain enough public support to secure his election, after which his supporters retorted, "Gone to the White House, ha, ha, ha!" This incident highlights an early instance of personal scandal in American presidential politics and showcases Cleveland's adeptness at managing political controversies.

During his presidency, Cleveland was known for his extensive use of the veto, particularly against hundreds of private pension bills for Civil War veterans he deemed unqualified, reflecting his dedication to reducing government spending. In foreign policy, he maintained a non-interventionist stance, withdrawing from the Pan-American Conference and showing restraint in extending U.S. influence overseas.

Domestically, Cleveland faced criticism for opposing critical civil rights legislation, such as the Lodge Bill or Federal Elections Bill of 1890, which aimed to protect African American voting rights in the South by ensuring federal oversight in elections to prevent fraud and intimidation. His opposition was crucial to the bill's failure in the Senate.

Cleveland was defeated for reelection in the 1888 election by **Benjamin Harrison** due to a faltering economy, strategic Republican focus on swing states, and allegations of electoral misconduct. Despite this setback, his wife, **Frances Cleveland**, confidently told the staff that they would return in four years, a promise that materialized when Cleveland defeated Harrison in the 1892 rematch. This victory was driven by widespread economic unrest, factionalism within the Republican Party, and Cleveland's sustained popularity, making him the first former president to reclaim the office after a defeat.

Despite these political victories, Cleveland's presidencies were tarnished by his inaction on the rampant lynching of African Americans in the South. His failure to publicly address these atrocities or support federal anti-lynching legislation essentially condoned the violence through his silence. This lack of advocacy for civil rights was a profound oversight in his administration, occurring in an era already marked by regressive policies and discriminatory attitudes toward racial equality.

In stark contrast, Republican President **Theodore Roosevelt** took a firm stand against lynching and made a significant gesture by inviting **Booker T. Washington** to the White House, making him the first African American to be invited to a formal dinner there. This event symbolized an unprecedented level of respect and recognition from the highest office in the land, but it also sparked considerable controversy and backlash, particularly in the South. Many white Americans were outraged by the implied social equality of a Black man dining with the President. The backlash was severe enough that Roosevelt never extended another meal invitation to Washington, though they continued to maintain a professional relationship.

Despite Roosevelt's generally progressive stance, his presidency was not without racial missteps. One such incident was the Brownsville Affair. On the night of August 13-14 in Brownsville, Texas, a shooting erupted, resulting in the death of a white bartender and the wounding of a white police officer. Despite a lack of evidence, local white residents immediately blamed the Black soldiers stationed at nearby Fort Brown, driven largely by racial prejudices.

The investigation into the incident was highly biased. Townspeople produced shell casings from army rifles, but there was no substantial proof linking the soldiers to the crime. Nevertheless, Roosevelt ordered the dishonorable discharge of 167 Black soldiers of the 25th Infantry Regiment without a trial. This decision stripped the soldiers of their pensions and barred them from reenlisting in the army. Roosevelt's action sparked widespread criticism, particularly from civil rights leaders and organizations, casting a shadow over his otherwise progressive administration.

The soldiers steadfastly maintained their innocence, and the case became a focal point for civil rights advocacy. After decades of persistent efforts to seek justice, the U.S. Army conducted a new investigation in 1972. This investigation concluded that the soldiers had been wrongfully accused, leading to their exoneration and the posthumous reinstatement of their honorable discharges. The Brownsville Affair remains a poignant example of racial injustice in the early 20th century, highlighting the enduring struggle against racial discrimination, even under a progressive administration.

During President **Woodrow Wilson**'s tenure, his administration saw a regression on racial issues, notably re-segregating multiple agencies within the federal government. Wilson also hosted a screening of "The Birth of a Nation" at the White House, a film that glorified the Ku Klux Klan and depicted African Americans in a deeply racist manner. Additionally, African American soldiers faced significant racial discrimination during World War I, reflective of Wilson's segregationist policies.

Despite over 350,000 Black men being drafted or enlisted, most were assigned to segregated units and relegated to labor and support roles. However, combat units like the 92nd and 93rd Divisions, particularly the 369th Infantry Regiment known as the Harlem Hellfighters, demonstrated exceptional bravery. The Harlem Hellfighters spent more time in continuous combat than any other American unit and were recognized with France's Croix de Guerre for their valor. One returning Harlem Hellfighter poignantly stated, "We returned fighting, not just for America but for the respect we deserved from our countrymen."

Wilson's failure to formally acknowledge the heroism of African American troops was consistent with his administration's broader policy of enforcing segregation in the military and other federal policies. This period of tension and injustice reached its zenith during the Red Summer of 1919, when a series of race riots broke out in over three dozen U.S. cities. These riots were often sparked by the return of Black veterans who, after defending democracy abroad, demanded equal rights at home and were increasingly unwilling to tolerate racial discrimination and violence. The economic competition, particularly in job and housing markets, further exacerbated these racial tensions. Notable riots in Chicago, Elaine, Arkansas, and Washington, D.C., marked this era as a critical and bloody chapter in American history, highlighting the enduring systemic racism that contrasted sharply with the battlefield valor of these soldiers.

Just as Black veterans sought the rights they had defended abroad, women, led by visionaries such as **Susan B. Anthony**, **Elizabeth Cady Stanton**, and **Lucy Stone**, fought tirelessly to dismantle another pillar of systemic inequality: the denial of their voting rights. The synchronization of these movements marked a period of intense social transformation, where both African Americans and women used their growing visibility and voices to challenge and redefine their roles within American democracy. Anthony, in her relentless pursuit of change, famously challenged male legislators who had long denied women's suffrage, stating, "Cautious, careful people, always casting about to preserve their reputations can never effect a reform." This bold declaration encapsulated the essence of the suffrage movement, mirroring the unyielding courage and willingness to challenge deeply ingrained prejudices that were also evident in the struggle of returning Black veterans, as both groups sought to reshape American society.

The movement was also marked by the emergence of other powerful voices like **Carrie Chapman Catt**, who founded the League of Women Voters and was instrumental in the eventual passage of the 19th Amendment. Another prominent figure, **Alice Paul**, organized the 1913 Women's Suffrage Parade in Washington, D.C., which became a key moment in publicizing the suffrage cause. Paul later formed the National Woman's Party, which pushed the boundaries of public protest by picketing the White House.

The suffrage movement faced considerable opposition and underwent many challenges, including internal divisions over strategy and racial inclusion, with African American suffragists like **Ida B. Wells** and **Mary Church Terrell** advocating for suffrage in the broader context of civil rights for all races. The movement's tactics evolved from peaceful demonstrations to more radical acts of civil disobedience and hunger strikes, particularly during World War I, which heightened the visibility of women's contributions to the war effort and underscored their argument for equal citizenship.

On the topic of women's suffrage, Wilson was initially skeptical but ultimately endorsed it, influenced by women's significant contributions during the war. The 19th Amendment, granting women the right to vote, was passed by Congress on June 4, 1919, and ratified by the required number of states on August 18, 1920. It was officially certified on August 26, 1920. This historic achievement was celebrated nationwide with parades, rallies, and public gatherings, notably a massive victory parade in New York City. Despite the celebrations, Wilson refrained from releasing any statement upon its passage and did not attend any of the celebrations, which marked a significant milestone in women's rights and set the stage for further advances in gender equality.

In the 1920 presidential election, **Eugene Debs**, a notable labor leader and socialist, campaigned for the presidency from his jail cell. Serving a ten-year sentence under the Espionage Act of 1917 for his anti-war stance during World War I, Debs' speech against the war had been judged as interfering with military recruitment. Despite his imprisonment, he managed to secure nearly a million votes, running under the memorable slogan "For President: Convict No. 9653." Debs was renowned for addressing themes of equality and justice in his speeches. His Canton speech, which directly led to his incarceration, is particularly famous for discussing the link between labor rights and civil liberties. Beyond speaking, Debs also contributed extensively to socialist publications, writing articles advocating for the end of racial discrimination and economic inequality.

His campaign and ongoing activism highlighted the growing emergence of labor unions, which would continue to advocate vigorously for workers' rights in the decades to follow. This movement saw significant strides in improving working conditions, establishing fair wages, and securing rights for the working class, shaping the labor landscape deeply into the 20th century. Until the 2024 presidential campaign of **Donald Trump**, Debs held the unique distinction of being the only felon to receive such a substantial number of votes. He was unconditionally pardoned in 1921.

President **Warren G. Harding** attended the dedication of the Lincoln Memorial on May 30, 1922, a poignant and majestic event held on Memorial

Day to underscore its national significance. The ceremony attracted thousands, including **Robert Todd Lincoln**, Abraham Lincoln's only surviving son. Although Robert Todd Lincoln did not speak, his presence added a deeply personal touch to the proceedings, bridging the past with the present. The ceremony was marked by solemnity, with military bands and choirs providing a stirring backdrop. They played the National Anthem and rendered military honors to Lincoln, acknowledging his critical role as Commander-in-Chief during the Civil War.

Harding celebrated Lincoln's enduring legacy as the savior of the Union and a steadfast advocate for freedom and equality. However, in an ironic twist, his administration censored the speech of Dr. **Robert Moton**, the principal of Tuskegee Institute and a prominent African American leader. Cautious about the political ramifications of allowing a Black speaker to address racial issues too directly in such a public and symbolic forum, the administration muted the original fervor of Moton's remarks. As a result, the speech that was delivered subtly addressed the ongoing struggle for equality and the significance of Lincoln's legacy for the current civil rights issues faced by African Americans.

The dedication of the memorial served as a powerful symbol of reunification and a tribute to the ideals that Lincoln championed, marking it as a significant event in the annals of American history.

During his presidency, Republican **Calvin Coolidge** signed the National Origins Act into law on May 26, 1924. This legislation, reflecting his belief in maintaining American homogeneity, significantly expanded upon measures such as the Emergency Quota Act of 1921. It instituted a more restrictive quota system that set annual admission limits to 2% of the population of each nationality as recorded in the United States during the 1890 census. This specific choice effectively curtailed immigration from southern and eastern Europe, regions that had seen high emigration rates to the U.S. in preceding decades.

Moreover, the Act continued the exclusion of Asian immigrants, reinforcing prohibitions that began with the Chinese Exclusion Act of 1882 and were extended by the establishment of the Asiatic Barred Zone in 1917. This continued exclusion was part of a broader national policy influenced by racial ideologies that favored immigration from northern and western Europe, reflecting widespread attitudes about race and desirability at the time.

This legislation solidified the exclusion of Asian immigrants, continuing policies set by earlier laws. The restrictive quotas imposed on Eastern and Southern Europeans drastically reshaped U.S. immigration policy. Heavily influenced by the eugenics movements and nativist sentiments of the era, the act not only curtailed immigration from regions deemed less desirable but also entrenched racial discrimination within immigration laws.

Speakeasy, Bootlegger & Teetotaler

The Temperance movement in the United States, which spearheaded the national cessation of legal alcohol consumption, reached its peak with the ratification of the 18th Amendment, establishing Prohibition. This movement began in the 19th century and was initially driven by figures like Reverend **Lyman Beecher**, an early leader of the American Temperance Society. Beecher equated drunkenness with moral failings akin to murder, highlighting the spiritual and societal decay linked to alcohol.

As the movement gained momentum, it attracted support from various organizations, including the Women's Christian Temperance Union (WCTU) and the Anti-Saloon League. These groups highlighted the moral and economic implications of alcohol, emphasizing the need for sober, reliable workers and the economic drawbacks of alcoholism on productivity and social stability. Deeply rooted in religious convictions, many Protestant churches advocated for temperance as a Christian duty, leading to widespread evangelical temperance meetings and revivals across the nation.

When Prohibition was enacted, it unveiled stark racial disparities in law enforcement. African Americans and other minorities often faced harsher penalties and more aggressive policing, reflecting the broader societal prejudices of the era. Political success for the temperance movement was solidified on December 18, 1917, when Congress, under Democratic President Woodrow Wilson, passed the 18th Amendment. Although Wilson vetoed the Volstead Act, which set the enforcement guidelines for Prohibition, his veto was overridden by Congress. His opposition stemmed more from concerns about the act's feasibility and enforcement rather than a fundamental disagreement with the temperance movement.

Prohibition officially began in January 1920, banning the manufacture, sale, and transport of alcoholic beverages across the United States. However, it led to unintended consequences and widespread noncompliance, epitomized by the proliferation of speakeasies—clandestine bars where alcohol was secretly sold and consumed. Law enforcement raids on these establishments were often corrupt and racially discriminatory, disproportionately targeting venues frequented by African Americans and immigrants, thereby exacerbating social tensions.

In the 1920s, the Ku Klux Klan experienced a resurgence, partly by positioning itself as an enforcer of Prohibition. The original Klan had dissolved during Reconstruction after government intervention, but it revived with a new focus closely tied to anti-immigrant and anti-Catholic sentiments. White,  Anglo-Saxon Protestants who viewed themselves as the only "real Americans" believed the country was under siege by Catholic immigrants from countries like Italy, who they claimed threatened American values with their drinking customs and saloons.

Thomas R. Pegram, a history professor at Loyola University Maryland and author of *One Hundred Percent American: The Rebirth and Decline of the Ku Klux Klan in the 1920s*, explains, "Prohibition became a way in which cultural supremacy could be enforced in local communities." This provided the Klan with a pretext to act as a vigilante force, ostensibly upholding the law against these immigrant groups. Membership skyrocketed, reaching between two to five million from 1920 to 1925.

During this period, organized crime expanded significantly, with notorious gangsters like **Al Capone** dominating the illicit alcohol trade. Capone, a central figure in the Chicago underworld, was implicated in numerous murders associated with his control of the liquor business. Although the exact number of killings he personally committed is unknown, newspapers from the time reported at least 522 gang-related deaths. Capone's era of dominance ended with his conviction for income tax evasion, and he ultimately died while still incarcerated.

During the 1920s, Republican Presidents Warren G. Harding and Calvin Coolidge approached the challenges of Prohibition differently. Harding, who privately opposed the policy, kept alcohol in the White House for personal use, underscoring the era's hypocrisy. In contrast, Coolidge supported Prohibition as a moral and social policy, maintaining a publicly dry White House and emphasizing the importance of law enforcement without actively campaigning against alcohol consumption.

Also in this decade, **Prince Edward**, who later became the Duke of Windsor, visited New York. Known for his charm and wit, he humorously commented on the seemingly ineffective Prohibition laws in the United States by asking, "Great, when does it begin?" This quip highlighted the widespread perception that despite legal restrictions, alcohol was readily available in the U.S., casting doubt on the law's effectiveness.

As the 1930s began, Republican President **Herbert Hoover** described Prohibition as a "great social and economic experiment, noble in motive and far-reaching in purpose." However, by the end of his term, the failure of Prohibition was apparent, prompting Hoover to call for a national commission to review its enforcement and effectiveness.

The repeal of Prohibition ultimately occurred under Democrat **Franklin D. Roosevelt**, who had openly opposed it during his presidential campaign. His administration facilitated the ratification of the 21st Amendment in 1933, officially ending Prohibition, which is often described as a "great disaster" by historians and scholars due to its wide-ranging negative consequences and the failure to achieve its intended goals. Roosevelt famously remarked, "I think this would be a good time for a beer," although he personally celebrated with a martini, reflecting his preference for this classic cocktail.

The day after legal liquor began to flow in 20 states, an Associated Press headline from New York appeared underwhelmed: "No drunks on Broadway, no roisterers anywhere." Prohibition lasted less than 15 years, but it left behind a significant legacy. When it ended, the U.S. government had a more powerful FBI and more prisons. As for the Klan, the upheaval and chaos that it created during the 1920s eroded its support in the following decade. Yet, the organization's history didn't end there. It experienced its third resurgence during the civil rights movement and saw an uptick in activity and increased national attention after the 2016 presidential election.

Jim Crow Era

While northern immigrants faced discrimination, African Americans in the South endured the harsh realities of Jim Crow laws. These state and local statutes institutionalized racial segregation and upheld white supremacist ideologies. Enacted by legislatures dominated by white Southern Democrats, Jim Crow laws systematically stripped away the political and economic gains Black Americans had achieved during Reconstruction.

Moreover, many Christian ministers and theologians propagated beliefs that reinforced racial hierarchies. They taught that white people were the chosen people, Black people were cursed to be servants, and that God endorsed racial segregation. This theological justification further entrenched racial inequality and supported the oppressive structures of the Jim Crow era.

Formal legal segregation was cemented by the landmark Supreme Court case Plessy v. Ferguson in 1896, which sanctioned racial segregation under the "separate but equal" doctrine. **Homer Plessy**, a man of mixed race, was arrested in 1892 for sitting in a "whites-only" car on a Louisiana train. Plessy deliberately violated the state's Separate Car Act to challenge the legality of segregation. He argued that the law violated the Equal Protection Clause of the 14th Amendment. However, both the lower court and the Louisiana Supreme Court upheld the law, and the Supreme Court affirmed these decisions.

The ruling legitimized state laws that institutionalized racial discrimination and segregation, profoundly affecting American society and civil rights. Jim Crow signs were placed above water fountains, door entrances and exits, and in front of public facilities. There were separate hospitals for Black people and white people, separate prisons, separate public and private schools, separate churches, separate cemeteries, separate public restrooms, and separate public accommodations.

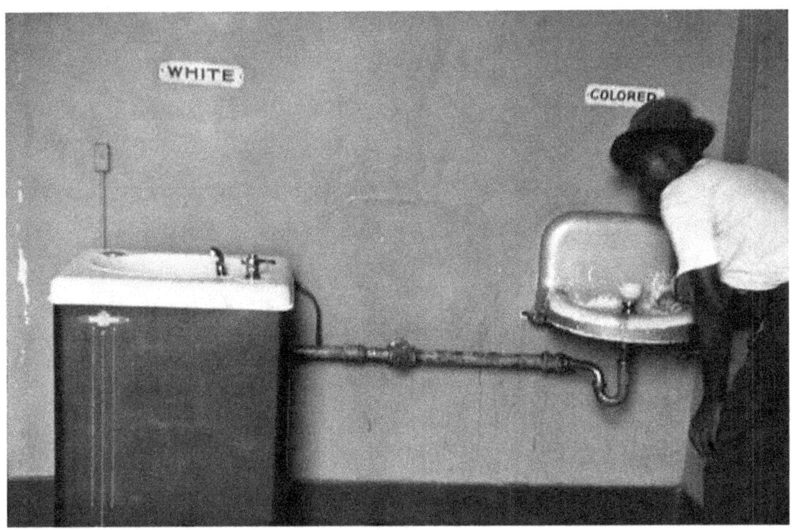

Jim Crow laws also severely restricted African American voting rights through the implementation of literacy tests, poll taxes, and grandfather clauses, effectively disenfranchising many. Frederick Douglass, in an 1887 letter, described the injustices in the South not merely as explicit legal measures but as "the hidden practices of people who have not yet abandoned the idea of mastery and dominion over their fellow man." Racism, violence, and vigilantism became tools to maintain this mastery, reinforcing a deeply ingrained social order of inequality.

Economically, many African Americans were confined to low-paying jobs or sharecropping, a system that often led to perpetual debt and poverty. Racial violence and lynching were rampant, frequently carried out with local law enforcement complicity or direct involvement.

Examples of Jim Crow laws across the United States illustrate this dark chapter:

- Texas: "The County Board of Education shall provide schools of two kinds; those for white children and those for colored children."
- Florida: "Any negro man and white woman, or any white man and negro woman, who are not married to each other, who shall habitually live in and occupy in the nighttime the same room shall each be punished by imprisonment not exceeding twelve months, or by fine not exceeding five hundred dollars."
- Tennessee: "All railroads carrying passengers in the state (other than street railroads) shall provide equal but separate accommodations for the white and colored races, by providing two or more passenger cars for each passenger train, or by dividing the cars by a partition, so as to secure separate accommodations."
- North Carolina: "The state librarian is directed to fit up and maintain a separate place for the use of the colored people who may come to the library for the purpose of reading books or periodicals."
- South Carolina: "No persons, firms, or corporations, who or which furnish meals to passengers at station restaurants or station eating houses, in times limited by common carriers of said passengers, shall furnish said meals to white and colored passengers in the same room, or at the same table, or at the same counter."
- Georgia: "It shall be unlawful for any amateur white baseball team to play baseball on any vacant lot or baseball diamond within two blocks of a playground devoted to the Negro race, and it shall be unlawful for any amateur colored baseball team to play baseball in any vacant lot or baseball diamond within two blocks of any playground devoted to the white race."
- Oklahoma: "The Conservation Commission shall have the right to make segregation of the white and colored races as to the exercise of rights of fishing, boating and bathing."
- Mississippi: "There shall be maintained by the governing authorities of every hospital maintained by the state for treatment of white and

colored patients separate entrances for white and colored patients and visitors, and such entrances shall be used by the race only for which they are prepared."

- Virginia: "The conductors or managers on all such railroads shall have power, and are hereby required, to assign to each white or colored passenger his or her respective car, coach or compartment. If the passenger fails to disclose his race, the conductor and managers, acting in good faith, shall be the sole judges of his race."
- Nebraska: "Marriages are void when one party is a white person and the other is possessed of one-eighth or more negro, Japanese, or Chinese blood."
- Missouri: "Separate free schools shall be established for the education of children of African descent; and it shall be unlawful for any colored child to attend any white school, or any white child to attend a colored school."
- Alabama: "It shall be unlawful for a negro and white person to play together or in company with each other in any game of cards or dice, dominoes or checkers."

Moreover, restrictive covenants in various communities barred African Americans, and sometimes other groups including Jews, Asians, and Latinos, from many neighborhoods, further cementing racial segregation. These oppressive conditions eventually spurred the Great Migration, as millions of African Americans moved north and west between 1916 and 1970, seeking better opportunities and escaping the harsh realities of the Jim Crow South.

Spiritually Surviving

Despite enduring generations of discrimination based solely on the color of their skin, African Americans have persevered and built robust religious, cultural, and social institutions. These institutions have been pivotal in providing education, spiritual support, and strategies for resisting oppression. Their resilience and communal spirit have enabled African Americans to sustain a rich cultural heritage and foster a strong sense of identity and community solidarity, which have been essential in their ongoing struggle for justice and equality.

A cornerstone of these institutions is the African American church, which has long served as a hub for social organization, education, and political activism. For instance, the African Methodist Episcopal (AME) Church, founded by **Richard Allen** in Philadelphia in 1816, has offered not only spiritual guidance but also served as a critical meeting place for civil rights activities and voter registration drives.

Education has also been a major focus, with the establishment of Historically Black Colleges and Universities (HBCUs) such as Howard University and Morehouse College, both founded in 1867. These institutions provided African Americans with access to higher education when most traditional routes were closed to them, fostering not only academic achievement but also a sense of identity and empowerment.

Civic engagement has also been crucial in advancing African American rights. Organizations such as the National Association for the Advancement of Colored People (NAACP), founded in 1909, have spearheaded efforts to combat lynching, segregation, and disenfranchisement. The National Urban League, established in 1910, focused on economic empowerment, helping African Americans gain access to jobs and educational opportunities.

Moreover, mutual aid societies like the Free African Society, founded in 1787, and fraternal organizations such as the Prince Hall Freemasonry, have provided financial and social support, fostering leadership and economic resources within African American communities.

Amazing Performances

In the world of sports and entertainment, African Americans continued to face and challenge systemic barriers. In 1910, retired undefeated heavyweight champion **Jim Jefferies** returned to the ring in Reno, Nevada, to challenge **Jack Johnson**, the first black heavyweight champion. Johnson, who had won the title in 1908, faced immense racism, exacerbated by his marriages to white women and his defiance of societal norms. Billed as the "Great White Hope," Jefferies was expected to reclaim the title for white America. However, Johnson defeated Jefferies in the 15th round, intensifying racial tensions and leading to severe backlash against him. Ultimately, Johnson was forced to flee the country due to dubious morals charges a few years later.

Similarly, **Jim Thorpe**, an Oklahoma-born American Indian, made history at the tiny Carlisle Indian School, elevating it to top status in football and track. At the 1912 Stockholm Olympics, Thorpe's remarkable versatility allowed him to win gold medals in both the pentathlon and decathlon. However, when it was revealed that Thorpe had played semi-professional baseball before the Olympics, violating the strict amateurism rules, his Olympic medals were stripped, and his achievements erased from the record books. While similar violations by other athletes were overlooked or handled less severely, Thorpe's punishment was swift and harsh, leading many to believe that racial prejudices played a part in the decision. His family did not see his medals restored until 1982, nearly 30 years after his death.

As these athletes confronted and challenged systemic barriers, baseball continued to embed itself deeply within American culture. The sport began taking its modern shape in the 1840s and 1850s, with the first officially recorded game under contemporary rules occurring in 1846 in Hoboken, New Jersey. By 1876, the National League was established, becoming the oldest existing Major League. This development set the stage for the upstart American League, which emerged to challenge the more established National League, leading to the inaugural World Series in 1903.

"Take Me Out to the Ball Game," a song penned by vaudevillian **Jack Norworth** in 1908, became famously associated with Katie Casey, a fictional protagonist who exemplifies the growing interest of women in baseball during the early 20th century. This song captures the spirit of American fans—both men and women—who enjoyed peanuts and Cracker Jacks as they cheered for their teams from the stands. By this time, baseball had firmly established itself as America's pastime, reflecting not just a sport but a cultural phenomenon that appealed across genders and social barriers, uniting a diverse nation through its sheer joy and competitive spirit.

In 1920, addressing the need for organized competition among African Americans who were barred from Major League Baseball due to racial segregation, **Andrew "Rube" Foster** founded the Negro National League. This league, along with others that followed, provided a platform for exceptionally talented players like **Josh Gibson**, who might otherwise have been overlooked. By 2024, Major League Baseball had formally recognized these contributions, amending its record books to include the achievements of Negro Leagues players—an acknowledgment long overdue of their skills and impact on the sport.

The struggle for racial equality in baseball reached a pivotal point in 1947 when Brooklyn Dodgers president **Branch Rickey** chose **Jackie Robinson** to break the color barrier. Aware of the significant challenges Robinson would encounter, including racial slurs and segregation, Rickey tested his resolve with hard-hitting questions. In a memorable interaction, Rickey questioned how Robinson would handle extreme racial insults, even hypothetically using a derogatory term to simulate the hostility he would face. Rickey's goal was clear: "I want you to be the first Negro player in the major leagues. I've been trying to give you some idea of the kind of punishment you'll have to absorb. Can you take it?"

Robinson's affirmative response underscored his bravery and resilience. His successful career not only advanced his personal achievements but also paved the way for the integration of other African American players, marking a significant step toward desegregating American sports and contributing to the civil rights movement. The integration of baseball symbolized broader societal shifts and the gradual movement toward racial equality, reflecting the critical role sports have played in cultural and social transformations.

The Jazz

The music of the Civil Rights era played a pivotal role in both reflecting and instigating societal shifts toward racial equality, shaping the narrative of the struggle for civil rights in the United States. Jazz, deeply rooted in African American history, emerged in the late 19th and early 20th centuries in New Orleans. This genre, which melded African rhythms, blues, and ragtime, showcased the cultural diversity of one of the South's most vibrant cities and became a medium through which African American musicians expressed both the joys and adversities of their lives. During the Harlem Renaissance of the 1920s, jazz spread beyond its birthplace, becoming a staple in American culture and influencing broader perceptions of race and culture. Jazz clubs, often among the few integrated spaces in America, allowed people of all races to unite through their shared appreciation of music.

Into the 1950s, **Elvis Presley**, dubbed "The King of Rock and Roll," became emblematic of the era's complex cultural dynamics. His frequent visits to black jazz clubs during his early years significantly influenced his musical style.

Growing up in Tupelo, Mississippi, and later in Memphis, Tennessee, Elvis was immersed in a diverse musical landscape. Memphis, a melting pot of blues, gospel, and jazz, offered a rich tapestry of African American culture that heavily influenced his musical development. The rhythms, melodies, and vocal techniques he observed in these clubs played a crucial role in shaping his own musical style, which eventually blended elements of pop, country, gospel, and rhythm and blues into the emerging genre of rock 'n' roll. Beyond just musical inspiration, these visits allowed Elvis to immerse himself in the cultural and social milieu that he loved, giving him a greater appreciation and respect for African American music and culture.

As Elvis rose to stardom, several African American singers who also achieved significant success faced considerable racial discrimination, yet their contributions helped shape the musical landscape of the era. **Chuck Berry**, often hailed as the father of rock and roll, brought innovative guitar playing and an energetic stage presence that made songs like "Johnny B. Goode" anthems of the new genre. Despite his immense influence, Berry contended with racial prejudice and legal injustices that marred his career.

Little Richard, known for his flamboyant performance style and powerful vocals, was a pioneer in rock and roll with hits like "Tutti Frutti" and "Long Tall Sally." Beyond the challenges of racial discrimination, he also struggled with societal acceptance of his identity and sexuality. **Nat King Cole** was a master pianist and velvet-voiced singer who became one of the first African Americans to host a national television show, "The Nat King Cole Show." Despite widespread acclaim, Cole faced racism that reached as far as physical attacks on stage and barriers to buying a home in an upscale neighborhood.

Sam Cooke, referred to as the "King of Soul," enchanted audiences with his smooth, soulful voice through hits like "You Send Me" and "A Change Is Gonna Come." Active in the Civil Rights Movement, Cooke navigated significant obstacles within a segregated music industry. **Ella Fitzgerald**, the

"First Lady of Song," was renowned for her purity of tone and impeccable diction. Despite her immense talent and acclaim, Fitzgerald faced the indignities of racial discrimination while touring, performing, and using public facilities.

Ray Charles, a pioneer of soul music, combined R&B, gospel, and blues into a compelling musical style. Blind from a young age, Charles triumphed over his disability and racial barriers with hits like "Hit the Road Jack" and "Georgia on My Mind," although he too faced the harsh realities of segregation. **Billie Holiday**'s song "Strange Fruit" became an anthem against lynching and racial violence, with its powerful imagery and her haunting delivery making it a critical piece in the fight for civil rights despite significant personal and professional risks.

James Brown, the "Godfather of Soul," had his music and performances resonate powerfully. Songs like "Say It Loud – I'm Black and I'm Proud" became anthems for the Black Power movement, directly addressing racial pride and the struggle for equality. **Mahalia Jackson**, a gospel singer with a powerful voice, significantly contributed to the Civil Rights Movement, with her rendition of "Take My Hand, Precious Lord" at the March on Washington in 1963 underscoring the role of gospel music in the movement.

Josephine Baker, although gaining fame in France, was an influential African American entertainer and civil rights activist. She refused to perform for segregated audiences in the U.S. and worked with the NAACP, speaking at the March on Washington in 1963. **Fats Domino**, a pioneer of rock and roll, faced segregation and discrimination while touring despite his significant contributions to the genre.

The **Freedom Singers**, established in 1962 in Albany, Georgia, by Cordell Reagon of the Student Nonviolent Coordinating Committee (SNCC), were a vital part of the Civil Rights Movement. The group, originally comprising

Cordell Reagon, **Bernice Johnson** (who later founded Sweet Honey in the Rock), **Charles Neblett**, and **Rutha Harris**, harnessed the power of music to drive the civil rights agenda. They aimed to educate and mobilize communities through performances that included spirituals, gospel songs, and freedom songs from the African American musical tradition.

Songs like "We Shall Overcome" and "This Little Light of Mine" became anthems of the movement, sung during marches, mass meetings, and on picket lines. **Nina Simone**'s politically charged performances, with songs like "Mississippi Goddam" and "To Be Young, Gifted and Black," also became anthems for the civil rights movement.

In the 1960s, **Bob Dylan**'s "The Times They Are a-Changin'" and Cooke's "A Change Is Gonna Come" both resonated deeply with those advocating for civil rights, providing not only solace but also a rallying cry for change.

Dylan's song, released in 1964, spoke directly to the urgency for change and the dynamism of the social movements of the time. With its compelling lyrics, it called on people from all walks of life to recognize and participate in the transformative currents sweeping through society. Dylan's message was clear: change was not only necessary but inevitable, and it was time for everyone to lend a hand.

On the other hand, Cooke's "A Change Is Gonna Come," released the same year, became an emblematic voice of hope and resilience. Inspired by personal experiences of racial discrimination and other Civil Rights movement stories, Cooke's song voiced the frustrations and aspirations of African Americans.

The soulful melody and poignant lyrics encapsulated the longing for justice and equality, making it one of the most influential songs of the era.

A poignant example of what black artists faced during this era involves **Dionne Warwick**, a prominent African American singer known for hits like "Walk On By" and "Say a Little Prayer." While touring through the American South, Warwick encountered the harsh reality of segregation. One night, she was performing in a club where a rope segregated white and black audience members. Opposed to such discrimination, Warwick took a courageous stand by walking over and removing the rope herself. This act of defiance was not only significant but also perilous, given the prevalent racial tensions and strict enforcement of segregation laws at the time. Warwick's actions angered the local authorities, and she was nearly arrested for her defiance. Although she ultimately avoided arrest, the incident underscores the challenges and discrimination African American artists faced while touring in the South during the civil rights era.

Overall, the music of the Civil Rights era not only bridged racial divides but also challenged social norms and provided a voice to the marginalized. This period highlighted the significant role that cultural expressions play in driving societal change, setting the stage for future musical innovations that continue to draw on America's diverse cultural influences, enriching its musical heritage even further.

Depression, World War & Civil Rights

In the 1930s and 1940s, President Franklin D. Roosevelt faced an unprecedented array of challenges during his presidency. In addition to his efforts on civil rights, he guided the nation through two of its most significant crises: the Great Depression and World War II.

When Roosevelt took office in 1933, the United States was mired in the depths of the Great Depression, with unemployment rates soaring to 25%. In response, Roosevelt launched the New Deal, an unprecedented series of programs, public work projects, financial reforms, and regulations. These initiatives aimed to restore dignity and prosperity to Americans, significantly expanding the government's role in the economy. They were designed to provide relief, recovery, and reform amidst the severe economic crisis. A landmark achievement of his administration came on August 14, 1935, when Roosevelt signed the Social Security Act into law. This legislation established a social insurance program that guaranteed a continuing income after retirement for workers aged 65 or older, marking a significant development in the nation's social welfare policies.

As Roosevelt focused on revitalizing the American workforce and economy, the global stage was set for further upheaval with the onset of World War II. Initially, Roosevelt was hesitant to involve the United States in the conflict. However, the attack on Pearl Harbor on December 7, 1941, marked a decisive turn when Roosevelt declared war on Japan, and shortly thereafter, on Germany and Italy. His leadership during the war was pivotal, encompassing significant military strategy and the domestic mobilization of the economy to support the war effort, effectively transforming the U.S. into the "Arsenal of Democracy."

Roosevelt's leadership was crucial in rallying public support and adeptly managing complex military alliances with key nations such as the UK and

USSR. His guidance helped navigate the U.S. through a comprehensive economic mobilization, transforming the nation into a vital support system for the Allied forces. These efforts were instrumental in confronting and ultimately overcoming tyrants like **Adolf Hitler** and **Benito Mussolini**, who were committed to spreading fascism and dictatorship globally, posing severe threats to democratic governance worldwide.

As the war unfolded, the world gradually became aware of Hitler's horrific actions, responsible for the murder of over six million Jews during the Holocaust. This genocide was part of a broader, cruel policy that also targeted Communists, Socialists, and other political opponents, who were among the first to be arrested and incarcerated in concentration camps. Additionally, gays, blacks, and an estimated quarter million physically and mentally disabled individuals suffered under Hitler's fanatical beliefs in racial purity and the supremacy of the 'Aryan' race. The Holocaust and the broader Nazi genocide represent one of the most extensive and systematic attempts in human history to exterminate entire groups of people based on ideologically driven definitions of race and purity. The devastating impact of these actions has left a lasting imprint on the world, underscoring the dangers of racist and exclusionary ideologies.

Roosevelt's strategic leadership and his ability to mobilize the American economy and military were instrumental in the Allied victory, marking a significant chapter in global history. His efforts not only contributed to the defeat of fascism but also set the stage for a new era of international cooperation and the advancement of human rights, shaped by the lessons of the war and the need to prevent such atrocities from recurring. These actions highlighted the stakes of the conflict and underscored the moral imperative of the Allied fight.

However, this era also came with significant costs, particularly for Japanese Americans. In response to the attack on Pearl Harbor, Roosevelt signed

Executive Order 9066 on February 19, 1942, which authorized the forced relocation and incarceration of approximately 120,000 Japanese Americans. These individuals, labeled as 'enemy aliens,' were primarily residents of the West Coast states like California, Washington, Oregon, and Arizona. The policy was driven by wartime hysteria, racial prejudice, and unfounded fears of espionage and sabotage. Entire families, including children, were uprooted and placed in internment camps situated in remote areas across states such as Utah, Colorado, Wyoming, Arkansas, and Idaho. Despite the absence of any evidence supporting security concerns, Japanese Americans were stripped of their civil liberties and subjected to harsh living conditions.

Lt. Gen. **John DeWitt**, head of the Western Defense Command, encapsulated the prevailing attitudes with his statement, "The Japanese race is an enemy race. And while many second and third-generation Japanese born on United States soil, possessing United States citizenship, have become 'Americanized,' the racial strains are undiluted."

This sentiment echoed decades of anti-Asian policies, such as the Chinese Exclusion Act of 1882 and the Immigration Act of 1924, which banned immigration from Asia and reflected the racial prejudice and xenophobia that characterized American attitudes toward Asians long before Pearl Harbor.

The internment led to severe economic impacts for Japanese Americans, who were forced to abandon their homes, businesses, and possessions, resulting in significant financial losses. Legal challenges to the internment reached the U.S. Supreme Court in cases like Korematsu v. United States (1944) and Hirabayashi v. United States (1943), where the Court upheld the internment and related curfews as wartime necessities. These decisions have been widely criticized and partially overturned in subsequent years.

Life in the internment camps was difficult, with internees living in hastily constructed barracks, suffering from limited privacy, and enduring inadequate facilities in harsh environments. Despite their internment, many Japanese Americans served in the U.S. military during the war, with the 442nd Regimental Combat Team becoming one of the most decorated units in U.S. military history.

First Lady **Eleanor Roosevelt** expressed concern about the internment policy. She visited the Gila River War Relocation Center in Arizona in 1943 and wrote about her visit in her "My Day" newspaper column, highlighting the resilience and patriotism of the internees and questioning the necessity of their confinement. Although not publicly vocal against the policy at the time, she worked behind the scenes to advocate for better conditions for the internees and supported efforts to secure their release. She believed the internment was a violation of civil liberties, reflecting her broader commitment to human rights and social justice.

Franklin Roosevelt did not publicly express remorse for the internment during his presidency, framing the decision as necessary for national security. Over the years, public perception of the internment has evolved, with many Americans recognizing it as a violation of civil liberties. The Civil Liberties Act of 1988 provided a formal apology and reparations of $20,000 to each surviving internee and established a public education fund to ensure that the lessons of the internment are remembered. Several states and institutions have also issued their own apologies and commemorations.

In April 2013, a Japanese American Internment Museum was established near the site of the former Rohwer internment camp in Arkansas. The opening ceremony was notably headlined by actor **George Takei**, famed for his role as

Lt. Hikaru Sulu on "Star Trek." Takei shared his personal experiences during the event, recounting how at age 5, he and his family were forcibly removed from their Los Angeles home at gunpoint by U.S. soldiers and sent to Rohwer, simply because they resembled the people who had bombed Pearl Harbor. He described his childhood years spent in harsh conditions: "in the swamps—fetid, hot, mosquito-laden. ... Block 6, Barrack 2, Unit F. We were little more than numbers to our jailers, each of us given a tag to wear like a piece of luggage. My tag was 12832-C." Takei's prominence significantly contributed to raising awareness about the internment.

Southern Lynchings

FDR's presidency, marked by the formidable challenges of the Great Depression and World War II, was also a significant period for civil rights, with **Eleanor Roosevelt** playing a pivotal role. Eleanor, a staunch advocate for equality, made a profound impact when she famously resigned from the Daughters of the American Revolution in 1939. This resignation came after the organization refused to allow **Marian Anderson**, a celebrated Black singer, to perform at Constitution Hall. Her commitment extended further as she joined the NAACP during FDR's first term and worked closely with NAACP leader **Walter White** to push for anti-lynching legislation. This advocacy made her the target of considerable animosity and death threats.

Critics of her husband, including **J. Edgar Hoover**, the influential director of the Federal Bureau of Investigation, spread racist rumors that she was of mixed race, attempting to undermine her credibility and influence. By the 1950s, her advocacy had made her enemies so vehement that the Ku Klux Klan placed a $25,000 bounty on her head. Eleanor Roosevelt's actions during this era underscore a complex chapter in the nation's history, highlighting both her courage and the severe resistance she faced.

Eleanor's steadfast pursuit of these causes also created tensions with President Roosevelt, who felt constrained by the political realities of the time. In early 1934, FDR confided in White about the delicate political balance he had to maintain. He explained his predicament, saying, "If I come out for the anti-lynching bill now, southern Democrats will block every bill I ask Congress to pass to keep America from collapsing. I just can't take the risk."

The urgency of this issue escalated in October 1934 following the horrific events involving **Claude Neal**, an African American farm worker in Florida. Neal was accused of raping and murdering **Lola Cannady**, a white woman. He was abducted from jail by a mob, which alerted the press that "justice" would be administered at the Cannady farm. The spectacle drew hundreds, but due to the chaos, Neal was secretly taken away, tortured, castrated, and killed. His mutilated body was then displayed outside the county courthouse. When sheriffs buried him, a riot ensued as a large crowd demanded to see the body, resulting in nearly 200 African Americans being attacked.

The National Guard was deployed to quell the disturbance. The lynching and subsequent riot received extensive media coverage, igniting public outrage, particularly outside the South. This incident heightened public support for anti-lynching legislation and increased the strain between White and Roosevelt.

Throughout January and February of 1935, Eleanor persistently urged Franklin to endorse the Costigan-Wagner Anti-Lynching Bill. However, when the bill was presented, southern Senators threatened a filibuster that would jeopardize the entire legislative agenda, including the vital Social Security Act. Despite an intense advocacy campaign by White and others, FDR remained silent during the filibuster, and the bill was ultimately shelved without a vote. The failure of the bill was a severe disappointment to White and the NAACP, leaving Eleanor deeply disheartened. She expressed her regret to White, writing, "I am so sorry about the bill. Of course, all of us are going on fighting, and the only thing we can do is hope that we will have better luck next time."

The fight for anti-lynching legislation continued to see setbacks, with another bill falling to a Senate filibuster in 1937. During this filibuster, Eleanor made a pointed statement by sitting in the Senate Gallery for days in silent protest against the shameful tactic. Unfortunately, the bill again died without a vote. It wasn't until 2005 that the U.S. Senate formally apologized for its historic failure to pass any anti-lynching legislation when it was most critically needed.

The era of the Roosevelts was a pivotal time for the Democratic Party, which began to experience a significant identity crisis. Eric Rauchway, a history professor at the University of California, Davis, observed the party's internal divisions following their 1932 electoral victories. He noted, "When the Democrats won both the presidency and a Congressional majority in 1932, you have this kind of split party." He explained how Southern Democrats wielded their power by holding New Deal legislation hostage, refusing to allow progress on these crucial reforms unless the party abandoned efforts to pass anti-lynching bills. This dynamic underscored the complex and often contentious nature of party politics even with an incredibly popular incumbent president.

The Failed Purge

On July 4, 1938, during an economic conference, Roosevelt highlighted the South as the nation's primary economic problem, pointing to its critical economic disparities. He noted the poor health and high mortality rates in the South compared to other regions, which underscored the dire conditions. Roosevelt emphasized the economic imbalances, revealing that although the South comprised 21% of America's population, it accounted for only 9% of the national income. This disparity was reflected in the wages of common laborers, who earned significantly less in the South—about $865 annually compared to $1,291 in other regions. Additionally, Southern wages were approximately 16 cents per hour lower than the national average.

The agricultural sector, a major component of the Southern economy, also faced challenges. The South had the largest number of farms, yet these were typically smaller and less profitable compared to those in other regions, contributing to the region's lower income levels. This economic underperformance was a symptom of broader systemic issues that Roosevelt aimed to address through his New Deal policies. These policies were designed to revitalize the American economy by boosting economic activity and improving living standards, particularly in economically disadvantaged areas like the South.

Roosevelt's sustained critique of the economic stagnation in the South paved the way for a major political maneuver during the 1938 midterm elections. He launched a bold and controversial effort to transform the Democratic Party by targeting conservative members, primarily from the South, who had collaborated with Republicans to block his New Deal policies. Roosevelt vigorously campaigned across states like Kentucky, Oklahoma, Arkansas, and Texas, supporting liberal candidates and denouncing the conservative incumbents as impediments to legislative progress. This initiative, known as "Roosevelt's Purge," sought to realign the Democratic Party with more progressive, reform-oriented values and reduce its reliance on Southern conservatives.

In a critical radio address before the primaries, Roosevelt expressed his frustration with obstructionist politics, stating, "We all know that progress may be blocked by outspoken reactionaries, and also by those who say 'yes' to a progressive objective, but who always find some reason to oppose any specific proposal to gain that objective. I call that type of candidate a 'yes, but' fellow." He further warned, "There will be a lot of mean blows struck between now and Election Day. By 'blows' I mean misrepresentation and personal attack and appeals to prejudice. It would be a lot better, of course, if campaigns everywhere could be waged with arguments instead of with blows."

During the purge campaign, **James Farley**, the chair of the Democratic National Committee (DNC), expressed strong objections, arguing that Roosevelt's involvement violated a fundamental principle of American politics: "that the President keep out of local matters." Despite the appeal of his New Deal policies, Roosevelt's campaign faced significant resistance. Southern voters, deeply resentful of his interference in local politics, largely rejected his initiatives. Critics accused Roosevelt of mimicking **Joseph Stalin**'s brutal purges, labeling his actions as attempts to establish a dictatorship. This resistance proved impactful: in the 1938 elections, almost all the incumbents he opposed managed to retain their seats, substantially limiting Roosevelt's ability to implement major new reforms. The elections resulted in notable gains for the Republican Party; while they did not achieve a majority in either house of Congress, the Republicans were strong enough to form a blocking coalition with conservative Southern Democrats, effectively halting any significant new initiatives from the White House.

Reflecting on this period, American political historian Laurence Jurdem noted, "It was not Franklin Roosevelt's finest hour." Historian Susan Dunn, in her book on Roosevelt's Purge, speculated that Roosevelt would have appreciated the eventual emergence of a polarized political landscape with parties holding mostly coherent ideological positions. "But it took decades. By being impatient and trying to force rapid realignment, he caused a backlash that stymied his agenda," Dunn explained. This episode underscored Roosevelt's constrained ability to influence and the deep-seated obstacles to political reform in the South. It also highlighted the challenges of aggressively pursuing civil rights policies, which, despite Eleanor Roosevelt's significant efforts, were not a strategic priority for FDR at the time.

Historians continue to speculate on the potential consequences had Roosevelt been successful in removing the original Jacksonian and Confederate-aligned members from the party in 1938. Such a victory might have shifted the party's base more toward the North and potentially accelerated civil rights legislation, potentially altering the landscape of American politics and possibly averting the civil rights turmoil of the 1960s or prompting an earlier ideological switch between the two major parties.

Despite the setbacks following the 1938 election, Roosevelt's administration continued to make significant strides toward racial equality, with the Works Progress Administration (WPA) playing a pivotal role by providing fair employment opportunities to African Americans and significant federal investment in Black schools and hospitals throughout the South. In 1941, Roosevelt advanced civil rights further by signing a nondiscrimination order for the national defense industry, a move that also increased the visibility of African Americans within his administration. These actions helped solidify African American support for the New Deal Coalition, transforming them into a crucial Democratic voting bloc.

From the perspective of Southern whites, these changes made the Democratic Party increasingly unappealing, a trend that continued to deepen over the following two decades. This shift marked a significant realignment within the

Democratic Party, as it gradually moved away from its traditional Southern base towards embracing a more inclusive and progressive national agenda. Roosevelt's handling of civil rights issues during a period when Americans were united behind the war effort began to subtly shift the direction of the traditionally Southern-based Democratic Party. This gradual change did not go unnoticed by powerful Southern Democrats, who were increasingly wary of the new trajectory. Many of these influential figures were not prepared to support this shift, signaling a brewing tension within the party that would eventually lead to significant political realignments.

FDR's Disability

During a tumultuous era marked by a world war and economic depression, most Americans were largely unaware of Roosevelt's struggles with disability. Diagnosed with polio in 1921 at the age of 39, Roosevelt was left paralyzed from the waist down. Despite this, he pursued a highly influential political career, serving as Governor of New York before becoming President.

To manage public perception, Roosevelt and his aides made considerable efforts to minimize the visibility of his disability. He used a wheelchair in private settings but was rarely photographed in it. Public appearances were meticulously planned to showcase him standing or walking with the aid of braces and support from aides. The media cooperated with these efforts, refraining from publishing images of him in his wheelchair or receiving assistance.

At public events, FDR often spoke from a specially designed podium that supported him upright, and he drove a custom-built car equipped with hand controls, maintaining his image as an active and capable leader. These adaptations contributed to his public persona of resilience and determination, which resonated deeply with Americans during the Great Depression and World War II.

Roosevelt's leadership through these challenging times, while managing his disability privately, bolstered his legacy. His famous assurance, "The only thing we have to fear is fear itself," epitomized his capacity to inspire and lead through personal and national crises. His role in founding the March of Dimes, originally the National Foundation for Infantile Paralysis, which significantly funded polio research and vaccine development, underscored his commitment to combating the disease.

Roosevelt often retreated to Warm Springs, Georgia, a resort he transformed into a rehabilitation center for polio patients, providing both personal relief and support for others afflicted by the disease. Eleanor Roosevelt played a crucial role during this period, supporting her husband significantly both in public and behind the scenes. While Roosevelt's presidency did not see significant advancements in disability rights, his effective leadership while managing a disability laid important groundwork for future disability advocacy and awareness. His enduring influence remains a source of inspiration within the disability rights movement.

As he sought a fourth term in 1944, Roosevelt was concealing a dire secret—he was dying. At 62, he battled severe symptoms: trembling hands, extreme fatigue, and incidents of fainting. His inner circle attributed his declining health to residual flu symptoms, even as his family pressed him to seek specialist care. At Walter Reed National Military Medical Center, cardiologist Howard Bruenn's findings were stark. Historian Jay Winik captures the moment: "Listening to Roosevelt's heart and lungs, Bruenn heard rales, telltale rattling sounds that indicated fluid buildup in the president's lungs—a sign of congestive heart failure." Roosevelt was told he might only have a year to live.

Despite facing serious health challenges, FDR decided to run for reelection, committed to leading the nation through the final stages of World War II. At the time, the media was more reserved in reporting personal details about political figures, allowing Roosevelt some privacy regarding his declining health. After winning the election, a visibly ailing Roosevelt attended the critical Yalta Conference in February 1945, alongside Britain's Prime Minister **Winston Churchill** and Russia's Joseph Stalin. This pivotal summit shaped key decisions about post-war Europe and strategies for the final defeat of Nazi Germany, laying the groundwork for the geopolitical dynamics that would usher in the Cold War.

At the conference, Churchill and others observed that Roosevelt's health was visibly deteriorating, though not all attendees fully grasped the severity of his condition. His energy had significantly diminished, raising concerns among those present. Churchill, in particular, was acutely aware of the changes in

Roosevelt's health. The British wartime leader would later refer to FDR as "the greatest American friend we have ever known."

In her memoir, *My Thirty Years Backstairs at the White House*, **Lillian Rogers Parks**, along with her mother **Maggie Rogers**, who collectively served over fifty years at the White House, offered intimate glimpses into the personal and professional life of Roosevelt. Parks described FDR as having "a remarkable presence" that "brought a sense of optimism and determination to the White House," which uplifted everyone around him. Despite his severe health challenges, she noted, "he remained cheerful and engaging," making his time in office a uniquely positive experience for the staff.

Parks also shared her high regard for Eleanor Roosevelt, recalling her as "one of the kindest women I ever met." Eleanor's genuine care for the staff was evident as she "went out of her way to make sure we were treated well," embodying the compassionate ethos of the Roosevelt administration.

Astonishment Of Many

In April 1945, Franklin D. Roosevelt, the only president ever elected to four terms, passed away during the first year of his fourth term in Warm Springs, Georgia. FDR had transformed the American presidency profoundly, leaving behind a legacy that significantly shaped the modern nation. His leadership during the Depression and World War II reaffirmed democracy at a time when many doubted its viability, and his New Deal legislation expanded the role of the federal government in ways that continue to influence the United States today.

Harry S. Truman, Roosevelt's successor, was a relatively unknown vice president from Missouri who had seldom interacted with Roosevelt during the previous campaign or in the Oval Office. The sudden death of Roosevelt plunged the nation into deep grief, confronting Americans with the uncertainty of leadership under a man they barely knew. Roosevelt thought so little of his new vice president that, during the 82 days before Roosevelt's death, the two met just twice. He did not even inform Truman about the U.S. development of the atomic bomb.

Truman's decision to use the atomic bomb twice on Japan during World War II was driven by a desire to swiftly end the war and minimize further American casualties. Despite devastating conventional bombing campaigns and a naval blockade, Japan showed no signs of surrendering. Military estimates suggested that a full-scale invasion of Japan could result in substantial Allied casualties, potentially extending the war by months or even years. In this context, Truman authorized the use of the atomic bomb on Hiroshima on August 6, 1945, and on Nagasaki on August 9, 1945, to compel Japan's unconditional surrender. The decision was also influenced by a desire to demonstrate American military superiority, particularly to the Soviet Union, as post-war geopolitical tensions began to surface. The bombings ultimately led to Japan's surrender on August 15, 1945, effectively ending the war. About 200,000 people died, although the exact number is difficult to determine due to the immediate and long-term effects.

While the decision to use the atomic bomb was primarily a strategic military one, it occurred within a broader context of racial prejudice. Anti-Asian sentiments, particularly against the Japanese, were prevalent during the war. Propaganda often dehumanized Japanese people, depicting them as barbaric and fanatical. This pervasive racism likely contributed to the perception of the Japanese as a suitable target for such an unprecedented weapon, although it was not the primary driving force behind Truman's decision.

Truman grew up in a home that openly reviled abolitionism, Reconstruction, and Abraham Lincoln. "Truman literally learned at his mother's knee to share the South's view of the War Between the States," wrote William E. Leuchtenburg, a professor emeritus of history at the University of North Carolina at Chapel Hill. "He also acquired an abiding belief in white supremacy." In a 1911 letter to his future wife, Bess, he wrote: "I think one man is as good as another so long as he's honest and decent and not a nigger or a Chinaman." Even Merle Miller, his reverential biographer, noted in the biography "Plain Speaking" that Truman privately continued to use the offensive terms "nigger" in conversations later in life and often referred to Jews as "kikes" privately. These documented statements reflect the deeply ingrained racial prejudices that Truman held from an early age, influenced by his family background—his grandparents on both sides were from Kentucky and owned slaves.

Raised in a segregated town in Missouri—a state marked by its pro-slavery history—Truman's perspective began to shift dramatically following World War II, particularly in response to the heinous treatment of African-American veterans. Despite the service of approximately 1.2 million Black Americans in the still-segregated U.S. armed forces, many faced murder and assault upon returning home. "My stomach turned over when I learned that Negro soldiers, just back from overseas, were being dumped out of army trucks in Mississippi and beaten," Truman said. "Whatever my inclinations as a native of Missouri might have been, as president I know this is bad. I shall fight to end evils like this."

Truman's decision to desegregate the U.S. military marked a pivotal moment in American civil rights history. On July 26, 1948, he signed Executive Order 9981, which mandated equality of treatment and opportunity for all persons in the armed services, regardless of race, color, religion, or national origin. This bold move paved the way for the end of racial segregation in the military and laid the groundwork for broader civil rights advancements in the United States. The implementation of Truman's executive order faced stiff opposition from within the military and across various segments of the public and Congress. Many military commanders were against integration, expressing concerns that it would lower morale, decrease efficiency, and undermine combat effectiveness. They argued that the military was no place for what they termed social experimentation with integration policies, fearing that it would lead to decreased cohesion and effectiveness at a time when the Cold War was heightening global tensions.

Critics also leaned on outdated racial theories, suggesting that Black soldiers were less capable or intelligent than their white counterparts. Furthermore, there was a significant portion of the American public, particularly in the South, that resisted any progress towards racial equality, reflecting the broader societal racism of the time. Despite these challenges, Truman's executive order gradually led to the integration of the armed forces. By the Korean War in the early 1950s, units had begun integrating, a process that would take years to fully realize but would ultimately be viewed as a significant advancement for civil rights in America. Truman recognized the hypocrisy of advocating for democracy abroad—while Black troops stood on the front lines fighting a tyrant like Adolf Hitler—while denying it at home based on race. This controversial yet courageous step set a precedent for future actions aimed at promoting civil rights and equality.

In 1998, on the 50th anniversary of Executive Order 9981, General **Colin Powell**, who later became America's first Black secretary of state, spoke about the impact of Truman's decision on his life: "The military was the only institution in all of America—because of Harry Truman—where a young Black kid, now 21 years old, could dream the dream he dared not think about at age 11. It was the one place where the only thing that counted was courage, where the color of your guts and the color of your blood was more important than the color of your skin."

On the same day, Truman also issued Executive Order 9980 to desegregate the federal workforce. This order aimed to ensure fairness in the employment and treatment of workers in the federal government, irrespective of their race, color, religion, or national origin. It represented a significant step towards racial equality, reflecting Truman's commitment to civil rights not just within the military but across all branches of the federal government. The Order established a Fair Employment Board to oversee the implementation of non-discriminatory hiring practices within federal agencies and to address complaints of discrimination. This move was crucial, as it tackled institutional racism and opened up opportunities for minorities who had been systematically excluded from certain roles within the government. Like the desegregation of the military, this policy faced resistance but ultimately helped to pave the way for more inclusive practices in the hiring and treatment of federal employees.

By issuing both orders on the same day, Truman signaled a comprehensive approach to civil rights, aiming to align the principles of democracy and equality within both the armed forces and federal employment.

Raymond H. Geselbracht, a historian on Truman's presidency, noted, "Truman never completely rose above his heritage, but he became the president of the United States who for the first time since the Reconstruction Period immediately following the Civil War committed the government of the United States to the realization of civil rights for African Americans." This profound statement encapsulates the significant legacy of Truman's presidency, marking him as a transformative figure in the pursuit of civil rights.

Truman's decision was not solely a matter of principle; it also reflected astute political pragmatism. Recognizing the growing importance of Black voters in northern cities, particularly with an election on the horizon, Truman aimed to secure their support through concrete policy changes. These actions by Truman marked a pivotal moment in the civil rights movement, setting the stage for further federal initiatives to combat racial discrimination and paving the way for more inclusive policies in America.

Throughout his presidency, Truman ardently advanced civil rights, taking significant actions such as ending economic discrimination, abolishing state poll taxes, and advocating for new federal anti-lynching laws. He also signed the bill establishing National Freedom Day, a commemoration of the 13th Amendment's signing, which abolished slavery in the United States. In these actions, Truman emerged as the first president since Lincoln to actively advocate for the equality of African Americans.

Notably, although Truman was a Democrat, he more effectively embodied and advanced Lincoln's vision of equality than any Republican president up to that point. This alignment with Lincoln's ideals marked a pivotal moment in American history, setting the stage for future civil rights advancements and solidifying Truman's legacy as a president who profoundly shaped the nation's approach to civil and human rights.

The Dixiecrats

As Truman promoted progressive themes, the Democratic Party was gradually adopting ideals that resonated with those of Lincoln, advocating for equal rights for all, including African Americans. This shift did not sit well with Southern Democrats. In a statement that marked a significant departure from a longstanding political tradition since Andrew Jackson's era, Mississippi Governor **Fielding Wright** notably warned his fellow Democrats that they could no longer take the South's electoral votes for granted. This caution underscored the growing tension within the party, signaling a profound change in the political landscape of the South.

In 1948, as Truman faced his first election as president and struggled in the polls, tensions reached a climax at the Democratic National Convention. After a heated debate, the party adopted a strong civil rights plank, inspired by Minneapolis Mayor **Hubert Humphrey**'s urging to "walk out of the shadow of states' rights, into the bright sunshine of human rights."

This inclusion of pro-civil rights language in the Democratic Party platform incensed **Strom Thurmond**, then the Democratic governor of South Carolina. He led a walkout of dozens of Southern delegates, highlighting the growing division within the party over civil rights issues. Following the walkout, Thurmond spearheaded the creation of the "Dixiecrats" party, which emphasized states' rights and segregation, positioning itself in stark opposition to Truman's civil rights agenda. This pivotal moment underlined the deepening rift within the Democratic Party over civil rights and signaled the beginning of a significant political realignment in the South.

Consider the potential consequences in today's fast-paced media environment if a group of delegates and elected officials openly defied the incumbent president and the leader of their party over racial issues at a national convention, and then proceeded to leave the convention to form a breakaway party. Given the immediacy and viral nature of digital and social media, such a bold move would likely create significant upheaval. The widespread publicity and intense public scrutiny could substantially damage the president's reputation and undermine the party's standing, potentially affecting its political fortunes for decades to come. This scenario would not only dominate

news cycles but could also deeply polarize party members and voters, leading to long-term ramifications in subsequent elections.

Thurmond's "States' Rights Democratic Party" aimed to maintain white supremacy and uphold Jim Crow laws. The Dixiecrats' platform explicitly supported racial segregation, proclaiming, "We stand for the segregation of the races and the racial integrity of each race," while also endorsing themes of anti-federal government sentiment, advocating for "home-rule, local self-government, and minimum interference with individual rights."

Thurmond became the symbol of this defiance, using the Confederate battle flag as a rallying icon for his new party. Although his campaign did not secure ballot access in enough states to realistically win, his rhetoric resonated deeply with many Southern voters. Thurmond infamously declared, "I wanna tell you, ladies and gentlemen, that there's not enough troops in the army to force the Southern people to break down segregation and admit the Nigra race into our theaters, into our swimming pools, into our homes, and into our churches."

Amid the Dixiecrat revolt, Truman openly criticized Southern Democrats who broke away from the party to support Thurmond, viewing their actions as detrimental to the Democratic Party and undermining the broader goals of civil rights and national unity. Nevertheless, Truman recognized the necessity of maintaining some support among Southern Democrats to achieve his policy objectives and secure a broader electoral base. Concurrently, he eyed Black voters, historically loyal to the Lincoln Republican Party, as the future of the Democratic base. In a surprising shift, given his background and previous positions, Truman steered the Democrats toward embracing Lincoln's vision for America, moving away from the states' rights that had been the hallmark and purpose of the Jackson Democratic Party, and toward a firm commitment to civil rights.

Although Thurmond lost the election to Truman, he secured over a million popular votes and won Louisiana, Alabama, Mississippi, and South Carolina, earning thirty-nine electoral votes. Historian David Goldfield noted, "It was the first time since before the Civil War that the South was not solidly Democratic. And that began the erosion of the southern influence in the Democratic Party."

Truman's narrow victory over Republican nominee **Thomas Dewey** was precarious; Dewey was less than 1 percent away from winning Ohio and Illinois, which would have forced the election to the House of Representatives. There, the Dixiecrats hoped to leverage their influence to roll back civil rights advancements.

Thurmond's strong performance in the election underscored a growing fissure within the Democratic stronghold of the South, and foreshadowed the political realignment that was underway.

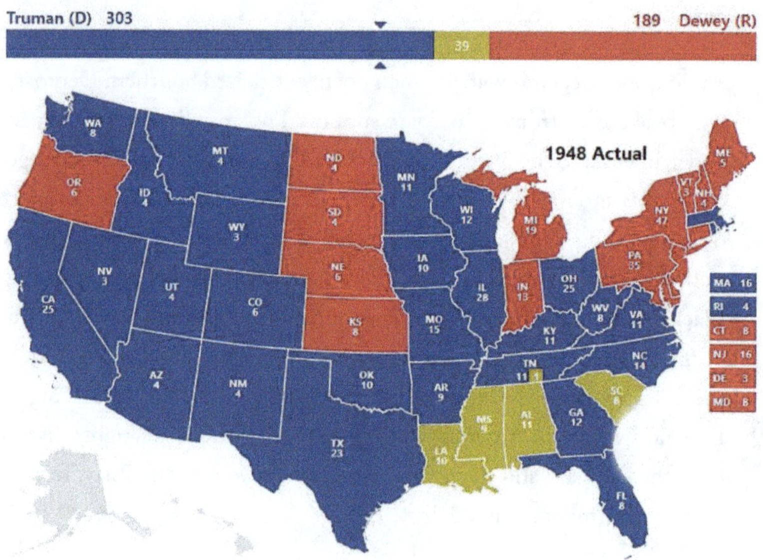

Cautious Ike

The post-war boom continued to lift the American standard of living to new heights. The suburban dream was in full swing, with families flocking to newly developed neighborhoods, lured by the promise of affordable homes and a better quality of life. The consumer culture flourished, fueled by an ever-expanding array of products designed to make life easier and more enjoyable. Yet, beneath this veneer of prosperity, there were underlying tensions and inequalities that would soon demand attention.

Despite the Republicans securing the White House in 1952 with President **Dwight D. Eisenhower**, he chose not to dismantle Franklin Roosevelt's expansive New Deal programs. Known as Ike, this Kansan and celebrated World War II hero was courted by both major political parties, reflecting his widespread popularity and proven leadership. However, his personal distaste for Harry Truman influenced his decision to run as a Republican rather than a Democrat. Despite his political affiliation, Eisenhower was not strictly conservative or ideological. Indeed, he supported a variety of policies initiated by Roosevelt, demonstrating a pragmatic approach to governance that often transcended party lines. His presidency, therefore, reflected a strong commitment to national unity and practical policymaking.

During his presidency, Eisenhower maintained and even expanded several key initiatives from Roosevelt's New Deal programs. Notably, he supported the continuation and expansion of Social Security, broadening its coverage to include additional workers and increasing the benefits provided. He also preserved and strengthened New Deal labor standards, ensuring that fair labor practices continued to be enforced. Additionally, Eisenhower was instrumental in developing the Interstate Highway System, echoing the New Deal's emphasis on large-scale infrastructure projects that provided jobs and boosted economic growth. This approach underscored his pragmatic governance, recognizing the value of these programs in promoting social welfare and national development.

Eisenhower's relationship with Southern politicians, including Strom Thurmond, was complex and underwent significant evolution throughout his presidency. Initially, Thurmond supported Eisenhower in the 1952 presidential election over his own party's nominee, **Adlai Stevenson**. Thurmond's support was driven by his hope that Eisenhower would oppose federal intervention in issues like segregation and civil rights, which many Southern Democrats felt should be managed by states without federal oversight.

However, as Eisenhower's presidency progressed and he began to support and sign civil rights legislation into law, the relationship between the two cooled significantly. Eisenhower's decisions to align the Republican Party with the legacy of Abraham Lincoln and to actively support civil rights legislation were seen as a betrayal by Thurmond and like-minded Southerners. This shift in policy and allegiance gradually diminished Thurmond's initial enthusiasm for Eisenhower and reduced his immediate desire to leave the Democratic Party, at least until the political landscape shifted further in the subsequent years.

During Eisenhower's presidency, significant events marked his administration as a time of cautious but consequential progress towards racial equality in America. The U.S. Supreme Court's decision in Brown v. Board of Education of Topeka in 1954 was a pivotal moment. It declared racially segregated public schools unconstitutional and mandated that schools integrate with "all deliberate speed." This landmark ruling sparked widespread resistance throughout the South, where many white residents vehemently opposed the dismantling of segregation.

Another seminal event in the civil rights movement occurred in 1955 when **Rosa Parks** famously refused to give up her seat on a segregated bus in

Montgomery, Alabama. While Parks' act was part of a larger, planned strategy by local civil rights leaders to challenge segregation, it led to the Montgomery Bus Boycott. This year-long protest, prominently led by Dr. **Martin Luther King Jr.**, successfully utilized nonviolent protest to challenge racial segregation. Despite the significance of this event, Eisenhower did not publicly comment on Parks' actions or the ensuing boycott, maintaining his administration's typically cautious stance on civil rights.

The Little Rock Crisis in 1957 compelled Eisenhower to adopt a more direct approach to civil rights. After Arkansas Governor **Orval Faubus** closed all public high schools in Little Rock to resist federal court orders for integration, Eisenhower decisively sent federal troops to enforce the integration of Little Rock Central High School. This action underscored a clear federal commitment to uphold civil rights, though it was controversial among Southern Democrats who saw it as an overreach of federal power and a threat to their local authority.

Despite the racial tensions and political risks, Eisenhower's presidency was marked by a significant, albeit gradual, shift towards addressing civil inequalities. This period was instrumental in setting the stage for future civil rights advancements, though Eisenhower's methods were often characterized by a strategic balancing act, aimed at reducing racial tensions without alienating key political constituencies in the South. His support for the Civil Rights Act of 1957, one of the first major pieces of civil rights legislation since Reconstruction, further demonstrated this cautious yet pivotal approach to civil rights during his administration.

Thurmond, incensed, conducted a marathon filibuster in the Senate that lasted 24 hours and 18 minutes, marking the longest filibuster in history. His opposition, while framed with legalistic and constitutional arguments, was deeply intertwined with the maintenance of the segregated status quo in the South. Although he might not have explicitly focused on race during the filibuster, the racial undertones and

implications of his stance were unmistakable, as the legislation directly addressed issues of racial segregation and discrimination. Despite his efforts, the Act passed with significant Republican support, including from conservative figures like Senator **Barry Goldwater**.

Although a legislative milestone, the Civil Rights Act of 1957 was notably diluted to ensure its passage through Congress, facing substantial resistance from Southern senators like Thurmond. Recognizing the Act's limitations, Eisenhower later signed The Civil Rights Act of 1960, which, although another compromise, helped establish the groundwork for the more comprehensive Voting Rights Act of 1965 by providing evidence of discriminatory voter-registration practices. This series of legislative efforts under Eisenhower's administration highlights a crucial era of civil rights advancement, albeit one marked by significant political challenges and compromises.

The Red Scare

During the 1950s, the civil rights movement found itself deeply entangled with the Red Scare, with Senator **Joseph McCarthy** as a dominant figure. McCarthy, a right-wing Republican from Wisconsin, launched aggressive accusations against numerous individuals in government, academia, and entertainment, labeling them communists or communist sympathizers. His approach, marked by sweeping allegations and scant evidence, cultivated an atmosphere of fear and suspicion across the nation. This period saw significant overlap between McCarthyism and the civil rights movement. The deliberate conflation of civil rights advocacy with communist ideologies was used by some detractors to undermine the movement. This not only increased political risks for activists but also complicated their struggle by linking the fight for racial equality with a highly charged anti-communist agenda.

The McCarthy era, notorious for the McCarthy hearings, involved investigations led by McCarthy to root out communists from the U.S. government and other sectors. These hearings, characterized by sensational accusations and often flimsy evidence, resulted in many unjustly ruined careers.

Eisenhower, a fellow Republican, had a complex and cautious relationship with McCarthy. Publicly, he avoided direct confrontation or even mentioning McCarthy's name, aiming not to lend him additional publicity. Privately, however, Eisenhower harbored a deep disdain for McCarthy's tactics, viewing them as destructive and unethical. Behind the scenes, Eisenhower's administration subtly supported efforts that eventually led to McCarthy's censure and decline.

Despite Eisenhower's public reticence, he played a pivotal role behind the scenes, strategically releasing information that discredited McCarthy and his circle, especially during the Army-McCarthy hearings in 1954. These televised hearings shifted public opinion against McCarthy, exposing his aggressive and baseless methods to a nationwide audience. A notable moment came when lawyer **Joseph Welch** challenged McCarthy with the now-famous question, "Have you no sense of decency, sir?" marking a critical turning point.

The McCarthy era concluded with the senator's censure by the Senate in December 1954. By then, the era had inflicted profound damage, impacting numerous lives and careers. It left a lasting legacy of fear and served as a stark reminder of the perils of unchecked political power and the infringement of civil liberties.

Under God

On June 14, 1954, amid the Cold War and fears of communism, Eisenhower signed legislation that significantly altered the Pledge of Allegiance, a fixture in daily school routines across the United States. The amendment added "under God," thus revising it to: "I pledge allegiance to the flag of the United States of America, and to the Republic for which it stands, one Nation under God, indivisible, with liberty and justice for all." This change deviated from the original 1892 version by **Francis Bellamy**, which read: "I pledge allegiance to my Flag and the Republic for which it stands, one Nation indivisible, with liberty and justice for all," and made no reference to religion.

The insertion of "under God" not only aimed to underscore the ideological differences between the U.S. and the atheistically portrayed Soviet Union but also represented a victory for cultural conservatives who challenged the prevailing interpretation of the separation of church and state. By integrating a religious element into the pledge, it affirmed the notion that American values were deeply intertwined with religious beliefs, differentiating the nation from its Cold War rivals. Despite various legal challenges, courts have maintained that reciting the pledge is voluntary, allowing students to opt out if the words conflict with their personal beliefs, thus mitigating concerns about religious coercion.

This period of American history, marked by ideological shifts and a reassertion of national values, set the stage for another significant event that united the nation. In February 1959, **Carl Sandburg**, a multifaceted American poet, historian, and biographer renowned for his lyrical and evocative writing style, accomplished two nearly impossible feats: he united the nation's two major political parties and, even more remarkably, rendered the members of Congress silent. The occasion was the sesquicentennial of Abraham Lincoln's birth, and Sandburg, whose massive biography "Abraham Lincoln: The Prairie Years and The War Years" had won the Pulitzer Prize in 1939, was the honored speaker.

As Sandburg sang Lincoln's praises on the floor of Congress, the usual distractions of yawns, whispers, and tapping pencils echoed through the hall. The white-haired Sandburg, unfazed, strode to the podium and let his lyrical cadences work their magic. He began with the opening sentence:

"Often in the story of mankind, there is a man who is both steel and velvet, who is as hard as a rock and as soft as drifting fog, who holds in his heart the paradox of terrible storm and peace."

An unspeakable hush fell over the congressmen, who seemed bewitched by Sandburg's address. Lincoln was still in the minds of politicians in both parties, even while his causes of civil rights and a strong union were transitioning from one party to another. Just as the Pledge of Allegiance had been altered to reflect the values of the time, Sandburg's address reminded the nation of Lincoln's enduring legacy and the timeless principles of unity and justice he represented.

Camelot for Civil Rights

During the 1960 presidential campaign, Eisenhower's Vice President, **Richard Nixon**, secured the Republican nomination and faced off against Democratic Senator **John F. Kennedy**. Both candidates had supported the Civil Rights Act of 1957, recognizing the growing importance of civil rights as a national issue. This shared stance led both Nixon and Kennedy to campaign vigorously for the African American vote, a strategic move given the increasing influence of this demographic.

In February 1960, black college students staged a sit-in at the whites-only lunch counter of a Woolworth store in Greensboro, North Carolina. Despite hostile looks and knowing they wouldn't be served, they remained seated all day. The following day, 20 more students joined them. Within two weeks, sit-ins were happening in 15 other cities. In Nashville, the protests reached a climax when a bomb destroyed the home of a lawyer involved in the movement. In response, about 6,000 people marched to City Hall, and Nashville Mayor **Ben West** ordered the lunch counters to be desegregated. JFK praised these sit-ins for challenging segregation in the South, highlighting them as an example of the "American spirit coming alive again" while Nixon remained quiet.

On October 19, Martin Luther King Jr. joined 51 other activists in a sit-in at a whites-only lunch counter at Rich's Department Store in Atlanta. King and other protesters were arrested for trespassing. Although such arrests were common during the civil rights movement, what made this incident particularly significant was what happened afterward. King was sentenced to four months of hard labor for a previous traffic violation after refusing to pay a fine, which many believed was a politically motivated decision to remove him from the civil rights struggle.

This arrest became a major issue in the 1960 presidential campaign. Kennedy reached out to **Coretta Scott King**, expressing his concern for her husband. Additionally, **Robert F. Kennedy**, JFK's brother and campaign manager, made a call to the judge in charge of King's case, which helped secure King's release. Kennedy, in particular, faced significant risks with his strong stance on civil rights, as he needed to balance the demands for social reform with the political realities of needing support from the still solidly Democratic South.

His campaign navigated this delicate balance by actively engaging with African American voters and leaders, while also trying not to alienate Southern white voters who were less supportive of rapid changes in civil rights laws.

Kennedy's intervention and support for King were widely publicized and helped him gain significant support from African American voters, although this calculated risk cost him support in the South. Still, in other states, like Illinois, it played a crucial role in his narrow victory over Nixon in the November 1960 election. In the tightly contested election, Kennedy won 303 electoral votes, 34 more than needed for victory, while Nixon secured 219. However, an unexpected result saw **Harry F. Byrd**, a Democratic senator from Virginia who was not actively campaigning, receive 15 electoral votes, including eight from Mississippi. Byrd, a staunch segregationist, was selected as a "favorite son" by some unpledged electors in the South, reflecting a broader strategy by certain Southern Democrats who were deeply dissatisfied with Kennedy's progressive stances on racial issues.

In his inaugural address, Kennedy, the youngest president ever elected, told Americans, 'Let the word go forth from this time and place, to friend and foe alike, that the torch has been passed to a new generation of Americans.'

Famous for its powerful and inspiring rhetoric, the speech challenged citizens with a call to action: 'Ask not what your country can do for you—ask what you can do for your country.'

Kennedy's presidency marked a critical period for civil rights in the United States. Initially, with his brother Robert appointed as Attorney General, Kennedy approached civil rights cautiously, aware of the political sensitivities of Southern Democrats in Congress who opposed sweeping reforms. However, as his term progressed, Kennedy became increasingly involved in the civil rights movement, propelled by growing civil unrest and a push for equality.

Just weeks into the Kennedy administration, the 23rd Amendment was ratified, granting residents of the District of Columbia the right to vote in presidential elections. This amendment provided the district with three electoral votes, equal to the number of electors it would have if it were a state, but no more than the least populous state. Kansas became the 36th state to ratify the amendment. Many found it astonishing that the district had to fight so hard for this right, attributing much of the opposition to racism, as the population was predominantly African American.

One of the next major challenges for civil rights activists was desegregating interstate bus terminals. **James Farmer**, director of the Congress of Racial Equality, organized the Freedom Rides in May 1961 to integrate seating on buses and facilities in bus terminals. These rides aimed to challenge segregation in the South, relying on the inevitable violent reactions to force government intervention. The Freedom Riders were met with hostility and violence; in the Deep South, a bus was bombed in Anniston, Alabama, and riders were beaten in Birmingham and Montgomery. Despite these perils, the Freedom Rides were a catalyst for other campaigns, leading to the desegregation of interstate travel by the end of the year. The rise of television played a crucial role during this period, broadcasting these brutal incidents nationwide and prompting widespread reflection on the morality of racial segregation.

In September 1962, after a protracted legal battle, the U.S. Supreme Court ruled in **James Meredith**'s favor, mandating his admission to the University

of Mississippi, an all-white institution. Meredith, an African American Air Force veteran, had applied to the university in 1961, but despite his impressive qualifications, his application was initially rejected. Supported by the NAACP, Meredith filed a lawsuit against the university, claiming racial discrimination. The Supreme Court's decision was met with fierce resistance from segregationists and led to violent riots in Oxford, Mississippi. These riots resulted in two deaths and numerous injuries, highlighting the intense opposition to desegregation in the Deep South.

Kennedy responded to the crisis by taking decisive action to uphold federal law and maintain order. He issued a series of executive orders to ensure Meredith's safe enrollment and protect his civil rights. Kennedy first sent federal marshals to escort Meredith to the university campus. When the situation escalated and violence erupted, Kennedy addressed the nation on television, emphasizing the importance of obeying the law and maintaining peace. Ultimately, Kennedy deployed thousands of federal troops to Oxford to quell the riots and restore order. On October 1, 1962, Meredith became the first African American student to enroll at the University of Mississippi, marking a significant victory for the Civil Rights Movement and a critical moment in the fight for desegregation in American education.

The following year, Alabama Governor **George Wallace** vowed to stand in the schoolhouse door to block integration. During his infamous stand in the schoolhouse door, Wallace proclaimed, "Segregation now, segregation tomorrow, segregation forever," a phrase that had become synonymous with his staunch opposition to desegregation since his inaugural speech as governor. This resistance was swiftly overcome as National Guardsmen, acting under federal orders, escorted African-American students **Vivian Malone** and **James Hood** into the University of Alabama's Foster Auditorium to register for classes. This marked a significant victory for the Kennedy administration in its ongoing struggle with Wallace.

In April, Robert Kennedy had met with Wallace, attempting to reach a peaceful resolution. However, he left in frustration as Wallace continued to defy federal integration orders. "It's like a foreign country," Kennedy complained, "There's no communication." The struggle in Alabama was far from over, with Wallace insisting he would continue to challenge the constitutionality of federal interference in state affairs.

Compelled by the escalating violence and driven by a moral imperative, Kennedy adopted a more assertive stance, fully aware that he was risking the support of Southern Democrats, whom the Republicans were now actively courting. On June 11, 1963, he delivered a landmark speech that robustly supported civil rights, beginning with a powerful declaration: "We are confronted primarily with a moral issue. It is as old as the Scriptures and is as clear as the American Constitution." He continued to address the nation, stating, "The heart of the question is whether all Americans are to be afforded equal rights and equal opportunities, whether we are going to treat our fellow Americans as we want to be treated." This statement underscored the principle of equality under the law and the basic fairness that should be afforded to every American.

Kennedy further challenged the conscience of the nation by posing a poignant question: "If an American, because his skin is dark, cannot enjoy the full and free life which all of us want, then who among us would be content to have the color of his skin changed and stand in his place?" With these words, he vividly highlighted the stark reality faced by African Americans. Culminating his address, Kennedy announced his intention to introduce comprehensive legislation aimed at eliminating racial discrimination, marking a significant commitment to advancing civil rights during his presidency.

On June 19, 1963, Kennedy reinforced this commitment by advocating for the passage of his comprehensive civil rights bill. He eloquently argued for the fundamental principle of equality, reminding the nation that no American had been barred on account of race from fighting or dying for the country, and thus should not face discrimination at home. "There are no 'white' or 'colored' signs on the foxholes or graveyards of battle," he pointed out, underscoring the shared sacrifices that unite all Americans.

Kennedy's increasingly assertive stance on civil rights, highlighted by his comprehensive legislation proposal, marked a critical evolution in his presidency and in the broader civil rights movement, setting the groundwork for future legislative and societal changes.

I Have A Dream

Just over a month after Kennedy's announcement, Martin Luther King, Jr., delivered his "I Have a Dream" speech, one of the most iconic and powerful addresses in American history. Delivered on August 28, 1963, during the March on Washington for Jobs and Freedom, the speech was a defining moment in the civil rights movement. Standing on the steps of the Lincoln Memorial, King spoke to an audience of over 250,000 people who had gathered to demand equality and justice for African Americans.

King began his speech by referencing Abraham Lincoln and the Emancipation Proclamation, which had declared freedom for slaves 100 years earlier. He noted that, despite this proclamation, African Americans were still not free due to pervasive discrimination and injustice. He stated, "Five score years ago, a great American, in whose symbolic shadow we stand today, signed the Emancipation Proclamation. But one hundred years later, the Negro still is not free. One hundred years later, the life of the Negro is still sadly crippled by the manacles of segregation and the chains of discrimination."

King's dream of a racially integrated and harmonious America resonated deeply with his audience. One of the most memorable quotes from his speech is, "I have a dream that one day this nation will rise up and live out the true meaning of its creed: 'We hold these truths to be self-evident, that all men are created equal.'" This powerful declaration captured the essence of the American ideal of equality and justice.

He also envisioned a future where people would be judged by their character rather than the color of their skin. He proclaimed, "I have a dream that my four little children will one day live in a nation where they will not be judged by the color of their skin but by the content of their character." This line has become one of the most quoted and celebrated passages in the fight for civil rights.

King's speech also emphasized the urgency of the moment, urging America to make real the promises of democracy. He warned against the dangers of gradualism and the need for immediate action, stating, "This is no time to engage in the luxury of cooling off or to take the tranquilizing drug of gradualism."

Another poignant part of his address was his vision of unity and brotherhood: "I have a dream that one day, on the red hills of Georgia, the sons of former slaves and the sons of former slave owners will be able to sit down together at the table of brotherhood."

Standing on the steps of the Lincoln Memorial, King drew on the legacy of Lincoln to call for a renewed commitment to the principles of freedom and equality. He invoked Lincoln's legacy to highlight the unfinished business of civil rights and the need for continued struggle to achieve true equality.

King concluded his speech with a hopeful and stirring call to action, invoking the patriotic song "My Country, 'Tis of Thee." He said, "And when this happens, and when we allow freedom to ring, when we let it ring from every village and every hamlet, from every state and every city, we will be able to speed up that day when all of God's children, black men and white men, Jews and Gentiles, Protestants and Catholics, will be able to join hands and sing in the words of the old Negro spiritual: 'Free at last! Free at last! Thank God Almighty, we are free at last!'"

Many in the audience were moved to tears, and the speech received thunderous applause and standing ovations. Media coverage was extensive and largely positive. Newspapers, television, and radio outlets across the country highlighted the speech, with many recognizing it as a defining moment in the civil rights movement. The speech was broadcast live, allowing millions of Americans to witness King's powerful delivery and the historic nature of the event. Commentators and journalists praised King for his eloquence and the moral clarity of his message.

While King championed a peaceful approach to resolving the racial divide, his contemporary **Malcolm X**, shaped by his involvement with the Nation of Islam, initially advocated for a more militant response to racial injustice. Malcolm X emphasized black pride and self-sufficiency, encouraging African Americans to establish their own businesses, schools, and communities to achieve economic independence and cultural pride. Unlike King, who promoted nonviolent resistance, Malcolm X believed in the right to self-defense, arguing that African Americans should protect themselves "by any means necessary" if attacked. Initially critical of the integrationist approach of the civil rights movement, he argued that seeking acceptance from white society was less important than building strength and unity within the black community.

However, later in his life, especially after his pilgrimage to Mecca, Malcolm X's views began to shift. He started advocating for racial unity and collaboration across racial lines, though he maintained his belief in self-defense and black empowerment.

Both leaders, despite their differing philosophies, profoundly impacted the civil rights movement and remain emblematic of the struggle for Black equality in America. Tragically, both leaders' lives were cut short by assassination—Malcolm X in 1965 and King in 1968. Their legacies, however, continue to inspire discussions and actions toward racial justice and equality.

Prepared for the civil rights battle ahead, Kennedy spent the summer of 1963 meeting with his brother Robert, the Attorney General, and civil rights leaders, demonstrating his dedication to these causes into the 1960s. Aware that his reelection the following year might be compromised, particularly with Southern Democrats turning against his agenda, Kennedy planned a politically charged trip to Texas. During a speech at a dinner in Houston on November 21, he underscored his administration's commitment to civil rights and the importance of the United States as a leader in equality and justice. He also revisited the ambitious space program, emphasizing the challenge he had set to put a man on the moon by the end of the decade. This was a poignant reminder in a city central to America's space efforts.

On the morning of November 22, just hours before his assassination, Kennedy spoke at a breakfast in Fort Worth, focusing on national values and progress in providing equal opportunities for all Americans. In what would be his final speech, Kennedy emphasized his ongoing commitment to civil rights, marking a poignant moment in history.

At around 11:30 am, while riding in an open-top convertible through downtown Dallas with his wife, **Jacqueline Kennedy**, his life was tragically cut short by **Lee Harvey Oswald**, an individual with documented Marxist and pro-Soviet leanings. Oswald was charged with the assassination but was killed two days later by **Jack Ruby** before he could stand trial, adding layers of complexity and fueling conspiracy theories that endure to this day. As the nation watched, glued to television sets, it entered a period of profound grief for its fallen young president.

The assassination profoundly shocked the nation, especially African Americans who were anxious about the implications for civil rights under Vice President **Lyndon B. Johnson**, a Texan. There were widespread concerns about whether Johnson would sustain Kennedy's momentum on civil rights or revert to regressive policies.

Conflicted Carolina

South Carolina is full of many charming features that represent its unique Southern character. The state tree, the Palmetto, adorns many streets, beaches, and historical sites with its tropical presence. Sweet tea, often called "the champagne of the South," is a staple beverage here, brewed strong, sweetened generously, and served ice cold, providing refreshing relief on hot Southern days. Known for its warm and welcoming spirit, South Carolina truly embodies Southern hospitality, with locals famous for their graciousness and eagerness to make visitors feel at home. The state's historic charm is palpable, with cobblestone streets in Charleston and antebellum plantations scattered throughout, preserving a rich, old-world allure. The Atlantic coastline is lined with beautiful sandy beaches, including the famous Myrtle Beach, known for its family-friendly atmosphere and vibrant boardwalk. Additionally, the culinary scene offers a delightful exploration of flavors; Lowcountry cuisine features dishes like shrimp and grits, she-crab soup, and fried green tomatoes, celebrating local ingredients and traditions.

Moving from Arizona to South Carolina to anchor the local news in Myrtle Beach, I was immediately introduced to significant cultural nuances. Among these was the local observance of Confederate Memorial Day every May 10, known regionally as the "War Between the States." This day, marked by the closing of state offices in South Carolina, Alabama, and Mississippi, honors those who fought for the Confederacy. A notable symbol of this legacy, the Confederate flag, had been a fixture over the South Carolina Statehouse since the 1960s, prominently used in Strom Thurmond's Dixiecrats campaign. It was removed in 2015, just weeks after a devastating act of domestic terrorism. A white supremacist and neo-Nazi murdered nine African American parishioners during a Bible study at the Emanuel African Methodist Episcopal Church in Charleston. This horrific act not only shocked the nation but also intensified the scrutiny of Confederate symbols. My tenure in the South granted me a firsthand experience of these cultural contrasts—some aspects beautiful, while others were profoundly disturbing.

Historically, South Carolina was a bastion of Democratic loyalty, a "blue" state where, for over a century, Democratic presidential candidates could nearly always count on its electoral support. This tradition dates back to 1829 with Andrew Jackson, who was from the Waxhaw region of the Carolinas. Throughout history, South Carolina consistently supported Democrats, whether they won or lost the presidency. The state backed candidates like Stephen A. Douglas, who lost to Abraham Lincoln, and **William J. Bryan**, defeated by **William McKinley** and **William Howard Taft**. It also supported **Alton Parker** and **Al Smith** in their unsuccessful bids and twice preferred Adlai Stevenson over Dwight D. Eisenhower in the 1950s. South Carolinians voted for victorious Democrats like Woodrow Wilson, John F. Kennedy, and **Jimmy Carter**. The state's unwavering support for Franklin D. Roosevelt, endorsing the New Deal four times, underscores its long-standing commitment to Democratic principles.

However, a significant shift toward Republicanism raises questions about the catalysts for this change, with Strom Thurmond playing a central role in the region's political realignment. Attributing a profound political shift to a single individual might seem simplistic, yet Thurmond's impact on the political landscape of the South is undeniable. His enduring influence has shaped generations. Thurmond's political career was extensive; he served as a U.S. Senator from 1954 until his retirement in 2003, one of the longest tenures in Senate history, and was Governor of South Carolina for four years before that. His public service began even earlier, serving as a county attorney for eight years before a five-year stint in the state legislature. Thurmond's dedication extended to his military service during World War II, where he earned eighteen decorations, showcasing his valor and commitment.

As a senator, Thurmond was notably effective at securing discretionary federal funds for South Carolina, receiving up to $10 for every $1 it paid in federal taxes. Known colloquially as "bringing home the bacon," this ability significantly boosted his popularity among his constituents. Despite his vocal criticism of federal overreach, Thurmond's knack for funneling federal dollars back to South Carolina underscored his influence and effectiveness as a lawmaker, reinforcing his appeal even as he championed smaller government and criticized the federal establishment. This paradoxical aspect of his career was a key element of his longstanding success and popularity in political life.

In the 1960s, the ideological battles between Thurmond and Lyndon B. Johnson highlighted a critical crossroads within the Democratic Party regarding equality and racial integration. Johnson, who started his political career as a senator from Texas and later served as Vice President, gradually embraced civil rights legislation, aligning with President Kennedy's progressive initiatives. In stark contrast, Thurmond, who had vigorously opposed such measures for decades, represented a significant ideological divide within the party. Their interactions were particularly pronounced during Johnson's tenure as Senate Majority Leader from 1955 to 1961, where Thurmond frequently used filibusters to block Johnson's efforts on civil rights legislation. This clash underscored the deep divisions within the Democratic Party and marked a pivotal moment in U.S. legislative history, mirroring the broader national debate over equality and integration.

When Johnson ascended to the presidency following JFK's assassination, he aligned himself with the more progressive elements within the Democratic Party that advocated for robust civil rights reforms. His administration marked a significant ideological shift as it aggressively pursued an ambitious civil rights agenda, sharply distancing itself from the staunch segregationist stance of figures like Thurmond. This shift signified a major realignment within the Democratic Party, decisively moving away from its segregationist roots toward a commitment to comprehensive civil rights reforms and dramatically altering the national political landscape. Meanwhile, Thurmond's gradual shift towards the Republican Party was met with seemingly little resistance from his constituents in South Carolina.

The scope of Johnson's legislative agenda extended beyond race to encompass the nation's health. As part of his broader "Great Society" initiative, aimed at reducing poverty, promoting equality, and enhancing the quality of life for all Americans, Johnson championed Medicare. He viewed the program as a necessary measure to ensure healthcare for the elderly, who often faced prohibitive medical costs and lack of insurance coverage. Believing it to be a moral obligation of the government, Johnson held that a society is judged by how it cares for its vulnerable populations.

On July 30, 1965, Johnson signed the Medicare bill into law at the Harry S. Truman Presidential Library in Independence, Missouri. This act was a symbolic nod to Truman's earlier efforts to establish a national health insurance program. Johnson's administration worked diligently to pass the legislation, overcoming significant opposition through his renowned persuasive skills and deep understanding of legislative politics.

In stark contrast, Thurmond vehemently opposed Medicare and similar social programs, viewing them as prime examples of government overreach that threatened personal freedom and fiscal responsibility. He argued that Medicare would lead to increased government intrusion into private lives. Moreover, Thurmond framed his opposition in terms of states' rights, asserting that healthcare initiatives like Medicare should be managed by local governments rather than mandated federally. He feared such federal involvement would set a precedent for an expansive welfare state, eventually encompassing Medicaid for low-income families, food stamps, and public housing programs.

Thurmond's resistance to Medicare was indicative of a broader conservative anxiety about the expanding role of the federal government, especially in sectors traditionally dominated by the private sector or left to individual initiative. Despite his staunch opposition, Medicare has evolved into a cornerstone of the American healthcare system, providing essential coverage to millions of elderly and disabled individuals. Today, Medicare, alongside Roosevelt's Social Security Act, is recognized as one of the most popular federal programs. It enjoys widespread support across a diverse range of demographics and political affiliations, a fact consistently confirmed by public opinion polls and surveys.

Not every South Carolina politician followed Thurmond's track. Senator **Ernest "Fritz" Hollings**, who was previously the governor, supported Thurmond for president in 1948 and the Dixiecrats' platform. Hollings, who passed away in 2019, admitted that early in his career, he shared Thurmond's segregationist views. However, his perspectives evolved significantly over the years, particularly after a pivotal moment in 1952. While arguing in favor of school segregation before the Supreme Court, Hollings was confronted by a lawyer who questioned how he could support Black soldiers fighting on the front lines in Europe but relegate them to the back of the bus when they returned home. As a World War II veteran, this question struck a chord with Hollings. He realized the inherent injustice in such a stance and began to reconsider his views on segregation.

After this moment of clarity, Hollings returned to South Carolina and began working toward integration in a gradual and non-violent manner. As governor, he played a crucial role in integrating state universities, a process he managed without the violent backlash seen in other parts of the South. This commitment to peaceful integration and civil rights marked a significant departure from his earlier segregationist views. Hollings' dedication to civil rights can be attributed to his personal experiences and reflections, particularly as a veteran who had witnessed the sacrifices of Black soldiers firsthand. This realization prompted him to pursue a more just and equitable path, committing to the cause years before the Civil Rights Act of 1964 was signed and before Thurmond left the Democratic Party.

While there might not have been direct, publicized clashes between Hollings and Thurmond over race, their respective actions and stances on civil rights clearly set them on different paths. During their nearly four decades in the Senate together, Hollings gradually supported integration and civil rights, whereas Thurmond remained a staunch opponent, symbolizing two divergent southern responses to the civil rights movement.

LBJ Legacy

During Freedom Summer in 1964, organizers launched a concerted effort to register black voters in Mississippi. Despite the loss of 15 volunteers during the campaign, it was the murders of three civil rights workers—two white volunteers, **Andrew Goodman** and **Michael Schwerner**, and black Mississippi resident **James Chaney**—that shocked the nation. On June 21, 1964, the three activists went to investigate the burning of a black church in Neshoba County, Mississippi. After leaving the church, they were arrested by local police on a traffic charge, detained for several hours, and then released that night into the hands of the Ku Klux Klan. Shortly after their release, the men were ambushed, abducted, and brutally murdered by Klansmen.

Their disappearance initially garnered significant media attention and a massive federal investigation led by the FBI. President Lyndon B. Johnson ordered a thorough search, and the case drew national outrage. The bodies of Goodman, Schwerner, and Chaney were discovered 44 days later, buried in an earthen dam.

The brutal killings highlighted the extreme violence and danger faced by civil rights activists in the South and underscored the lethal opposition to racial equality. The fact that two of the victims were white Northerners brought the reality of Southern racism and the civil rights struggle into sharper focus for many Americans who had previously been indifferent or unaware of the severity of the situation.

At the same time, Southern Democrats had just conducted an unpopular 75-day filibuster against the Civil Rights Act of 1964. Leading the opposition once again was Senator Strom Thurmond, known for his staunch segregationist views. Thurmond, who had previously set a record for the longest individual filibuster against the Civil Rights Act of 1957, was determined to block the 1964 legislation. Joining him in the effort were other

Southern senators, including **Richard Russell** of Georgia, **Robert Byrd** of West Virginia, and **James Eastland** of Mississippi. These senators were part of a long-standing tradition of Southern resistance to civil rights advancements and were motivated by a desire to maintain racial segregation and white supremacy.

The rhetoric used by these senators during the filibuster was often inflammatory and derogatory, reflecting their deeply ingrained racist beliefs. They argued that the Civil Rights Act infringed upon states' rights and personal liberties, a common justification used to perpetuate racial discrimination. Their speeches frequently emphasized the supposed dangers of racial integration and equality, aiming to incite fear and resistance among their constituents. Public perception of the filibuster was overwhelmingly negative, especially as media coverage highlighted the senators' racist rhetoric and Americans watched the horrific stories coming from the South.

The Civil Rights Act of 1964, passed by the Senate and signed into law by Johnson on July 2, 1964, represented a pivotal moment in the fight against racial segregation and discrimination in the United States. As the most comprehensive civil rights legislation in U.S. history, it aimed to eliminate segregation and discrimination across the nation. The Act prohibited discrimination based on race, color, religion, sex, or national origin in public accommodations, employment, and federally funded programs.

In the same year, another significant advance was made with the ratification of the 24th Amendment, which rendered the use of poll taxes in federal elections unconstitutional. A controversial symbol of racial discrimination in the South, the poll tax was abolished by this amendment. Johnson celebrated the ratification as a "triumph of liberty over restriction," marking further progress toward equality in voting rights.

Following the assassination of President Kennedy, there were many uncertainties about the type of leadership Johnson would provide. However, any doubts were quickly dispelled by his instrumental role in the passage of the Civil Rights Act. His political acumen and dedication were crucial in navigating the complexities of Congress to ensure the bill's passage, marking a significant achievement in advancing civil rights and social justice in America.

Martin Luther King Jr. praised Johnson for his efforts, acknowledging his significant contribution to civil rights, stating, "I want to tell you how grateful I am to the President for the action he has taken in this field. He has done more for civil rights than any other President since Abraham Lincoln."

Johnson himself reflected on the historical significance of his actions, remarking, "I shall never forget that it was more than 100 years ago when Abraham Lincoln issued the Emancipation Proclamation—but it was a proclamation; it was not a fact." In the Civil Rights Act of 1964, Johnson affirmed that "men equal under God are also equal when they seek a job, when they go to get a meal in a restaurant, or when they seek lodging for the night in any State in the Union. Now the Negro families no longer suffer the humiliation of being turned away because of their race." His administration vigorously enforced the Act, using federal authority to fight discrimination and promote equality nationwide.

On the night he signed the Act, his special assistant **Bill Moyers** found Johnson in a melancholic state. Moyers later recounted that Johnson remarked, "I think we just delivered the South to the Republican party for a long time to come." While this might have seemed a somber reflection following such a landmark event, it was also a prescient observation. An angry Thurmond, nearly two decades after storming out of the Truman Democratic Convention to lead the Dixiecrats, finally renounced his membership in the Democratic Party and joined the Republican Party. This move signaled the start of one of the most significant political realignments in American history.

In a statement that employed codewords like socialism and states' rights—terms long associated with Southern Democrats—Thurmond declared: "I have been increasingly concerned over the past few years with the trend in the national Democratic Party toward more and more socialism, or what they call government for everybody and the doctrine that government owes everybody a living. I believe that the Democratic Party is leading the evolution toward a socialistic state. On the domestic front, the leaders of the Democratic Party have sought to bring about the social and economic regimentation of the American people. Moreover, they have done this against the desires and wishes of the vast majority of the people as evidenced in the 1962 elections. I am not prepared to surrender this great country of ours to the leadership of those who advocate the course of defeatism and appeasement."

This ideological shift had been simmering for decades, starting with the administrations of FDR and Truman. Yet, it was Johnson's staunch commitment to integrating racial equality into the Democratic Party platform that led many Southerners, including figures like Thurmond, to switch to the Republican Party—the party of Abraham Lincoln, whom they had long reviled.

In Your Heart

In the 1964 election, Senator Strom Thurmond endorsed Arizona Senator Barry Goldwater for president. Although President Lyndon Johnson won the election in a landslide, Goldwater achieved a notable victory by carrying five states in the Deep South, a notable achievement as it was the first significant shift of this region to the Republican Party in the 20th century. Goldwater's success in the Deep South caused leaders from both parties to take notice and left Thurmond, who had recently switched to the Republican Party, with a sense of vindication.

Goldwater's campaign is often characterized as appealing to racial tensions, especially in the context of his opposition to the Civil Rights Act of 1964. However, it's important to understand that Goldwater's campaign strategy and his personal views on race were more complex. His vote against the Civil Rights Act of 1964 played a significant role in his campaign's appeal to certain segments in the South, where resistance to federal civil rights legislation was strong. Goldwater's stance attracted the support of many white voters in Southern states who were opposed to integration and federal civil rights mandates. This phenomenon was part of a broader shift in the political landscape of the South, which saw many white voters moving away from the Democratic Party in reaction to its increasing support for civil rights.

During the campaign, Goldwater made a personal commitment to Johnson that he would not engage in negative campaigning. This pledge was deeply rooted in Goldwater's belief in upholding dignity and respect in political discourse, even amid the often intense election battles. Goldwater frequently reminisced about discussions with Jack Kennedy regarding a joint campaign tour using the same airplane, a plan disrupted by Kennedy's assassination. Following this tragedy, Goldwater recognized the nation's reluctance to face the prospect of three different presidents within a single year. Despite this, and the highly charged political atmosphere of the time, Goldwater remained focused on campaigning on issues like small government, individual liberty, and his critique of the expanding federal power under Johnson's administration.

However, Johnson did not adhere to a similar standard. His campaign frequently cast Goldwater in a negative light through the media, particularly with the infamous "Daisy" ad, which suggested Goldwater's policies could trigger a nuclear war. This commercial, recognized as the first major negative television advertisement, along with other tactics from Johnson's team, proved highly effective in negatively framing Goldwater, despite his commitment to maintain a positive and issue-focused campaign.

In October 1986, as a twenty year old college student, I had the distinct honor of organizing and emceeing the final appreciation dinner for Goldwater in Lake Havasu City, Arizona. This event was more than a ceremonial farewell; it marked the end of the public life of the 1964 Republican presidential nominee, a figure both revered and controversial. Goldwater had profoundly shaped both the trajectory of the Republican Party and the national discourse on conservatism.

As I stood at the podium addressing the audience and the man of the hour, I felt a deep responsibility to honor a legacy as complex as it was transformative. Goldwater's steadfast principles and his courage to stand against the prevailing currents made this evening a poignant reflection on the nature of political bravery. Seated next to him at the dinner, I seized a rare opportunity to engage him directly. I asked about his infamous vote against the 1964 Civil Rights Act—a decision that had cast a long shadow over his legacy—and whether, with the benefit of hindsight, he harbored any regrets. His response was thoughtful and reflective, shedding light on the complexities of a man who often found himself at the crossroads of American ideology and politics.

Goldwater acknowledged his support for earlier civil rights legislation, such as the 1957 Act which Thurmond famously filibustered. He also pointed out that Johnson had not supported these earlier civil rights bills. By 1964, however, he believed that the inherent intelligence and fairness of the

American people would naturally overcome racial prejudices without the need for further legislation. He argued that astute business owners wouldn't turn away customers based on race, foreseeing a self-regulating economic environment. Reflecting on this, he shook his head and admitted that perhaps he had been overly optimistic.

Goldwater's opposition to the Civil Rights Act of 1964 was not rooted in racial prejudice but was based on his libertarian views concerning the roles of state and federal government in matters of race and religion. Being half-Jewish on his father's side, Goldwater had a personal disdain for segregation, a sentiment that led him to end segregation in his family's department stores. He was neither a segregationist nor a racist; rather, he was a staunch opponent of racial discrimination throughout his life. During his early political career as a city councilman, Goldwater actively promoted the desegregation of Phoenix public schools and spearheaded the integration of the Arizona Air National Guard. Notably, his first staff assistant in the Senate was an African American woman, underlining his commitment to equality. Additionally, his membership in the NAACP further exemplified his dedication to civil rights and his ongoing efforts to combat racial discrimination.

The 1964 presidential campaign, however, revealed that conservative philosophical language could be misinterpreted as a stance against forced integration, and Goldwater struggled to distance himself from an alliance with those who resisted civil rights—a connection he had never sought. By 1968, Goldwater had openly distanced himself from figures like Thurmond, notably declining to write a foreword for Thurmond's book due to disagreements over key racial issues like the Brown v. Board of Education decision.

In his later years, Goldwater emerged as a forward-thinking advocate for issues not typically associated with his conservative roots. He supported a woman's right to choose an abortion and became an early advocate for gay rights, along with backing the legalization of marijuana—positions that were notably progressive compared to the stances of most politicians from either side of the aisle at the time. Additionally, Goldwater was known for his confrontations with the religious right within his own party, famously challenging figures like conservative preacher **Jerry Falwell**, whom he saw as threats to individual freedom within the Republican Party.

When Goldwater died in 1998, he was recognized across the political spectrum for his influential role in American politics. Among those who paid tribute was Democratic Senator **Edward Kennedy**, brother of former President Kennedy, whom Goldwater had hoped to challenge in the 1964 presidential election instead of Johnson. Reflecting on Goldwater's impact, Kennedy noted, "Clearly, Barry understood what was happening in the country before many others did; he played a very important and significant role in this country's history."

Goldwater's unwavering adherence to his principles, as articulated in his seminal work "The Conscience of a Conservative," firmly established him as a leader more guided by conviction than by political expediency. His readiness to challenge his party's shift toward the religious right and his staunch advocacy for personal freedoms on cultural issues underscored his reputation as a statesman of extraordinary integrity and vision.

Born and raised in the West, Goldwater's distinct background set him apart from the eastern establishment prevalent at the time. His robust moral compass distinguished him from many other political figures I have encountered and interviewed over the years. Indeed, Barry Goldwater remains one of the finest statesmen I have ever met, embodying a commitment to principle over popularity that is exceedingly rare in the political arena.

Marching to Vote

The March from Selma to Montgomery in 1965 was a defining moment in the American civil rights movement, underscoring the push for voting rights and highlighting the racial injustices in the South. This movement included three pivotal protest marches organized by civil rights activists to confront the discriminatory practices preventing African Americans from registering to vote.

In early 1965, Martin Luther King Jr. strategically chose Selma, Alabama, as the focal point to intensify the campaign for black voter registration. Understanding the volatile atmosphere, King anticipated that the strong-arm tactics of Sheriff **Jim Clark** would capture national attention, much like the events in Birmingham a year earlier. In Birmingham, Commissioner of Public Safety **Bull Connor** had responded to peaceful protests with excessive violence, deploying police dogs and high-pressure fire hoses against demonstrators, many of whom were children and teenagers. These brutal encounters were broadcast on national television and covered extensively in newspapers, revealing the harsh realities of racial segregation and police brutality to a broader audience. As King prepared for the march in Selma, he drew a parallel between past and upcoming events, famously remarking, "Connor gave us the civil rights bill and Jim Clark is going to give us a voting rights bill."

The first march, famously known as "Bloody Sunday," took place on March 7, 1965. Approximately 600 protesters, led by **John Lewis** and **Hosea Williams**, set out from Selma, Alabama, aiming for the state capital, Montgomery. Their peaceful march was met with violent opposition as they crossed the Edmund Pettus Bridge. State troopers and local police attacked the marchers with billy clubs and tear gas, an act of brutality that was broadcast on national television, sparking outrage across the nation.

In response to this violence, King led a second march on March 9. The marchers reached the Edmund Pettus Bridge and held a brief prayer session before turning back, complying with a court order that prohibited them from continuing. This act of nonviolent resistance demonstrated the protesters' commitment to their cause and their respect for the rule of law.

The resolve of the protesters led to a third march on March 21, this time under the protection of federal forces, including National Guard troops and FBI agents. Starting with about 3,000 participants, the marchers traveled the 54-mile route to Montgomery over five days, their numbers swelling to about 25,000 by the time they reached the capitol on March 25.

On March 15, 1965, President Lyndon Johnson went before Congress to urge the passage of a voting rights bill, stating that Selma exemplified the struggles of African Americans to secure the full blessings of American life. He declared, "We shall overcome," invoking the battle cry of the civil rights movement. The march and the violence in Selma, particularly the events of "Bloody Sunday" on March 7, when peaceful marchers were attacked by law enforcement, garnered widespread media coverage and public sympathy.

These marches played a crucial role in galvanizing public support for civil rights reform and compelling the federal government to act. The national reaction to the violence of "Bloody Sunday" was instrumental in prompting Johnson to champion the Voting Rights Act of 1965. This significant legislation, which aimed to eradicate racial discrimination in voting, faced strong opposition from several Southern leaders, notably Strom Thurmond. The Act was designed to ensure voting rights for African Americans, challenging the established norms and deepening ideological divisions within the Democratic Party.

King heralded the Voting Rights Act as "a triumph for freedom as huge as any victory that has ever been won on any battlefield." He had seen firsthand the systemic efforts to disenfranchise African American voters through literacy tests, poll taxes, grandfather clauses, and other obstructive measures. King regarded the Act as a vital step toward removing these barriers, promoting fairer access to the voting process. He believed that the success of this legislation, achieved through nonviolent protest and advocacy, validated the effectiveness of peaceful resistance.

Historian David Goldfield noted that "the southern Democrat defections became a flood" after the enactment of the Civil Rights and Voting Rights Acts, signaling a significant reorganization of the political parties. This shift not only transformed the political landscape of the South but also had lasting implications for national politics, shaping the dynamics for decades to come.

The Urban Riots

During the 1960s, despite significant advancements in civil rights legislation, growing frustration over the slow pace of change led to heightened discontent, particularly in major cities. This sentiment sparked a series of urban riots, driven by young urban Black men who felt that Martin Luther King Jr.'s nonviolent approach was too passive for their immediate challenges. Prominent "Black power" advocates like **Stokely Carmichael**, newly elected head of the Student Nonviolent Coordinating Committee (SNCC), and **Floyd McKissick** of the Congress of Racial Equality (CORE), expressed not only dissatisfaction with the achievements of the Johnson administration's civil rights program but also contempt for its goal of racial integration. This burgeoning militancy manifested vividly throughout the decade as urban riots swept across the nation, marking a significant shift toward more radical and assertive forms of protest within the Civil Rights Movement.

In July 1964, Harlem in New York City became an epicenter of racial tension when a white police officer shot 15-year-old African American student **James Powell**. The incident sparked six days of looting and violence, resulting in extensive property damage and heightened racial tensions. The riots in Harlem were widely televised, shocking many white Americans insulated from the daily struggles faced by African Americans and bringing the stark realities of racial strife into living rooms across the nation.

The following year, the Watts neighborhood of Los Angeles erupted after a routine traffic stop escalated into a full-scale riot following accusations of police brutality. The conflict lasted six days, during which 34 people died, over 1,000 were injured, and extensive property damage occurred, estimated at $40 million. The dramatic scenes broadcast nationwide painted a stark picture of America's deep-seated racial divisions and underscored the urgent need for change in racial relations.

In July 1967, Newark, New Jersey, saw similar unrest after the arrest and beating of a black taxi driver by police, leading to 26 deaths and decades of urban decay. Later that month, the Detroit riots, also known as the 12th Street Riot, erupted in Detroit, Michigan, from July 23 to July 27, 1967, and stand as one of the most devastating urban riots in United States history. This event was marked by severe violence and had a profound socio-political impact on both the city and the nation.

The riots were primarily fueled by deep-seated racial tensions and economic inequalities that African Americans faced in Detroit. By the 1960s, the city had become highly segregated, with stark disparities in housing, education, and employment between black and white populations. Discrimination in public services was rampant, and economic opportunities for African Americans were severely limited.

The immediate trigger for the riots occurred in the early morning of July 23, when police conducted a raid on an unlicensed, after-hours bar known as a "blind pig" on 12th Street. The bar was hosting a welcome-back party for two Vietnam War veterans at the time. Typically, the police would arrest everyone present at such gatherings, a practice that had particularly targeted African American communities. On this occasion, the crowd outside the bar grew agitated and began throwing objects at the police, igniting the riots.

As the violence spread, it quickly escalated into a citywide civil disturbance characterized by widespread looting, arson, and violent confrontations with law enforcement. The situation deteriorated to such an extent that Governor **George Romney** ordered the Michigan Army National Guard into Detroit, and President Johnson sent in U.S. Army troops. Over the course of five days, the riots led to 43 deaths, over 1,000 injuries, and extensive property damage, leaving a lasting impact on the city of Detroit. The Detroit riots highlighted the urgent need for reform and prompted a national reflection on the racial and economic disparities that continue to influence American society.

As news of these riots reached the White House, Johnson expressed both perplexity and frustration, despite his significant efforts to advance civil rights legislation. Historian Doris Kearns Goodwin captured a dramatic shift in Johnson's sentiments. Initially elated by his landslide reelection, Johnson found himself despairing over the riots, lamenting, "How is it possible that all those people could be so ungrateful to me after I had given them so much?" This quote underscored the complexity of the social and racial issues of the time, which persisted even in the face of legislative achievements aimed at addressing systemic inequality.

The 1968 Olympic Games in Mexico City provided a global stage for civil rights activism. Black athletes, searching for a platform to protest racial injustice in the United States, found their moment during the medal ceremony for the 200-meter dash. **Tommie Smith** and **John Carlos**, having clinched first and third places respectively, transformed their moment of victory into a silent but powerful statement. As the national anthem played, each athlete raised a black-gloved fist—an emblem of Black Power—while bowing their heads and steadfastly refusing to look at the American flag. This act of protest, though silent, echoed loudly across the world, bringing immediate and harsh consequences: Smith and Carlos were suspended from the U.S. Olympic team and summarily expelled from the Olympic Village. Their gesture of defiance was a stark reminder of the racial tensions simmering within their home country, overshadowing their athletic achievements with political controversy.

Despite the absence of a broader boycott, which had been contemplated but never realized, the impact of their stand was profound. The U.S. team's success at the games, underscored by winning 45 gold medals, highlighted the contradiction of a nation capable of greatness in the global arena yet grappling with profound social injustice at home. This trend of using sporting events as platforms for protest would continue, as white police shootings of black individuals persisted into the next century, reminding the world of the ongoing struggle against racial injustice and inequality.

Intraracial Love

In a landmark decision in 1967, the Supreme Court case Loving v. Virginia struck down all state laws banning interracial marriage across the United States. **Richard** and **Mildred Loving**, an interracial couple previously sentenced to a year in prison simply for marrying, successfully challenged Virginia's anti-miscegenation statute. This victory marked a significant triumph in the civil rights movement, highlighting the tension between federal authority and states' rights and symbolizing a milestone in the fight for equal rights.

In the backdrop of the 1950s, interracial marriage faced vehement opposition across the United States. A 1958 Gallup poll demonstrated this resistance, showing negligible approval rates among southern whites and only slightly higher rates outside the South. Resistance to interracial marriage persisted, and even after the Loving decision, Alabama did not officially overturn its ban until 2000, with a substantial 40% of voters opposing the repeal.

Despite the Supreme Court's clear ruling, resistance to interracial marriage lingered, though societal attitudes gradually evolved. By 2013, Gallup polling indicated that opposition to marriages between blacks and whites had significantly decreased.

Remarkably, the stability of certain civil rights issues remains uncertain. In 2022, conservative justices overturned Roe v. Wade, returning the question of a woman's right to choose an abortion to the states after a half-century of legal precedent. In a concurring opinion, Justice **Clarence Thomas**, who is Black and married to a white woman, suggested that the high court should also reevaluate other established rulings, including those on interracial marriage.

In a prompt response to emerging legal uncertainties, Congress passed and President **Joe Biden** signed the Respect for Marriage Act in late 2022. This significant legislation enshrines protections for same-sex marriages, originally recognized by the Supreme Court in 2015, as well as for interracial marriages. By doing so, it reaffirms rights that have been well-established for decades, ensuring that these marriages are safeguarded against potential legal challenges in the future.

Historian Ana Edwards, who is Black, and her husband, Phil Wilayto, who is white, have been married nearly 20 years. Both have been community activists for years and said they didn't consider interracial marriage a potentially vulnerable institution until the Supreme Court overturned Roe v. Wade. "It's a little unnerving that these things where we made such obvious progress are now being challenged or that we feel we have to really beef up the bulwark to keep them in place," said Edwards.

Vietnam

The turbulence of the late 1960s in America cannot be comprehensively understood without addressing the Vietnam War's profound impact on society and politics. The involvement began under President John F. Kennedy, who initially deployed American troops to support South Vietnam against the Communist North. In a revealing interview with **Walter Cronkite**, Kennedy expressed doubts about the war, hinting he might withdraw troops before his presidency ended. Unfortunately, his assassination in 1963 left these plans unfulfilled.

Following Kennedy, President Lyndon B. Johnson significantly escalated U.S. involvement, which fundamentally altered the conflict's nature. This escalation disproportionately affected young black men who were overrepresented on the front lines. Early in the war, African Americans, making up about 11% of the U.S. population, accounted for approximately 16% to nearly 25% of the combat deaths. This stark disparity led to significant criticism and demands for changes in military policies by the late 1960s.

The war's impact varied dramatically across different segments of American society, illustrating a profound disparity in how individuals responded to the call for military service. Some young men felt a deep sense of patriotic duty to wear the uniform. **John McCain**, for example, served valiantly, being shot down and spending five years as a prisoner of war. In stark contrast, a vast number of elite, wealthy young men, including Donald Trump, found ways to avoid service. Trump received deferments for bone spurs in his feet, a common avoidance tactic among the affluent. This stark difference highlighted not only the socioeconomic inequalities but also the differing senses of obligation and sacrifice during the Vietnam War era.

The ongoing conflict fueled extensive student protests across the United States, intensifying around 1967 with significant events such as the confrontation at the Pentagon in October of that year. Over 10,000 people marched from the Lincoln Memorial to the Pentagon, initially in a peaceful demonstration that quickly escalated as activists clashed with military police.

The National Mobilization Committee to End the War in Vietnam had declared its intention to shut down the Pentagon, and for a brief moment, a small group managed to breach the building. However, their intrusion was short-lived as they were quickly expelled by security forces. The clash resulted in injuries to more than a dozen protesters and led to the arrest of hundreds, including notable figures such as **Dave Dellinger**, one of the era's most influential radical pacifists and activists, along with the novelist **Norman Mailer**.

This wave of protests was not isolated to Washington, D.C.; it was part of a broader wave of anti-war demonstrations that swept through major cities including San Francisco, Los Angeles, New York, and Madison, Wisconsin. These events marked a significant escalation in the domestic opposition to the United States' involvement in Vietnam, highlighting a growing national discontent that would continue to influence American politics and society.

In November 1969, an unprecedented demonstration unfolded in Washington D.C., marking the largest anti-war protest in the city's history. A quarter of a million people marched peacefully from the Capitol to the Washington Monument, united by their call for an end to the Vietnam War. The chants "All we are saying is give peace a chance" echoed through the crowd, symbolizing a nation's growing weariness with the conflict. Simultaneously, nearly 200,000 individuals gathered in San Francisco's Golden Gate Park, further amplifying the message across the continent.

Amidst this powerful display of public sentiment, President Richard Nixon chose to largely ignore the demonstrations. Instead, he spent the week solidifying support for his Vietnam policy, emphasizing the stakes involved. "The security of America is involved, peace for America and the world is involved, and the lives of our young men are involved," Nixon declared, framing the conflict as a pivotal moment for the nation regardless of political affiliation. "We are not Democrats. We are not Republicans. We are Americans," he stated, attempting to unify the country under his continued pursuit of the war effort.

The convergence of the Vietnam War and the civil rights struggle intensified societal discord during the late 1960s. For many, the war mirrored the racial and social inequalities they fought against within the United States, making the battle for civil rights resonate even more profoundly. As the decade progressed, the combined impact of the war abroad and the fight for equality at home created a potent mix of disillusionment and determination, driving the era's defining movements and leaving an indelible impact on American history.

It's important to recognize the shifting political dynamics around the Vietnam War. Initially, it was Democratic Presidents Kennedy and Johnson who escalated U.S. involvement. However, as the war dragged on, a significant transformation occurred within the Democratic Party. By the end of the conflict, progressives and liberals strongly opposed the war, aligning themselves with the growing anti-war sentiment across the country. In contrast, many Republicans continued to support the war effort, driven by a staunch anti-communism that favored a military victory.

The war ultimately concluded under dramatic and chaotic circumstances that marked a profound moment in American history. In the final days of the conflict, as North Vietnamese forces closed in on Saigon, American helicopters were famously pictured evacuating the last remaining U.S. personnel and at-risk Vietnamese from the rooftop of the U.S. Embassy. President **Gerald Ford** is often credited with putting an end to American involvement in Vietnam, closing one of the most turbulent chapters in American foreign policy.

1968 - Year of Turmoil

The 1968 presidential election remains one of the most dramatic and volatile in modern American history, marked by the assassinations of Martin Luther King Jr. and Democratic presidential candidate Robert F. Kennedy. These tragedies, alongside the escalating Vietnam War, ignited widespread unrest and fear across the nation. The political scene was further destabilized when President Lyndon B. Johnson unexpectedly announced he would not seek reelection, deepening the national crisis.

The assassination of King on April 4, 1968, by **James Earl Ray** marked a profound and devastating moment in American history. Ray, a white man, initially confessed to the killing but recanted three days later, claiming it was part of a conspiracy. The lack of a clear motive and the ambiguous details surrounding the assassination have left many questions unanswered, despite Ray's conviction. King's death ignited widespread grief and anger, sparking riots and civil disturbances in over 100 cities across the United States. The intensity of these riots reflected the deep frustrations and despair among many African Americans over the slow pace of racial progress and the loss of a leader who had fervently advocated for nonviolent change.

On the night of King's assassination, RFK was campaigning for president in a predominantly black neighborhood in Indianapolis. In an impromptu speech, he delivered the heartbreaking news of King's death to the crowd. Kennedy spoke of his own brother's assassination five years earlier and called for reconciliation rather than violence. His empathetic and conciliatory words helped calm a potentially explosive situation. Remarkably, while other cities erupted in violence that night, Indianapolis remained peaceful.

This tragic event injected new urgency into the civil rights movement, compelling politicians to act decisively. Just a week after King's assassination, Johnson signed the Civil Rights Act of 1968, also known as the Fair Housing

Act. This legislation, strongly supported by King, aimed to eliminate discrimination in housing based on race, religion, or national origin. It mandates equal access to housing opportunities and covers most housing transactions, ensuring individuals cannot be denied housing based on discriminatory reasons. It also protects against retaliation for filing fair housing complaints or assisting in investigations. The Fair Housing Act still exists today and remains a fundamental piece of civil rights legislation, promoting fair housing practices and combating discrimination.

Furthermore, King's assassination solidified his status as a martyr for the civil rights cause, ensuring that his legacy would be celebrated and remembered for generations. His death, while tragic, became a rallying point that reinforced the resolve of civil rights advocates to continue the struggle for justice and equality. Fifteen years later, in recognition of King's profound contributions and enduring legacy, a federal holiday was established in his honor. Signed into law in 1983 and first observed in 1986, Martin Luther King Jr. Day is celebrated every third Monday of January, offering a time for reflection on the ongoing fight for racial equality.

Kennedy's decision to run for president emerged from a complex backdrop of ambition, rivalry, and ideological commitment. After serving as Attorney General under his brother, and then under Johnson following JFK's assassination, Kennedy's relationship with Johnson was marked by deep personal and professional animosity. Despite their shared party affiliation, the two men often clashed over policy and personal style, with Kennedy viewing Johnson as an unworthy successor to his brother's progressive vision.

In 1966, while traveling in South Africa, RFK delivered his famous 'Ripple of Hope' speech at the University of Cape Town, advocating for civil rights and his belief in individual action contributing to societal change. He stated, "Each time a man stands up for an ideal, or acts to improve the lot of others, or strikes out against injustice, he sends forth a tiny ripple of hope, and crossing each other from a million different centers of energy and daring, those ripples build a current which can sweep down the mightiest walls of oppression and resistance."

Kennedy, now a U.S. Senator from New York, was increasingly seen as a voice for the disenfranchised and an advocate for social justice, appealing especially to young people, African Americans, and the poor. In March 1968, Kennedy took a strong stance against the Vietnam War, criticizing its moral implications and the enormous cost in human lives and economic resources. He argued that the funds devoted to the war would be better spent addressing domestic issues like poverty and inequality, contending that the war distracted from critical needs at home.

Kennedy's pointed critique had a profound impact, contributing significantly to Johnson's decision not to seek reelection—a decision Johnson announced in a live broadcast two weeks later. Viewed as a self-styled agent of sweeping political transformation, Kennedy had become a symbol of change, while Johnson, overshadowed by the Vietnam War, had become a symbol of the status quo. This perception, combined with mounting opposition, led him to believe he could no longer effectively unite the country. As Johnson confided to Vice President Hubert Humphrey in the spring of 1968, "I could not be the rallying force to unite the country and meet the problems confronted by the nation ... in the face of a contentious campaign and the negative attitudes towards me of the youth, Negroes, and academics." Despite the tumult of his presidency, overshadowed by Vietnam, Johnson's contributions to civil rights remained a defining legacy.

Kennedy's deep commitment to civil rights was highlighted by his outreach to African American communities. His visits to impoverished areas of black America were not just political but emotional engagements, where he spoke directly to the suffering and injustice experienced by minorities.

RFK's presidential campaign in 1968 gained momentum, marked by significant victories that suggested he could secure the Democratic nomination. His campaign was tragically cut short when, on the night of June 5, after winning the California primary, Kennedy was assassinated in Los Angeles. His assassin, **Sirhan Sirhan**, a Palestinian Arab, was deeply angered by Kennedy's strong support for Israel. The immediate trigger for his actions appears to have been Kennedy's pro-Israel stance and his promise to send 50 fighter jets to Israel if elected. Kennedy's death was a profound shock to the nation and the world, deeply felt by his supporters who believed that he could have led the nation toward reconciliation and peace in a time of great division and conflict. His assassination, coming so soon after the death of King, underscored the volatility and violence of the period, marking 1968 as one of the most tumultuous years in American history.

That year, a sobering assessment of American society was delivered by the President's National Advisory Commission on Civil Disorders, commonly known as the Kerner Commission. Their report presented a stark portrayal of a nation deeply divided along racial lines, stating that the United States was "moving toward two societies, one black, one white—separate and unequal." This landmark document linked the recent widespread rioting directly to entrenched white racism and highlighted systemic failures that perpetuated racial disparities.

The Kerner Commission was unequivocal in its call for sweeping reforms to bridge these divides. It advocated for comprehensive programs aimed at job creation, the abolition of discriminatory practices in employment and housing, and a major reorganization of the welfare systems to address the underlying causes of urban unrest. Moreover, in recognition of the immediate contexts that had led to recent violence, the commission also recommended the implementation of new riot control techniques and fairer processes for dealing with incidents of civil disorder.

The report was a critical moment in the civil rights movement, urging the nation to confront and rectify systemic injustices or face the consequences of increased racial tension and conflict. Its recommendations, although visionary, were met with mixed responses, highlighting the challenges of reforming deeply ingrained societal structures.

The 1968 Democratic National Convention in Chicago was a significant flashpoint of violence and unrest, influenced deeply by the divisive Vietnam War. The war had disproportionately impacted African American soldiers; during its early years, African Americans made up about 11% of the civilian population but accounted for nearly 20% of combat-related deaths. This stark disparity highlighted racial inequities within military conscription and deployment, fueling the broader civil rights movement's demands for equality and justice, including fair treatment within the military.

Amidst growing criticism from civil rights activists and the black community, the military eventually implemented changes to address these disparities. This issue, combined with the broader implications of the war, split the nation and spurred a vigorous anti-war movement demanding an end to U.S.

involvement in Vietnam. In response, thousands of anti-war demonstrators, including significant participation by groups like the Students for a Democratic Society (SDS), the Youth International Party (Yippies), and the National Mobilization Committee to End the War in Vietnam (The Mobe), converged on Chicago. The Mobe, in particular, was instrumental in organizing protests and included a diverse coalition of activists, including African Americans.

Mayor **Richard Daley**, maintaining his tough law-and-order reputation, mobilized thousands of police officers and the National Guard. The authorities' aggressive tactics, such as the use of tear gas, billy clubs, and mass arrests, led to violent clashes with protesters. The media's extensive coverage brought these confrontations into American living rooms with startling footage of police brutality, underscoring the country's deep divisions.

Inside the convention hall, the Democratic Party was bitterly divided. Supporters of anti-war candidate **Eugene McCarthy** were in stark opposition to those backing Humphrey, the eventual nominee linked to the Johnson administration's controversial policies. This internal conflict resulted in palpable tension, leading to heated debates and confrontations among delegates. Humphrey's acceptance speech, delivered at 2:30 am and met with boos and heckles, occurred when most of America was asleep, highlighting the strained atmosphere.

In his speech, Humphrey, who had famously challenged Southern Democrats to embrace human rights over states' rights at the 1948 Democratic National Convention, now aimed to unify a fractured nation. Twenty years after his pivotal challenge contributed to a significant exodus of Southern Democrats, and against the backdrop of the Vietnam War and profound civil rights issues, he addressed the widespread pain and anger afflicting America. Calling for unity and healing, he declared, "The tests of leadership for me would be to fulfill the needs of the American people and to unite us as a nation." His plea sought to bridge the deep political and social chasms that were threatening to destabilize the country further.

Thus, the 1968 Democratic National Convention became emblematic of the broader societal conflicts of the era, including opposition to the Vietnam War, civil rights struggles, and a pronounced generational divide. The chaotic scenes in Chicago symbolized the intense political and social divisions in the United States during the late 1960s.

The Wallace Effect

Republican presidential nominee Richard Nixon, reinvigorated after his defeat in the 1960 presidential election and an unsuccessful bid for governor of California in 1964, subtly aligned himself with former Alabama Governor

George Wallace, who was running as an Independent. Both Nixon and Wallace emphasized themes of "law and order" domestically and "peace with honor" in Vietnam, resonating with the so-called Silent Majority. This demographic, nostalgic for traditional family values, felt increasingly alienated by decades of New Deal policies and the radical counterculture movements of the era. Their campaigns effectively tapped into this sentiment, seeking to capitalize on the public's desire for a return to a more conservative social order.

At the onset of his campaign, Wallace made a statement that would define his political stance and justification for running as an independent: "There's not a dime's worth of difference between the Republican and Democratic parties."

This proclamation highlighted his dissatisfaction with both major parties, which he criticized for their similarities, especially on issues he considered crucial like states' rights and opposition to federal intervention in matters such as desegregation.

Wallace's appeal was particularly strong among voters who felt disenfranchised by the national policies of the major parties. During his infamous 1963 inauguration as Alabama's governor, he established himself as a staunch segregationist, famously declaring, "Segregation now, segregation tomorrow, segregation forever!" This stance positioned him as a pivotal figure in the resistance against civil rights progress.

Wallace's campaign deftly harnessed the social and racial tensions of the era, using groups like the Black Panther Party—which advocated for Black empowerment and racial justice—as examples of the radical elements he claimed were causing chaos and violence in American cities. By highlighting these groups, Wallace sought to position himself as the candidate who would restore order and protect white Americans from the perceived dangers of radical activism and federal overreach.

His campaign style was characterized by visceral populism, marked by raucous rallies and a confrontational approach that included belittling opponents. He adopted the slogan "Stand Up for America," responding to the riots sweeping the nation's cities with extreme rhetoric, such as, "Bam! Bam! Bam! Shoot 'em dead on the spot."

Wallace, much like Andrew Jackson before him and Donald Trump after him, portrayed himself as a champion of the common man, standing against what he depicted as an out-of-touch federal government and elite establishment. This resonated with many who felt marginalized or overlooked by the mainstream Democratic and Republican parties, particularly among poor and working-class whites in the South and Midwest. His use of provocative language and straightforward directness appealed to those disillusioned with political niceties and hungry for simple solutions.

His extreme rhetoric on law and order played well with his base, who were deeply concerned about what they saw as a breakdown of societal norms. The existence of the Black Panther Party provided a stark contrast to Wallace's platform. While the Panthers pushed for systemic changes to address racial inequality, Wallace leveraged the visibility of such groups to amplify fears and prejudices among his audience, positioning himself as a bulwark against the perceived threats of radical change.

Despite initially being viewed as a fringe candidate, by 1968 Wallace had successfully capitalized on the widespread discontent among white Americans who felt abandoned by the government. His support extended beyond his traditional Southern base to include significant portions of the Midwest and the North, regions also confronting the challenges posed by desegregation. Wallace's ability to tap into these sentiments indicated a significant shift in American politics, as he drew substantial attention to the divisions and dissatisfaction with the established political order.

Wallace's opposition to Kennedy, and later Johnson, was rooted in a broader ideological battle over the direction of the country, particularly concerning racial integration and the expansion of federal power. His resistance to Kennedy and Johnson's policies elevated his status among those who opposed civil rights legislation and feared federal overreach, bolstering his national profile among conservative and segregationist groups.

Wallace's intuitive political style resonated deeply with many Americans disenchanted with the rapid social changes of the 1960s. He positioned himself as a champion of traditional values, standing against what he depicted as the moral decline represented by student radicals, anti-war protestors, and civil rights activists. While his rhetoric often employed subtlety, it clearly played on racial anxieties, resonating with white voters who were uncomfortable with the civil rights advancements that were reshaping society.

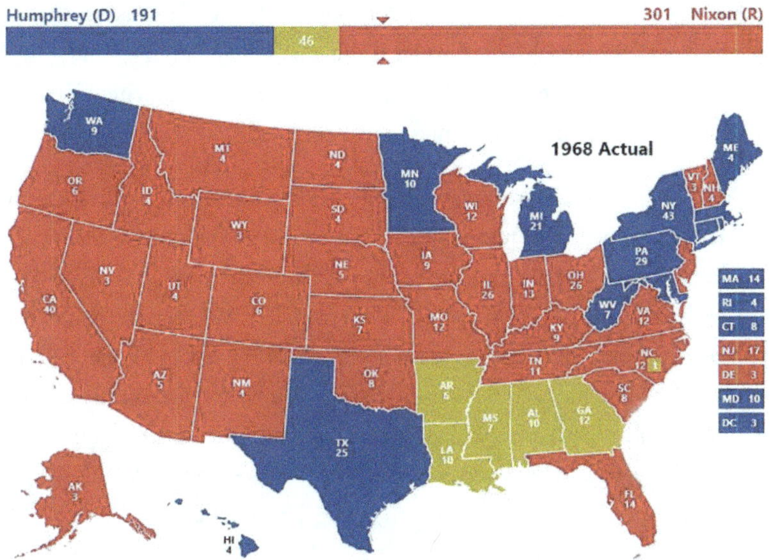

In the 1968 presidential election, Wallace's campaign dramatically reshaped American political dynamics. Securing 46 electoral votes and approximately 9.9 million popular votes, which accounted for about 13.5% of the total, Wallace's electoral success was concentrated in five Southern states—Alabama, Arkansas, Georgia, Louisiana, and Mississippi. His segregationist message resonated strongly among many white voters in these areas, highlighting deep-seated regional support for his policies.

Wallace's campaign left a profound and enduring impact on American politics. While he did not win the presidency, he effectively tapped into the discontent among white voters who felt alienated by the progressive changes of the 1960s. This demographic, later known as "Reagan Democrats," began shifting away from the Democratic Party, marking a significant realignment that would influence political strategies for decades. The influence of Wallace's campaign highlighted the deep divisions and strong resistance to social change emerging in American society at the time. His ability to galvanize such support not only reflected the highly polarized state of the nation but also foreshadowed the political realignments that would become more pronounced in the years to follow, marking a pivotal moment in the evolution of American political dynamics.

Wallace's political career was marked by both controversy and transformation. He ran for president four times, including in 1972 when he was severely injured in an assassination attempt by **Arthur Bremer**, a 21-year-old busboy, while campaigning in Maryland. The attack left Wallace paralyzed from the waist down, confining him to a wheelchair for the rest of his life. Despite his physical limitations, he was re-elected to a fourth and final term as Alabama governor in 1982 after publicly renouncing his earlier segregationist views and admitting he had been wrong about race. Wallace died in 1998, leaving behind a complex legacy intertwined with America's struggle over civil rights and political realignment.

Nixon's Southern Strategy

The "Southern Strategy" was a calculated political approach employed by the Republican Party, notably by Richard Nixon during his 1968 presidential campaign, to garner political support in the Southern United States. This strategy was similar to George Wallace's appeal as an Independent candidate, in that both aimed to capitalize on racial tensions and the growing dissatisfaction among white Southern voters with the Democratic Party's advocacy for civil rights and racial integration.

The GOP's new strategy was spearheaded by **Kevin Phillips**, a political strategist and analyst, who provided the intellectual foundation for the strategy with his work "The Emerging Republican Majority," which posited that the Republican Party could gain a majority by capitalizing on the dissatisfaction among Southern whites with the Democratic Party's civil rights reforms and social changes.

Unlike Wallace's more overt racial rhetoric, Nixon's Southern Strategy was characterized by the use of coded language and a focus on issues that indirectly resonated with racially conservative attitudes. This included promoting "states' rights," advocating for "law and order," and opposing forced busing for school integration—terms that acted as dog whistles. These phrases, created by Nixon adviser and speechwriter **Pat Buchanan**, also played a significant role by refining the campaign's rhetoric around issues like "law and order" and "states' rights," which resonated strongly with the target demographic.appeared neutral but conveyed specific, racially charged messages to target audiences. Such language allowed Nixon's campaign to appeal to white voters who were uneasy with the rapid pace of racial integration and the civil rights movement, without alienating moderate constituents.

During a pivotal moment in the summer of 1968, with Richard Nixon struggling to secure the Republican nomination against California Governor **Ronald Reagan** and lacking the necessary delegates, he met privately with a relatively new but increasingly influential GOP Senator, Strom Thurmond. This meeting highlighted Thurmond's growing clout within his new party. At

this crucial gathering, Nixon made several commitments that would shape his presidential campaign and policies. He promised to appoint "strict constructionists" to the federal judiciary—judges who would likely interpret the Constitution conservatively, especially on issues related to states' rights and civil rights. Additionally, Nixon agreed to consider Southern candidates for the Supreme Court, though his initial nominees, Clement Furman Haynsworth Jr. from South Carolina and George Harrold Carswell from Georgia, were ultimately not confirmed. However, he later successfully appointed **Lewis Powell** of Virginia.

Nixon also pledged to oppose court-ordered busing, a highly contentious issue at the time that was primarily used to achieve desegregation in public schools. Further, he consented to consider vice-presidential candidates from a list provided by Thurmond, ultimately selecting Maryland Governor **Spiro T. Agnew** as his running mate. These commitments were pivotal in helping Nixon secure 264 of the 356 Southern delegates, which clinched the nomination for him.

Agnew played a significant role in this strategy, promoting the misleading notion that the riots of the late 1960s were not a reaction to black Americans' frustration with urban unemployment, discrimination, and police brutality, but rather the result of manipulation by black leaders. In his acceptance speech at the Republican National Convention in Miami, he declared, "The first civil right of every American is to be free from domestic violence." Agnew's appeal to the 'common man' may have been a key factor in tipping the balance in swing states like Tennessee and North Carolina.

Furthermore, Thurmond bolstered Nixon's campaign by lending him his former aide, **Harry Dent**. Dent's deep understanding of the South's political landscape was instrumental in courting Southern voters and effectively implementing the Southern Strategy.

This alliance, however, faced significant criticism. Jackie Robinson, who broke Major League Baseball's color barrier and faced racial abuse, segregation, and even death threats en route to earning the league's MVP award and a World Series championship in 1955, had supported Nixon in 1960 due to his civil rights stance. Yet, he publicly withdrew his support in 1968, accusing Nixon of betraying civil rights principles to curry favor with Southern segregationists like Thurmond. Nixon's strategic focus on securing the Southern white vote resulted in a dramatic decline in his support among Black voters, plummeting from 32 percent in 1960 to just 12 percent in 1968, even as his popularity in the Southern states surged. This shift highlighted a profound realignment in American politics, emphasizing regional and racial considerations over broader ideological commitments, and marked a pivotal moment in the nation's political history.

By November, Hubert Humphrey enjoyed a dramatic late-campaign surge after he distanced himself from the unpopular Johnson administration, notably with a speech in Salt Lake City where he suggested a possible halt to the bombing of North Vietnam to foster peace talks. This move, alongside increased support from labor unions determined to counteract the "Wallace infection," helped Humphrey regain some of the blue-collar vote that had been drifting away.

Despite these efforts, many suburban voters leaned towards Nixon's toned-down version of law and order, which seemed less extreme compared to George Wallace's overtly segregationist rhetoric. Nixon won by less than one percent of the popular vote, but by a more comfortable margin in the electoral college despite Wallace carrying five states. Nixon's presidency would later reflect elements of Wallace's ideology, albeit in a more sanitized form, as observed by Humphrey who remarked that a "perfumed, deodorized" version of Wallace had won the presidency.

The Southern Strategy has been credited with transforming the political landscape of the South but has also been criticized for exacerbating racial divides and capitalizing on the fears and prejudices of white voters. In recent years, some leaders within the Republican Party have acknowledged the divisive nature of this strategy, reflecting a broader reassessment of the role of race in American politics and the dynamics of voter bases. The Southern Strategy remains a controversial yet crucial aspect of understanding the evolution of political affiliations and racial dynamics in the United States, highlighting the complex interplay between race relations and political strategy.

In reviewing the dynamics at play during 1968, my sense is that conservative Nixon advisers, in developing the Southern Strategy, naively believed they could maintain their identity as the party of Lincoln and uphold their roots in civil rights while exploiting the rift between Southern and progressive Democrats. However, in siding with Southern Democrats, they indeed compromised their principles and made a Faustian bargain. In a short time, Southern Democrats infiltrated the Republican Party, gradually eroding Lincoln's legacy on civil rights.

Summer of Love

There were few breaks during the 1960s from the turmoil and unrest, but the Summer of 1967, immortalized as the Summer of Love, marked a cultural and social turning point. In San Francisco, the epicenter of this countercultural revolution, about 50,000 young people converged, drawn by a shared yearning for peace, love, and a radical departure from conventional society. Many of these youths, sporting hair even longer than the Beatles', dressed in a riot of colors that mirrored their break from the drab conformities of the early 1960s.

Amidst this vivid spectacle, **Jim Morrison** of The Doors captured the mood perfectly when he chanted, "We want the world and we want it now!" This wasn't just a lyrical demand; it was a profound expression of the aspirations that many felt. Haight-Ashbury transformed into a vibrant commune of like-minded souls—artists, activists, and adventurers alike. The air was thick with the scents of incense and marijuana, and the sounds of groundbreaking music filled the streets. Icons of the era, including **Janis Joplin**, Jefferson Airplane, and The Grateful Dead, performed, fueling the atmosphere with their revolutionary sounds.

This period was not just a celebration but also a form of protest. Many young people, disillusioned by the nightly news depicting violence and racial injustices, sought refuge in this hippie haven, hoping to construct a society based on different values. The pervasive use of psychedelic drugs like LSD offered an escape from reality and an expansion of consciousness, further influencing the generation's outlook. Legendary concerts and impromptu performances were common, with musicians like **Jimi Hendrix** and The Mamas and the Papas making appearances, solidifying the summer as a musical and cultural milestone.

The Summer of Love was also influenced by key events like the Monterey Pop Festival in June 1967, which featured groundbreaking performances by

Hendrix, The Who, and Otis Redding, setting the stage for the summer's musical landscape. The "Human Be-In" in January 1967 at Golden Gate Park, organized by countercultural leaders like **Allen Ginsberg** and **Timothy Leary**, served as a prelude, bringing together thousands of people and spreading the ethos of love, peace, and communal living.

The Summer of Love, though brief, left an indelible mark on American culture and politics. It was an audacious declaration of a desire for a new way of living, one that was profoundly shaped by the social upheavals of the time. The events and ethos of this summer would reverberate through the decades, influencing everything from music and art to politics and social movements, embodying a quintessential moment of 1960s idealism and rebellion. Despite its idealism, the influx of thousands into Haight-Ashbury strained local resources and led to a backlash, highlighting the challenges of sustaining such a utopian vision.

As the 1960s drew to a close, the cultural landscape of America was marked by a series of pivotal events that captured the spirit of a generation and cemented the legacy of the counterculture movement. In August 1969, the Woodstock Music and Art Fair, colloquially known as Woodstock, epitomized this spirit. Held on a 600-acre farm outside the small town of Bethel, New York, owned by dairy farmer **Max Yasgur**, this unprecedented gathering attracted 400,000 people. United by a shared ethos of peace, music, and liberation, attendees experienced a weekend filled with the iconic sounds of artists like Hendrix, Joplin, The Band, and Jefferson Airplane, among others. Despite logistical nightmares such as overwhelming traffic jams, widespread substance use, and torrential downpours that turned the grounds into thick mud, the festival remained remarkably peaceful. The crowd, diverse in every sense—black and white, straight and gay, anti-war activists and pacifists—created a harmonious community, showcasing a unified front against the establishment while embracing peace and music.

Only a month before Woodstock, another significant event unfolded that would also profoundly impact American society. On June 28, 1969, the Stonewall riots began with a police raid on the Stonewall Inn, a gay bar in New York City's Greenwich Village. This raid sparked a series of demonstrations by the bar's patrons and broader LGBTQ+ community, protesting against longstanding police harassment and discrimination. These protests marked the first major instance of LGBTQ+ individuals collectively standing up against oppression in the United States. Unlike the peaceful scenes at Woodstock, Stonewall was marked by nights of unrest and resistance, which became a catalytic event for the LGBTQ+ rights movement. The legacy of the Stonewall uprising is celebrated annually during Pride month, symbolizing the ongoing struggle for equality and the empowerment of LGBTQ+ communities worldwide.

These events, occurring within weeks of each other, highlighted the era's complex tapestry of social change, where the calls for peace, love, and personal freedom were interwoven with demands for recognition and equality. As such, Woodstock and Stonewall stand as enduring symbols of the counterculture era, each fostering a legacy of change and influence that resonates to this day.

Landslide to Misery

President Richard Nixon's civil rights record is characterized by a complex interplay between political strategy and substantive policy actions. His administration's Southern Strategy appealed to conservative elements resistant to civil rights advancements. Nevertheless, Nixon also enacted several significant policies that furthered civil rights.

Notably, Nixon signed crucial legislation like the extension of the Voting Rights Act in 1970 and supported the Equal Employment Opportunity Act, bolstering civil rights protections. His administration expanded affirmative action programs, initially introduced under President Johnson, with the "Philadelphia Plan" of 1969. This required federal contractors to meet specific quotas for minority workers, marking a significant federal move to combat racial inequalities in employment. Although Nixon's political strategies sometimes seemed to counter civil rights progress, he enforced desegregation court orders, notably advancing school desegregation in the South. Additionally, Nixon focused on urban policy and support for minority-owned businesses, establishing the Office of Minority Business Enterprise to provide financial aid and other support.

A pivotal aspect of Nixon's legacy was the establishment of the Environmental Protection Agency (EPA) in 1970, reflecting a commitment to environmental justice. Recognizing clean air, water, and land as fundamental rights, the EPA signified a major shift in managing environmental issues in the United States, ensuring public health and the preservation of natural resources. This move also addressed the disproportionate impact of environmental degradation on minority and low-income communities by consolidating federal research, monitoring, and enforcement activities into a single agency.

By launching the EPA and endorsing crucial environmental legislation like the Clean Air Act of 1970 and the Clean Water Act of 1972, Nixon contributed to a legacy that recognized the right to a clean and healthy environment as a civil right for all Americans. His commitment to environmental policy remains one of the enduring positive aspects of his tenure, illustrating a form of civil rights that ensures governmental protection of the environment for the benefit of the entire population.

By 1972, Nixon's popularity was high with voters. Meanwhile, the Democratic Party was grappling with the exodus of Southern Democrats and internal divisions. Amidst this turmoil, Democratic Representative **Shirley Chisholm** from New York launched a historic and groundbreaking presidential campaign. As the first African American woman to run for the Democratic Party's presidential nomination, Chisholm's campaign was guided by her motto, "Unbought and Unbossed," which also served as the title of her autobiographical book. Chisholm had already made history in 1968 by becoming the first Black woman elected to the United States Congress.

Her presidential campaign symbolized her lifelong commitment to justice and equality, aiming to give a voice to the "voiceless." Her platform included advocating for civil rights, women's rights, the poor, and opposition to the Vietnam War. Chisholm sought to challenge the political status quo and address the needs of marginalized groups across America.

Despite facing discrimination as both a woman and an African American, Chisholm's campaign managed to secure 152 delegates before she withdrew. She encountered numerous obstacles, including limited funding, scant media coverage, and opposition from within the established political structure, including some African American leaders. Nonetheless, her bid for the presidency paved the way for future generations of women and minority candidates, leaving a lasting impact on American politics. Chisholm's campaign was not just about trying to win the presidency—it was about challenging the nation to be more inclusive and just.

South Dakota Senator **George McGovern** clinched the Democratic nomination for the 1972 presidential election through a grassroots campaign that capitalized on his strong anti-war stance and appeal to the progressive wing of the Democratic Party. McGovern's success in securing the nomination was due in part to his campaign's effective organization, especially in caucus states, and his ability to mobilize young voters and activists who were disillusioned with the Vietnam War and the political establishment.

The 1972 Democratic National Convention in Miami Beach was marked by significant chaos and controversy. The convention was a scene of factional infighting and procedural disputes, reflecting the deep divisions within the Democratic Party. Supporters of various candidates, including Hubert Humphrey and George Wallace, clashed with McGovern's backers. The credentials committee had to deal with challenges to delegate slates, leading to prolonged debates and delays.

McGovern's acceptance speech was notably delivered in the early hours of the morning, around 3:00 AM, when most Americans were asleep. This unusual timing was a result of the prolonged and contentious proceedings earlier in the day. As a consequence, his message did not reach a wide television audience, which hampered his ability to capitalize on the moment.

The Nixon campaign effectively defined McGovern as an out-of-touch liberal, a characterization that resonated with many voters. Nixon's team portrayed McGovern as too radical and disconnected from mainstream American values, emphasizing his positions on issues like amnesty for draft evaders, decriminalization of marijuana, and a significant reduction in defense spending. These portrayals contributed to a perception of McGovern as outside the political mainstream, which Nixon exploited to his advantage.

McGovern's handling of his running mate also became a significant issue. Initially, McGovern chose Missouri Senator **Thomas Eagleton** as his vice-presidential candidate. However, it was soon revealed that Eagleton had a history of mental health treatment, including electroshock therapy. The media and political opponents seized on this information, creating a crisis for the McGovern campaign. After initially standing by Eagleton, McGovern eventually decided to replace him on the ticket with **Sargent Shriver**, a former ambassador and Peace Corps director. This incident damaged McGovern's campaign, contributing to the perception of disorganization and poor judgment.

Nixon's 1972 reelection triumph over McGovern was decisively overwhelming, illustrating a sharply divided Democratic Party, exactly as the Republicans had predicted. During this time, significant shifts within the Democratic Party saw Northern liberal Republicans, disenchanted with the GOP's rightward tilt, gradually replacing the rapidly departing Southern Democrats. Nixon secured a resounding victory, carrying 49 states and amassing 521 electoral votes, with only Massachusetts and the District of Columbia supporting McGovern, who received a mere 17 electoral votes. This marked the first Republican landslide in the traditionally Democratic South since Reconstruction, and the first time since 1944 that the South had unanimously supported a single candidate. Nixon's dominance extended across all 11 states of the old Confederacy as well as all the border states. Notably, his win in Arkansas was the first Republican presidential victory there since 1872.

A pivotal factor in McGovern's defeat was the erosion of the traditional Roosevelt coalition of black, Jewish, and Catholic voters. Election day surveys revealed that Nixon captured the Catholic vote by 59 to 33 percent, a significant shift from the 55 to 70 percent typically secured by Democrats in prior elections. Additionally, Nixon made substantial inroads by securing 58 percent of the urban vote, traditionally a Democratic stronghold.

High-profile African American entertainers such as **Sammy Davis Jr.**, James Brown, and **Jim Brown**, the former football star turned actor, publicly endorsed Nixon. At an Operation PUSH expo, Davis faced considerable backlash for his endorsement, resulting in boos from the crowd. Reverend **Jesse Jackson**, president of PUSH, intervened, calming the audience to allow Davis to perform. Despite these high-profile endorsements for Nixon, McGovern still received 87% of the black vote, albeit a decline from Hubert Humphrey's 90% four years earlier, while Nixon's share increased by three percentage points to 13%.

The introduction of the 26th Amendment in 1971, which lowered the voting age from 21 to 18, significantly impacted the electoral dynamics of the period. Pollster **George Gallup** observed a notable shift among young voters; initial enthusiasm for McGovern on college campuses waned as the election neared. Ultimately, Nixon captured nearly half of the votes from these young, first-time voters. This broad-based national support indicated that the Republicans were well-positioned to dominate the political landscape throughout the 1970s and beyond, barring any major scandals.

Watergate

On June 17, 1972, just before Nixon's landslide reelection victory, the Watergate office complex in Washington, D.C. was the site of a break-in at the Democratic National Committee (DNC) headquarters. This operation was quickly linked to officials from the Nixon administration and his re-election committee. As the investigation progressed, it became clear that this break-in was not an isolated incident but part of a broader pattern of political espionage and sabotage on behalf of Nixon's campaign.

The scandal deepened with the revelation that Nixon had installed a tape recording system in the Oval Office, which captured numerous conversations, including evidence implicating his administration in both the initial break-in and the efforts to cover it up. Nixon resisted releasing these tapes despite a subpoena from a special prosecutor, resulting in a series of court battles that peaked with the Supreme Court's decision in United States v. Nixon (1974), which mandated the release of the tapes.

In the thick of these events, **Fred Thompson**, serving as chief Republican counsel for the Senate committee investigating the scandal, gained prominence. Reflecting on Thompson's crucial role during my preparation for a 2008 interview with him, I recalled Senator Barry Goldwater's harsh assessment of Nixon as "the most dishonest individual I've ever met in my life." The contents of the Watergate tapes were damning, showing Nixon's direct involvement in the cover-up and eroding his support among key party members, including Goldwater.

Thompson's questions to **Alexander Butterfield**, the deputy assistant, were pivotal. He asked, "Mr. Butterfield, are you aware of the installation of any listening devices in the Oval Office of the president?" Following a lengthy pause, Butterfield confirmed, "I was aware of listening devices, yes sir." Thompson continued, probing the authority under which the devices were installed, to which Butterfield responded, "On the president's authority, by way of Mr. Haldeman [then-chief of staff H.R. "Bob" Haldeman] and Mr. Higby [Lawrence Higby, a Haldeman aide]." Butterfield's acknowledgment was a critical turning point that would ultimately lead to Nixon's historic resignation—the only U.S. president ever to do so.

During the interview, Thompson, who later starred in films like "The Hunt for Red October" and TV shows such as "Law & Order," transported us back to that pivotal summer of 1973: "I was thirty years old, right in the heart of our country's most significant events. Sitting next to a statesman, **Howard Baker**, with **Sam Ervin** just a seat away, I witnessed history unfolding," he recounted. He also recognized the gravity of his role during the hearings: "I started and remained a loyal Republican, but we were aware of the taping system, and it was our responsibility to expose it."

Nixon had been skeptical about Thompson's role, reacting to his appointment with disbelief and dismissal, as evidenced in his recorded remarks, where he called Thompson 'dumb as hell.' Just three months later, Thompson's crucial questioning would trigger the events leading to Nixon's disgraceful departure from office.

On August 8, 1974, facing the near certainty of impeachment and conviction, President Richard Nixon resigned from office. The repercussions of the Watergate scandal were profound and long-lasting, particularly for the Republican Party. The scandal led to significant losses in the 1974 midterms, as voters strongly rebuked Nixon's Republican Party, now tainted by corruption. This not only eroded public trust in political leaders but also stamped the GOP with a legacy of scandal that would take years to shed. The term 'Watergate' itself became synonymous with political corruption, casting a long shadow over the party's image for decades.

The scandal further deepened the existing divisions within the Republican

Party. Moderates and liberals within the party sought to distance themselves from Nixon's actions and the conservative faction, leading to internal conflicts and a battle over the party's future direction. Nixon, who had previously built a broad political coalition, watched it disintegrate into turmoil—mirroring the chaos the Democratic Party had faced.

Nixon had been a towering figure in American politics—serving eight years as Vice President, engaging in a historic electoral battle with John F. Kennedy, making a dramatic comeback to win the presidency in 1968, and securing a landslide reelection in 1972. He was the first sitting president to visit China and engaged Soviet leaders from Nikita Khrushchev to Leonid Brezhnev. Yet, his presidency, marked by significant achievements, ended in disgrace, leaving a lasting impact on the nation's political landscape.

Carter Country

After Nixon's resignation, Vice President Gerald Ford ascended to the presidency, famously declaring that the nation's "long national nightmare" was over. Ford had been appointed less than a year prior to replace Spiro T. Agnew, who had resigned as vice president following an investigation into multiple allegations, including conspiracy, extortion, and bribery. Agnew avoided prison by pleading no contest to a single charge of federal income tax evasion. Taking office amid a period of deep political scandal and national disillusionment, Ford faced the formidable task of healing a divided nation. Known for his integrity and openness, the new president from Michigan, a moderate Republican, worked diligently to restore trust in the executive branch and unify the country, all while another presidential election rapidly approached.

During his 1976 presidential campaign, Ford employed a markedly different strategy than Nixon had previously used. Ford consciously avoided the racially charged and conservative messaging that had been central to Nixon's strategy for winning over disaffected Southern Democrats. Instead, Ford adopted a more nuanced and inclusive approach, aiming to attract a broad spectrum of voters, including moderate Democrats and Republicans. This strategy was reflected in his campaign slogan, "He's making us proud again," which aimed to restore national pride and highlight his administration's efforts to stabilize an economy suffering from inflation and unemployment, as well as to emphasize his strong stance on national defense.

Despite these efforts, Ford encountered significant obstacles in the South, where he faced former Georgia Governor Jimmy Carter. Carter leveraged his deep regional connections and a genuine personal appeal that resonated strongly with Southern voters, gaining a crucial advantage. Additionally, Ford's decision to grant Nixon a full pardon, absolving him of any potential criminal charges, alienated millions of Americans. This controversial decision deeply wounded his campaign, as many voters were unable to forgive him, significantly impacting his chances in the election.

Carter's successful bid for the presidency in 1976, especially his triumph in Southern states, was a nuanced accomplishment that harmonized his profound Southern roots with progressive stances on human rights. As a Georgian peanut farmer and former governor, Carter's intrinsic Southern identity appealed to regional voters. His image as a devout Christian and family man further enabled him to connect deeply with Southern voters, appealing to their traditional values during a period when the nation was still reeling from the disillusionment of the Watergate scandal.

Carter's approach to civil rights was also pivotal. He supported civil rights broadly, but he was careful in how he articulated these positions, focusing on universal themes of fairness and justice rather than framing his support as part of a radical agenda. This allowed him to maintain credibility with both progressive and moderate voters. His progressive stances were balanced with his advocacy for a strong federal government, yet he presented these views in a manner that emphasized efficiency and compassion rather than coercion.

Moreover, Carter's campaign capitalized on the public's desire for new leadership and moral integrity in the White House, themes that resonated strongly in the post-Watergate era. His promise of a government as competent and trustworthy as the American people struck a chord with voters eager to move past the cynicism and corruption that had marred the national government.

However, Carter's campaign faced a significant challenge when he admitted in a 1976 Playboy magazine interview to having "committed adultery in my heart many times." This confession scandalized devout Christians and diverted public and media attention from his policies to his personal life. Reflecting on the incident, Carter noted, "It was a devastating blow to our campaign when this Playboy interview was published. The news reporters and the general public just totally forgot about all the issues, what I stood for, what I might do as president when they became absorbed with the Playboy interview."

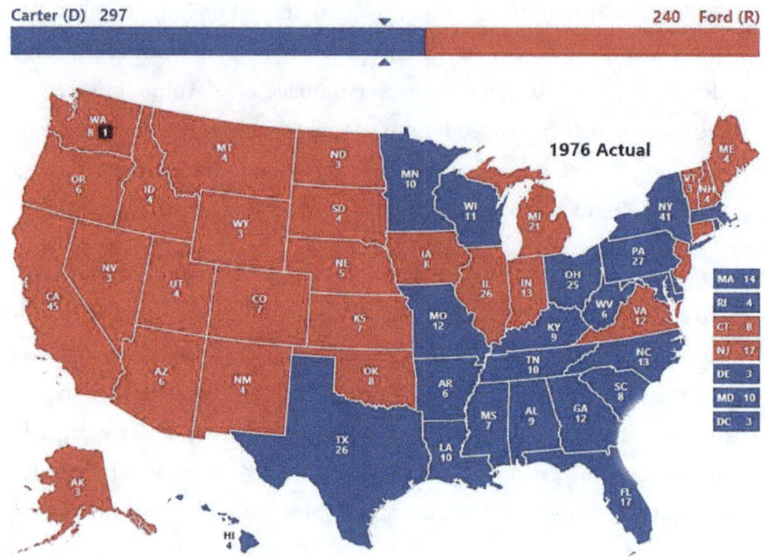

Despite this controversy, Carter's campaign vision of inclusion and fairness extended beyond the traditional confines of Southern politics. His ability to maintain regional loyalty while embracing progressive governance countered the trend of Southern Democrats drifting from the party during the turbulent post-civil rights era. This balance was crucial in connecting with a broader electorate, though the race was tight, with Carter securing only 51% of the popular vote to Ford's 48%. In key states, the margin was about 1%, leaving many in Ford's camp to ponder the "what ifs," particularly regarding the Nixon pardon.

After taking office, Carter vigorously advanced civil rights both at home and abroad. He was dedicated to diversifying the federal government, appointing an unprecedented number of women and minorities to significant positions. His notable appointments included **Andrew Young** as the United States Ambassador to the United Nations and **Patricia Roberts Harris** as the Secretary of Housing and Urban Development. In 1977, Carter also championed the Community Reinvestment Act (CRA), aimed at combating redlining—the discriminatory practice where banks avoid providing financial services based on community demographics. This law pressed banks to serve the credit needs of all community segments, particularly those in low- and moderate-income neighborhoods.

Carter's commitment to civil rights was paralleled by his strong human rights record. He placed human rights at the forefront of his foreign policy, challenging oppressive regimes and supporting initiatives that promoted human dignity and freedom worldwide. This stance marked a significant shift in American foreign policy, emphasizing moral principles alongside national interests.

In the cultural sphere, Carter made notable efforts to include African American artists in White House events. In 1978, he hosted a jazz concert at the White House featuring prominent black musicians like **Dizzy Gillespie**, **Max Roach**, and **Sarah Vaughan**, recognizing the importance of jazz and the contributions of African American musicians at a time when the genre was often marginalized. According to Carter biographer Kai Bird, one of Carter's chief presidential objectives was "to mend the racial divide." Under his administration, food aid was significantly expanded, providing substantial relief to many impoverished Black residents in rural areas. Moreover, his administration implemented stricter regulations to prevent racially discriminatory schools from claiming tax-exempt status, further demonstrating his dedication to racial equality.

Carter's presidency relied heavily on support from Black voters, who were crucial in propelling the underdog Democrat to the White House in 1976. Despite facing numerous challenges during his term, this loyal base largely remained steadfast; four years later, Black voters supported Carter nearly as uniformly, even as many white voters shifted their allegiance to his Republican challenger, Ronald Reagan.

Following the 1976 election, First Lady **Rosalynn Carter** sent a personal note to Reverend **Jim Jones**, a political and religious figure in San Francisco, expressing gratitude for his support. Jones had risen to prominence in the 1950s as a charismatic preacher dedicated to racial equality and desegregation within his church, the Peoples Temple. During the '76 campaign, Jones, alongside Rosalynn Carter, captivated nearly 5,000 of his followers at a rally in support of her husband.

Two years after the election, Jones embarked on a radical plan, leasing over 3,800 acres of remote jungle from the Guyanese government to establish Jonestown, a supposed utopia for his California-based followers. However, beneath the utopian facade, disturbing realities simmered. In late 1978, concerns about these conditions prompted Democratic Congressman **Leo Ryan** to lead an investigative delegation to Jonestown, spurred by allegations from disenchanted former members who claimed it was a cult.

The situation escalated rapidly after a tense dinner at the compound when a journalist received a note from a desperate follower seeking to escape. The next day, a fraught confrontation ensued between an agitated Jones and Ryan, who demanded additional planes to evacuate those wishing to leave. The tension peaked at the airport, where Ryan and about 40 defectors were ambushed by Jones' security team, resulting in the fatal assassination of Congressman Ryan.

Later that day, in a horrific culmination of his control, Jones led 918 of his followers, including children, to participate in a mass suicide, ingesting a cyanide-laced drink of Flavor Aid. This event tragically coined the now famous phrase 'don't drink the Kool-Aid,' used to warn against unquestioningly following charismatic leaders who propagate clearly false beliefs.

"Jim Jones spoke with the fiery passion typical of Baptist and Pentecostal ministers, especially from the black church tradition. His sermons on civil rights and societal injustices demanded attention," noted follower Tim Carter (no relation to Jimmy and Rosalynn). Describing the aftermath, Carter revealed the heartrending toll: he lost his wife and baby in the mass-murder-suicide orchestrated by Jones.

This tragic event highlights the perilous influence of charismatic leadership and the devastating impact of cult dynamics that can ensnare and distort the perceptions of hundreds, even millions, blurring the lines between faith, politics, and rationality.

Backwards Nobody

By 1980, Jimmy Carter's presidency was besieged by a series of economic hardships—high inflation, soaring interest rates, and an energy crisis—that contributed to widespread dissatisfaction. Adding to these challenges was the Iran Hostage Crisis, a prolonged ordeal where American diplomats were held captive in Iran, which severely undermined Carter's image as a decisive leader. This crisis dominated the final year of his presidency, highlighting a perceived ineffectiveness and indecision.

Carter also faced significant criticism from the religious right, particularly when his administration enforced Internal Revenue Service (IRS) rules that revoked the tax-exempt status of racially segregated, private Christian schools.

Although these rules reinforced policies initiated during the Nixon administration, the religious right accused Carter of targeting Christian institutions. This controversy became a pivotal moment for the evangelical community, as many of these schools had been established to circumvent court-ordered desegregation, effectively functioning as havens for maintaining racial segregation under the guise of religious freedom.

Richard Viguerie, a prominent Republican activist, described the IRS actions as the "spark that ignited the religious right's involvement in real politics." The underlying issue in this IRS controversy was race. Many of these private Christian schools had been established as part of a strategy to circumvent court-ordered desegregation, effectively functioning as havens for maintaining racial segregation under the guise of religious freedom.

All of these attacks on Carter prompted a formidable primary challenge from Senator Edward Kennedy, the progressive brother of former president John F. Kennedy. On the campaign trail, Kennedy vocally criticized the sitting president, declaring at rallies, "I say it's time to say: No more American hostages. No more high interest rates. No more high inflation, and no more Jimmy Carter."

Reflecting on the dynamics of the primary, author Jon Ward noted, "I think Kennedy just saw Carter as sort of a backwoods nobody who was going to be gone, you know, in a couple of months. And he really had contempt for him as having not a lot of accomplishments and not a lot of pedigree. So they were just from alien worlds." Carter managed to secure the nomination over Kennedy, but unity within the party was notably absent during their convention.

The lack of unity within the Democratic Party was starkly visible during their convention, with Kennedy evasively moving around the stage, avoiding a photo opportunity with Carter that was meant to symbolize party unity.

Once again, the Democrats were perceived as disorganized and fractured, struggling to present a united front in a critical election year.

The Time Is Now

Amid the challenges of the late 1970s, Ronald Reagan's presidential campaign capitalized on the opportunity to promise economic revival through deregulation, tax cuts, and reduced government spending. His campaign slogan, "Let's make America great again," provided a hopeful contrast to the grim economic realities of the Carter years, resonating with voters experiencing economic stagnation. This message appealed broadly across the electorate, playing a significant role in the shifting political landscape that would eventually usher Reagan into the presidency.

Reagan also adeptly connected with the cultural and ideological preferences of Southern voters. His emphasis on conservative values, strong national defense, and states' rights deeply resonated in the South. These themes, coupled with his charismatic appeal and a promise of robust American leadership, effectively drew many Southern voters away from Carter.

Reagan's embrace of the Moral Majority in 1979 marked a pivotal moment in his political career and in American politics overall. Founded by Jerry Falwell, a Baptist minister and religious broadcaster from Lynchburg, Virginia, the Moral Majority was an explicitly political organization committed to a "pro-life, pro-family, pro-morality, and pro-American" agenda. By decrying what they perceived as the decline of the nation's morality, the organization quickly amassed a significant following and played a crucial role in solidifying the influence of the New Christian Right in American politics. This shift significantly altered the political landscape, pushing it further to the right and leaving behind Carter, an evangelical himself, who could not secure the same level of support from this burgeoning conservative movement.

Reagan's success in the 1980 election was underpinned by his adeptness at tapping into economic, cultural, and ideological concerns that resonated deeply with American voters. His famous assertion, "I didn't leave the Democratic Party, the Democratic Party left me," underscored a broader transformation in the South from a Democratic stronghold to a Republican base. This statement reflected a sentiment felt by many voters in the South who felt alienated by the Democratic Party's shift towards more progressive policies, which they felt no longer represented their values.

Reagan's ability to connect with these voters was not simply about exploiting Carter's vulnerabilities; it was about effectively dismantling Carter's hold on his home turf. By aligning his campaign with the values promoted by organizations like the Moral Majority, Reagan was able to pave the way for a sweeping victory that reshaped the political alignment in the South for decades to come. This realignment was not only a testament to Reagan's strategic campaign efforts but also indicative of the shifting ideological and cultural landscapes of American society during that period.

Not the Bigots

Ronald Reagan's 1984 reelection campaign stands as a historical outlier in the annals of American politics, not just for its overwhelming success but also for the nature of its appeal. Reagan's 1980 campaign might have drawn on elements of Richard Nixon's 'Southern Strategy', which targeted disaffected white voters in the South, but by 1984, Reagan's broad appeal across demographic and geographic lines rendered such a focused strategy unnecessary.

During his first term, Reagan cultivated a charismatic and optimistic leadership style that deeply resonated with the American public. Known as the "Great Communicator," Reagan's ability to articulate his vision played a pivotal role in transcending traditional political boundaries. His rhetoric frequently evoked a sense of renewed American pride and optimism, starkly contrasting with the economic malaise and international tensions of the Carter years.

However, Reagan's presidency, while significant for its economic and foreign policy impacts, presents a more nuanced and often controversial legacy regarding civil rights. He steered a distinct shift towards a conservative agenda that not only sought to reduce the size and influence of the federal government but also deeply influenced civil rights policies and enforcement. Reagan was notably critical of affirmative action, which he termed "reverse discrimination," arguing that such policies unfairly favored specific groups at the expense of others.

While Reagan did renew the Voting Rights Act in 1982, he did so with reluctance and reservations, reflecting a complex stance on civil rights legislation. Despite these hesitations, it became increasingly clear that Reagan was growing personally concerned about the right-wing fringe elements beginning to infiltrate the Republican Party. The Ku Klux Klan (KKK), notorious for its white supremacist beliefs and a violent history against African Americans, Jews, immigrants, leftists, and other marginalized groups, had experienced a resurgence following the civil rights advancements of the 1960s.

Recognizing the potential damage such associations could inflict on the Republican Party's image and core values, Reagan took a definitive stand during his 1984 Republican National Convention speech. In a clear and forceful manner, he reaffirmed the party's foundational principles, emphasizing inclusivity and a rejection of bigotry. He stated, "We don't lump people by groups or special interests, and let me add, in the party of Lincoln, there is no room for intolerance and not even a small corner for anti-Semitism or bigotry of any kind." Reagan's stern rejection of extremism was unequivocal as he declared, "Many people are welcome in our house, but not the bigots."

This moment in Reagan's presidency highlighted his efforts to steer the Republican Party away from divisive and extremist elements, reinforcing a commitment to the foundational values of tolerance and inclusiveness that he believed should define the party of Lincoln.

Reagan's ability to resonate with a broad audience was evident in his significant inroads among traditionally Democratic groups like Black and Hispanic voters. His campaign's focus on economic opportunity, national strength, and an optimistic vision for America's future appealed across racial and ethnic lines. Although this did not permanently shift these groups' political allegiances, it did impact the 1984 election results significantly.

Reagan's reelection campaign against former Vice President **Walter Mondale** spotlighted critical issues such as trade and immigration. Reagan championed a free trade agreement between the U.S. and Mexico, asserting, "Our trade policy rests firmly on the foundation of free and open markets. I recognize the inescapable conclusion that all of history has taught: The freer the flow of world trade, the stronger the tides of human progress and peace among nations." Mondale countered this view, criticizing the imbalance in trade relationships: "We've got many countries that enjoy largely unlimited access to the American market but won't let us in their markets. I'm not a sucker. I think the American people want their president to stand up for the American workers, American businesses, and American farmers again."

Immigration also became a focal point, reviving historical debates and exposing systemic prejudices akin to those encountered by other ethnic groups. Hispanic communities, especially Mexicans and Central Americans, faced distinct discrimination—both social, seen in stereotypes and cultural misunderstandings, and economic, reflected in disparities in employment and wages. This period also saw significant immigration driven by economic crises and civil unrest in Central America, which intensified xenophobic attitudes in the U.S. Concerns about shifts in "American identity" due to non-European immigrant cultures and economic uncertainties of the early '80s recession further fueled these sentiments, leading to fears about job competition and cultural changes.

In a 1984 presidential debate, Reagan supported amnesty for undocumented immigrants who had established lives in the U.S., stating, "I believe in the idea of amnesty for those who have put down roots and lived here, even though sometime back they may have entered illegally." He criticized American employers for exacerbating illegal immigration: "These are employers down through the years who have encouraged the illegal entry into this country because they then hire these individuals at starvation wages and with none of the benefits that we think are normal and natural for workers in our country, and the individuals can't complain because of their illegal status." Reagan also emphasized the importance of strong relations with Latin American nations, noting, "No administration that I know has established the relationship that we have with our Latin friends. But as long as they have an economy that leaves so many people in dire poverty and unemployment, they are going to seek that employment across our borders."

Mondale criticized Reagan's amnesty approach, advocating for comprehensive immigration reform that included stronger border enforcement. He argued that granting amnesty without securing the borders could worsen the immigration problem and incentivize more illegal immigration, potentially exacerbating job competition for lower-income Americans and those already economically vulnerable.

Forty years later, Donald Trump would introduce positions similar to Mondale's on both trade and immigration into his Republican platform, reflecting a notable shift from Reagan's policies. Trump's skepticism about free trade agreements and emphasis on stringent border security marked a significant departure from Reagan's more open trade and immigration stances.

Reagan's amnesty policy culminated in the Immigration Reform and Control Act of 1986, which legalized approximately 2.8 million undocumented workers and was noted for the significant increase in legal immigration during Reagan's administration—the most since Teddy Roosevelt. The law also strengthened border security and imposed penalties on employers who hired undocumented workers. Reagan consistently defended this legislation post-presidency, never expressing regret, despite contrary claims by his former attorney general, **Edwin Meese**.

In more recent times, intensified anti-Hispanic sentiments have been fueled by policies and rhetoric. Laws like Arizona's SB 1070, known as the "show me your papers" law, have led to racial profiling and increased scrutiny of Hispanic communities. The separation of families at the U.S.-Mexico border and conditions in detention centers have drawn significant criticism for their human rights implications. Furthermore, the economic exploitation of Hispanic immigrants in low-wage, hazardous jobs, coupled with cultural and social discrimination, underscores the persistent nature of racial and ethnic discrimination in the U.S., echoing the experiences of earlier immigrant groups discussed in this book.

Keep Hope Alive

During the 1984 Democratic primaries, Walter Mondale faced significant challenges in securing a solid base of support, particularly during the South Carolina Democratic Primary where he was defeated by civil rights leader Reverend Jesse Jackson. Jackson's victory in South Carolina was a pivotal moment in American politics, emphasizing the growing influence of African American voices within the Democratic Party. This win represented more than just a personal triumph for Jackson; it symbolized a beacon of hope for many who had previously felt marginalized by the political establishment.

In 2011, I interviewed Jackson in Columbus about his two historic White House bids. He reflected on the 1984 race, saying, "We ran a campaign that was inclusive, a rainbow coalition—multiracial, multicultural. Starting in Iowa, we learned about campaigning there amid a lot of milking cows. Then we went to New Hampshire, which felt a lot like Mississippi—cold and poor—and  we built alliances. By Super Tuesday, we had momentum and won South Carolina, and we could taste victory."

Jackson, following in the footsteps of Shirley Chisholm, also confronted racial discrimination during his campaign. Recalling an incident in New Hampshire, Jackson shared, "One local official was patronizing, suggesting I skip a foreign policy discussion. I responded that I was looking forward to it, explaining that slavery was a foreign policy issue. I had a global view; he saw me through racial limitations and assumptions. We faced headwinds, the media dismissed us and there were many violent threats."

At the 1984 Democratic National Convention, Jackson delivered a compelling speech, where, after securing some concessions in the party platform, he endorsed Mondale and his running mate, Rep. **Geraldine Ferraro** of New York. This was a historic moment as Ferraro was the first woman to be nominated as the vice presidential candidate on a major party's ticket. Despite this milestone, Reagan's charismatic leadership and the successful perception of his presidency had endeared him to a broad segment of the American electorate. This widespread appeal led to a commanding electoral victory, with Reagan winning 49 of the 50 states and decisively defeating Mondale by a margin of 525 electoral votes to 13.

The day after the 1984 election, Mondale disclosed to reporters that he had anticipated the loss throughout much of the campaign. The election served as much an endorsement of Reagan's persona as it did of his platform, symbolizing a confident and prosperous America. This campaign marked a significant shift from reliance on regional strategies, such as the Southern Strategy, to a more personality-driven approach. It showcased how a charismatic leader could unify a diverse electorate through optimistic rhetoric and the perception of economic success. Reagan's landslide victory also underscored the power of presidential incumbency and its ability to dominate the national conversation.

In today's highly polarized and media-saturated political landscape, the kind of sweeping electoral success Reagan achieved in 1984 seems increasingly unlikely. The American electorate has become more demographically and culturally diverse, leading to heightened ideological divisions. Future candidates are likely to face a more segmented voting public, making the unifying electoral victories like Reagan's more challenging to replicate. Reagan's '84 campaign remains a historical benchmark, reminding us of a time when a president's personality and policy success could transcend entrenched political divides.

Lurch to the Right

The Reagan era marked a significant rightward shift for cultural conservatives, moving away from the more progressive trends of the Civil Rights era. This period also witnessed the devastating emergence of AIDS in the early 1980s, disproportionately affecting the nation's gay community. The Reagan administration's initial response was widely criticized for its indifference, with Congressman **Henry Waxman** suggesting that the response would have been more robust had the disease affected a demographic like Americans of Norwegian descent. Amid the crisis, conservative figures like Patrick Buchanan viewed the epidemic as a consequence of the sexual revolution, criticizing the gay lifestyle.

In response to the lack of governmental support, the gay community mobilized. Notable activists like **Larry Kramer** founded the Gay Men's Health Crisis to advocate for a more proactive governmental response. The creation of the AIDS Memorial Quilt in 1985 aimed to humanize the affected individuals, highlighting their dignity and the profound scale of loss. Activists also collaborated with researchers and doctors to expedite the development and testing of new drugs. This partnership helped lead to the development of antiretroviral therapies that transformed HIV from a death sentence into a manageable chronic condition.

Ryan White, a teenager who contracted AIDS from a contaminated blood treatment for his hemophilia, became a national symbol after being barred from attending school in 1985 due to his illness. Despite conservatives often labeling AIDS as the "gay disease," White's situation underscored that the disease could affect anyone and brought significant public attention to the broader issues of discrimination and stigma associated with AIDS. Reagan remained silent as White faced discrimination, a silence many viewed as a moral failure during a period when awareness and leadership were critically needed to combat both the spread of the disease and the surrounding misinformation. White died on April 8, 1990, from complications related to AIDS. He was just 18 years old at the time of his death.

The death of actor **Rock Hudson** in October 1985 marked a turning point in Reagan's public acknowledgment and response to the AIDS crisis. Hudson's diagnosis and subsequent death brought significant public attention to the disease, due to his celebrity status and his close ties to Reagan and his wife, Nancy. Before Hudson's death, the Reagan administration had been criticized for its slow and indifferent response to the AIDS epidemic. Reagan finally mentioned AIDS the year Hudson died. Hudson's public battle with AIDS and his death raised awareness and urgency about the epidemic, making it harder to ignore.

At that point, the federal response to AIDS became more serious. Surgeon General **C. Everett Koop** called for increased federal funding for AIDS research. Although funding reached $500 million by 1987, experts contended it was only 25% of what was necessary. That year, Reagan's presidential commission on AIDS recommended antidiscrimination laws to protect those with AIDS and advocated for more federal research spending, marking a notable shift in policy but years too late to prevent the deaths and suffering of countless individuals affected earlier in the crisis.

Simultaneously, Reagan actively promoted the reintroduction of organized prayer in public schools, a practice restricted since the Supreme Court's 1962 Engel v. Vitale decision, which deemed official school-sponsored prayer a violation of the First Amendment. Reagan framed his advocacy for school prayer as a defense of religious freedom and moral necessity, appealing broadly to evangelical Christians.

Continued endorsement from subsequent Republican presidents influenced a significant rightward shift in the Supreme Court's composition by 2022. This shift was evident in the Court's decision in Kennedy v. Bremerton

School District, which upheld a high school football coach's right to pray on the field post-games. This ruling represented a substantial change in the interpretation of the First Amendment, allowing greater individual expressions of faith in public schools and moving away from previous rulings that limited such activities to prevent perceived government endorsement of religion. The court's current stance tends to favor religious freedoms, even in contexts traditionally requiring a strict separation of church and state to avoid coercion or endorsement.

Reagan profoundly influenced the Republican Party's stance on abortion, integrating anti-abortion language into the 1980 GOP platform and opposing the 1973 Roe v. Wade decision. This marked a significant shift from the more moderate views held by his predecessors, such as Richard Nixon, who had enacted Title X federal funding for family planning, and Gerald Ford, who believed decisions about abortion should remain a private matter between a woman and her doctor.

Driven by the rising influence of socially conservative Christians like Jerry Falwell and **Pat Robertson**, this shift toward a stronger anti-abortion stance culminated decades later. After several Republican appointments to the court, the same Supreme Court that relaxed restrictions on public school prayer voted to overturn Roe in 2022. This decision not only delivered a major victory to cultural conservatives but also stood as a triumph for states' rights advocates, granting individual states the power to regulate abortion—a significant retraction of federal oversight.

Amid claims of moral superiority and attacks on the gay community while calling for more prayer and Christian conservatism, the world of televangelism in the 1980s was rocked by a series of scandals involving some of its most prominent figures, notably **Jim Bakker**, **Jimmy Swaggart**, and **Bill Haggard**. These scandals exposed the underside of a sphere that had gained enormous influence and financial power.

Bakker, a prominent figure in televangelism known for his prosperity gospel and broadcasts alongside his flamboyant wife, **Tammy Faye Bakker**, experienced a dramatic fall from grace. His career was marred by a highly publicized scandal that involved financial misconduct and allegations of rape by church secretary **Jessica Hahn**. Revelations emerged about Bakker's misuse of funds raised for his PTL (Praise The Lord) ministry, as well as attempts to cover up his sexual indiscretions, ultimately leading to his resignation and subsequent imprisonment.

Simultaneously, Swaggart, another influential televangelist, was implicated in a sex scandal involving prostitutes, revealed after he was caught by a private investigator hired by rival preachers. His tearful on-air confession became infamous, and although he initially seemed to rebound, the damage to his reputation was severe, and his ministry suffered significant financial and follower losses.

Haggard, although his major fall occurred slightly later, faced similar issues. As a prominent leader in the evangelical movement, Haggard's downfall came when accusations of drug use and encounters with a male prostitute surfaced. His public responses, a mix of denials and admissions, created confusion and eroded trust among his followers.

Oral Roberts, another prominent televangelist and key figure in the charismatic Christian movement, made a dramatic claim in 1987: he needed to raise $8 million for the university that bore his name or he would be "called home to heaven." Roberts informed his massive TV audience that he had received a vision from God indicating that his life would be taken if the funds were not raised by a specific deadline. The appeal received significant media attention and public scrutiny, ultimately resulting in the required funds being raised by the deadline. Thus, he lived on, even as many criticized the tactic as disgraceful.

The stark contrast between the public personas and private actions of these televangelists highlighted pervasive hypocrisy within high-profile ministries, even as they raked in millions of dollars. The scandals not only damaged their individual ministries but also cast a long shadow over the broader evangelical movement. This led to calls for greater accountability and transparency within religious organizations. This tumultuous period emphasized the complexities and challenges within the evangelical community, which continues to grapple with the dichotomy between preached values and practiced realities.

Despite Reagan's popularity, reflected in a national victory, his presidency was marked by contradictions for African Americans. While there were significant cultural and socioeconomic advancements, disparities remained stark, with the poverty rate among African Americans alarmingly higher than that of whites by the end of Reagan's presidency—31.6% compared to 10.1%. His nomination of **Robert Bork** to the Supreme Court, who opposed the 1964 Civil Rights Act and affirmative action, and his economic policies, which involved substantial tax cuts and reduced social program spending, were seen as exacerbating these inequalities.

Reagan defended his civil rights record just days before leaving office, asserting that his economic programs were not detrimental to African Americans and highlighting his early support for civil rights. However, figures like Jesse Jackson criticized him as "the worst civil rights president in recent memory," pointing to his lack of support for fundamental civil rights initiatives and his refusal to engage with civil rights leaders. Despite these controversies, Reagan left office having put into motion cultural issues that would deeply divide Americans for decades to come.

Throughout his presidency, Reagan, the oldest president to have served up to that time, maintained consistently high approval ratings—even during challenging periods like the Iran-Contra affair. During this scandal, he admitted to misleading the American public about secretly selling arms to

Iran, which was under an arms embargo. His administration hoped these sales would help secure the release of several American hostages held by Hezbollah groups in Lebanon. The proceeds from these arms sales were then illegally used to support the Contras, a rebel group fighting the Sandinista government in Nicaragua, despite a congressional ban on military aid to the Contras. Reagan's initial denial and subsequent apology months later raised concerns about his mental fitness for office.

With former Senator Howard Baker returning to Washington, D.C., to serve as his new chief of staff, and with First Lady **Nancy Reagan** fiercely guarding his legacy, Reagan traveled to the Soviet Union in his final year in office. There, he walked the streets of Moscow, meeting the Russian people, and signed nuclear weapons ban treaties with the reformist Soviet leader **Mikhail Gorbachev**. The actions of these leaders, through pivotal meetings in the late '80s, significantly contributed to the historic fall of Soviet communism the following year.

A few years after leaving office, amid concerns expressed by his son Ron and others close to him regarding his mental health during his final years as president, Ronald Reagan reached out to the nation again—this time revealing his diagnosis of Alzheimer's disease. In a deeply personal letter, he shared, "I now begin the journey that will lead me into the sunset of my life. I know that for America there will always be a bright dawn ahead." This heartfelt disclosure resonated widely, profoundly touching many people and increasing awareness of a disease that was becoming increasingly prevalent among older individuals.

Willie Horton Campaign

As the 1988 presidential election approached, Senator **Gary Hart** of Colorado was widely regarded as the frontrunner for the Democratic nomination. Known for his Kennedy-esque charisma, Hart had been a formidable contender in the 1984 Democratic primaries against Walter Mondale.

In 1987, amid swirling rumors of marital infidelity, Hart famously challenged the press to scrutinize his private life, declaring, "Follow me around. I don't care. I'm serious. If anybody wants to put a tail on me, go ahead. They'll be very bored." This defiance dramatically backfired when reporters from the *Miami Herald*, acting on a tip, observed a woman, later identified as model **Donna Rice**, visiting Hart's Washington, D.C., townhouse. The controversy escalated when photographs of Hart and Rice aboard the yacht *Monkey Business* were published.

The ensuing scandal dominated headlines, igniting intense public scrutiny over Hart's character and judgment. Despite initially resisting calls to withdraw, the mounting pressure and erosion of political support compelled Hart to suspend his presidential campaign, marking a rapid and dramatic collapse of his once-promising bid. At his withdrawal, he poignantly invoked Thomas Jefferson to underline the serious implications of his departure and the pressures on public and private morality in American politics. Hart said, "I tremble for my country when I think we may, in fact, get the kind of leaders we deserve." This quote, adapted from a letter written by Jefferson, reflected Hart's profound concern about the intersection of media scrutiny, personal conduct, and the quality of American leadership.

Similarly, Senator Joe Biden's 1988 presidential campaign ended abruptly amid its own controversy. Biden entered the race buoyed by significant enthusiasm, but soon faced allegations of plagiarism. It was revealed that

Biden had used parts of speeches by British Labour Party leader **Neil Kinnock** without proper attribution. Further scrutiny uncovered additional instances of plagiarism in his law school records and earlier political speeches. Facing growing criticism, Biden admitted his errors and the lapses in judgment regarding his use of others' words. This controversy severely undermined his credibility and viability as a candidate, leading to his early withdrawal from the race.

Meanwhile, Reverend Jesse Jackson was solidifying his position as a formidable contender for the Democratic nomination. He refined his campaign strategies and broadened his appeal across the party's diverse spectrum. "We could command presence on stage, and 'Free Mandela' became one of my battle cries," Jackson recounted in an interview. "We advocated for a two-state solution in the Middle East, where Palestinians and Israelis coexist. Our campaign focused on breaking the cycle of drugs and guns. There was a certain readiness in '88 that wasn't there in '84. We kept on growing, and of course, we won Michigan."

Jackson's victory in the 1988 Michigan Democratic primary was a significant and somewhat unexpected triumph that highlighted his appeal across a diverse voter base. He garnered strong support from both African American and white working-class voters, showcasing his ability to unite a broad coalition. This victory significantly boosted his campaign and solidified his status as a serious contender for the Democratic nomination. Though Jackson's impressive run ultimately fell short against Massachusetts Governor **Michael Dukakis**, who clinched the nomination, his influence was profound and transformative. He brought critical issues affecting minorities and the working class to the forefront, pressing the Democratic Party to actively address systemic inequalities.

The late civil rights leader **Roger Wilkins** once remarked, "I think that when the story of the 20th century in the United States is written, Jackson will have to be one of the ten or fifteen most important contributors to the development of America in that century. Because if he had done nothing else, his two runs for the presidency were national civics lessons. They expanded the imagination of Americans about who could aspire to be President."

On the Republican side, Reagan's vice president, **George H.W. Bush**, who came from a moderate establishment political background, adopted a highly aggressive campaign strategy against Dukakis, who was not widely known outside of New England. South Carolina's **Lee Atwater**, a protégé of Strom Thurmond, refined the old Southern Strategy during the 1980s. While highly effective in securing votes, these tactics were also noted for their racial undertones and divisive nature, drawing significant criticism. This strategy played a crucial role in shaping the tone and tactics of the campaign.

Atwater, in a revealing 1981 interview, outlined the evolution of the GOP's offensive campaign rhetoric and its indirect impacts on African Americans: "You start out in 1954 by saying, 'Nigger, nigger, nigger.' By 1968 you can't say 'nigger' — that hurts you, backfires. So you say stuff like forced busing, states' rights, and all that stuff, and you're getting so abstract. Now, you're talking about cutting taxes, and all these things you're talking about are totally economic things and a byproduct of them is, blacks get hurt worse than whites. And subconsciously maybe that is part of it. I'm not saying that, but I'm saying that if it is getting that abstract, and that coded, that we are doing away with the racial problem one way or the other. You follow me — because obviously sitting around saying, 'We want to cut this' is much more abstract than even the busing thing, and a hell of a lot more abstract than 'Nigger, nigger.'" This admission by Atwater confirmed that old strategies of racism were being used but with different phrases and code words.

During the 1988 presidential campaign, Atwater, serving as Bush's campaign manager, masterfully applied abstract and coded strategies with notorious effectiveness. He exploited the significant contrast in public familiarity and perception between Bush and Dukakis. Atwater portrayed Dukakis as overly liberal and weak, strategically linking him to **Willie Horton**, a black man who committed a violent crime while on a weekend furlough from a Massachusetts prison. This connection was notably controversial, considering a similar furlough program had existed under the Reagan administration.

The focus on the Horton case crystallized in a series of infamous advertisements that profoundly damaged Dukakis's candidacy. These ads tapped into racial fears and prejudices, echoing the darker elements of the Southern Strategy by using coded language and imagery that suggested threat and criminality associated with race.

Atwater's unapologetic and aggressive approach during the campaign was vividly captured in his own words. He infamously stated his goal for Dukakis was to "strip the bark off the little bastard" and "make Willie Horton his running mate." This ruthless strategy not only showcased the effectiveness of Atwater's methods but also marked the evolution of the Southern Strategy into more subtle, yet equally impactful forms. Representative **Pat Schroeder** famously called Atwater "the most evil man in America" due to these tactics.

Atwater's approach underscored a continuing trend in American politics where racial and social fears could be manipulated for electoral gain, reflecting a complex and often troubling facet of political strategy and messaging.

During the second presidential debate in 1988, Dukakis was confronted by CNN anchor **Bernard Shaw** with a highly charged question about Willie Horton. Shaw challenged Dukakis on whether he would support the death penalty if his wife, **Kitty Dukakis**, were raped and murdered, thereby spotlighting his controversial stance against the death penalty in light of a furlough program that allowed Horton to commit additional crimes. Dukakis's response, more analytical than emotional, was widely criticized for lacking the passion expected in such a personal and emotionally charged context. This likely played a significant role in undermining his chances of winning the election.

Susan Estrich, Dukakis' campaign manager, accused the Bush campaign of stoking racial tensions. "If you were going to run a campaign of fear and smear and appeal to racial hatred," she told The New York Times, "you could not have picked a better case to use than this one."

Bush subsequently defeated Dukakis in a significant landslide, marking the first time since Franklin Roosevelt that one party had secured the White House in three consecutive elections. Despite the decisive victory, Bush's campaign was not particularly noted for its policy mandates. The most memorable element of his campaign emerged from his acceptance speech at the Republican Convention, where he famously declared, "Read my lips: no new taxes." This phrase struck a chord with voters and became the six most famous words of that election cycle.

Stefan Forbes, who produced the documentary *Boogie Man: The Lee Atwater Story*, emphasized Atwater's significant impact on the GOP. He stated, "Atwater reshaped the Republican Party; he completed the process Nixon had begun of moving the party away from the old Eastern seaboard elite and transforming it into a Southern party." Forbes further elaborated, "He brought so-called value issues to the forefront, and the culture war took over. He proved you could win on these issues if you made 'Liberal' a dirty word, and that you could make it the party of the working man—even though it was traditionally seen as the party of the rich—if you could connect deeply with people on an emotional level and tap into their resentment of the elite, their fears, or even a strong sense of patriotism."

By 1991, as he faced terminal illness, Atwater, then chairman of the Republican National Committee, revisited his tactics and publicly apologized to Dukakis, expressing regret for his actions, stating, "I am sorry for both statements: the first for its naked cruelty, the second because it makes me sound racist, which I am not." Dukakis accepted the apology, but the historical impact of the Horton strategy had already contributed significantly to Bush's resounding victory in both the popular and electoral votes, reflecting a pivotal moment in American political history.

Read My Lips

President Bush entered his 1992 re-election campaign facing a drastically different set of circumstances compared to the peak of his popularity following the successful liberation of Kuwait from Iraq's **Saddam Hussein** the preceding year. Initially, Bush enjoyed high approval ratings, bolstered by his foreign policy successes. However, as the nation headed into an election year, a severe recession took hold, significantly weakening Bush's standing in the polls.

Compounding Bush's challenges was a political decision that came to haunt him. In his 1988 campaign, Bush had famously declared, "Read my lips: no new taxes." Yet, faced with a burgeoning deficit, he later reached a compromise with Democrats that involved tax increases. This reversal not only damaged his credibility but also incited a primary challenge from conservative Pat Buchanan. Buchanan's campaign, while ultimately unsuccessful in capturing the nomination, significantly weakened Bush by intensifying divisions within the Republican Party.

Perhaps due to pressure from conservatives like Buchanan, Bush had a mixed legacy on civil rights. This seemed at odds with his family's long history of opposing discrimination—his father, **Prescott Bush**, a Connecticut senator, worked to desegregate schools and protect voting rights—and with his own work raising money for the United Negro College Fund. However, in 1990, he vetoed a civil rights act that would have expanded job protections. He and Ronald Reagan were the only presidents to veto a civil rights measure since the start of the civil rights era. Bush argued that the bill would have introduced the "destructive force of quotas into our national employment system." This move garnered criticism from civil rights leaders and liberals, including Edward Kennedy, the Democratic Senator from Massachusetts, who said the veto showed Bush was "more interested in appeasing extremists in his party than in providing simple justice."

"It was not a good look to be vetoing a civil rights bill when you are trying to offer a kinder, gentler version of Reagan," said David Greenberg, a professor of history and journalism and media studies at Rutgers University, noting that the backlash led Bush to work on a compromise bill, the Civil Rights Act of 1991, which passed the following year.

The Civil Rights Act of 1991, which Bush signed, aimed to strengthen and improve federal civil rights laws. It overturned several Supreme Court decisions that had made it harder for employees to prove discrimination, strengthened the enforcement of anti-discrimination laws, provided more substantial remedies to victims, and clarified many contentious aspects of civil rights law.

Bush also signed the Americans with Disabilities Act (ADA), a landmark law that prohibited discrimination based on disability. The ADA profoundly impacted millions of Americans by providing greater access to buildings, transportation, and communication, and ensuring their rights in workplaces and public spaces. It also raised awareness and improved the inclusivity and accessibility of public infrastructure and services.

Bush's most lasting legacy in race relations may stem from his nomination of Supreme Court Justice Clarence Thomas. By selecting the conservative Thomas, an ardent opponent of affirmative action, to replace the liberal **Thurgood Marshall**, the first Black Supreme Court justice who championed equal rights and challenged discrimination, Bush stalled or set back progress on civil rights issues for decades, said Jason Johnson, a professor of politics and journalism at Morgan State University, who likened the choice to "trolling."

Bush was also criticized for his role in the war on drugs, which began in the Reagan administration and carried on into the Clinton years, leading to the mass incarceration of many African-American men. In his first significant policy speech as president, on Sept. 5, 1989, Bush chose to focus on drug policy and the cocaine epidemic. Sitting in the Oval Office, Bush lifted up a plastic bag.

"This is crack cocaine seized a few days ago by Drug Enforcement agents in a park just across the street from the White House," he said. "It could easily have been heroin or PCP. It's as innocent-looking as candy, but it's turning our cities into battle zones, and it's murdering our children."

He called for a $1.5 billion increase in drug-related federal spending to law enforcement and pushed to "enlarge our criminal justice system across the board, at the local, state and federal levels alike. We need more prisons, more jails, more courts, more prosecutors." That approach, along with the mandatory minimum sentences passed under Reagan, contributed to the so-called 100-to-1 drug sentencing discrepancy, in which the penalty for crack possession and sale was 100 times greater than that for powder cocaine, said Joshua Clark Davis, a University of Baltimore history professor. This discrepancy has been widely criticized for its racial implications, as crack cocaine was more prevalent in predominantly African American urban communities, while powder cocaine was more commonly associated with white, suburban users.

The speech was notable not only for its substance but because the crack sale mentioned by Bush had been set up by the Drug Enforcement Administration. Agents manipulated a 19-year-old high school student, a low-level dealer, into conducting a sale near the White House. Keith Jackson, who did not know where the White House was and had to be given directions, was arrested and sentenced to 10 years.

In a tweet posted in 2018, Davis noted, "It's what his War on Drugs did to just one person. But it shows the human costs of that war in miniature detail.

A high schooler was lured to the WH to sell crack and spent 7+ years in prison, so that the President could make a point on TV."

The judge in the case pointed out that Jackson, who had no prior criminal record, had been used as a prop. Much like the Willie Horton ad during Bush's campaign, this incident highlighted the manipulation of individuals for political gain. "We can say Bush was horrendous on civil rights but that he was a good father and treated people decently," said Johnson.

Twenty years later, the Fair Sentencing Act of 2010 was signed into law by President **Barack Obama**, reducing the sentencing disparity between crack and powder cocaine from 100-to-1 to 18-to-1, acknowledging the need for more equitable drug laws. However, the legacy of the original disparity continues to impact communities of color.

The Rise of Clinton

Arkansas Governor **Bill Clinton**, George Bush's challenger in 1992, brought a unique set of qualities that temporarily disrupted the Republican Party's Southern Strategy. Clinton's appeal stemmed from his Southern roots as a native of Arkansas and his moderate political stance as part of the "New Democrat" movement. This movement aimed to shift the Democratic Party away from its more liberal postures of previous decades. By choosing Senator **Al Gore** from Tennessee as his running mate, the Democrats fully embraced their version of a Southern Strategy, targeting similar demographics and leveraging their Southern connections.

Clinton's strategy emphasized economic issues, aiming to attract a broad coalition that included traditional Democrats and moderate Republicans disenchanted with the existing economic policies. His focus on economic recovery, job creation, and welfare reform resonated well with Southern voters, who were experiencing economic shifts and growing concerns about social policies. Moreover, his charismatic personality and ability to connect with everyday Americans across the cultural divides further enhanced his appeal, making him a formidable candidate who could reclaim parts of the South.

As the general election approached, Bush faced challenges not only from Clinton but also from third-party candidate **Ross Perot**. Perot's independent campaign didn't win any electoral votes but captured a notable 19 percent of the popular vote. His significant support among voters disillusioned with the traditional parties is widely believed to have diverted votes from Bush, aiding Clinton's victories in several Southern states including Louisiana, Tennessee, Kentucky, Georgia, and Clinton's home state of Arkansas.

Clinton focused his campaign on domestic issues, particularly the economy, tapping into the electorate's concerns amid economic distress. He effectively neutralized Bush's attempts to undermine his character based on his lack of military service during the Vietnam War, a strategy that did not gain traction with voters more preoccupied with economic matters. During a critical presidential debate, Perot came to Clinton's defense on the character issue, emphasizing the importance of context and timing of past mistakes, contrasting youthful errors with those made by mature government officials in positions of significant power.

Ultimately, a combination of factors including the economic downturn, backlash over tax increases, an intra-party challenge from Buchanan, and the impact of Perot's candidacy, created a perfect storm that Bush could not weather. Despite his notable foreign policy achievements and his role in ending the Cold War, these domestic challenges and electoral dynamics contributed to Bush's defeat, marking him as one of America's more competent one-term presidents. He is remembered for his prudence in international affairs but his presidency was overshadowed by these domestic and electoral challenges during his re-election campaign.

Domestic Terrorism

In 1992, while Bush was president, a deadly confrontation known as Ruby Ridge occurred in Idaho. This standoff involved **Randy Weaver**, his family, and federal agents, and began due to Weaver's failure to appear in court on firearms charges. The situation escalated when an FBI sniper killed Weaver's wife, and the 11-day standoff resulted in three deaths, including a U.S. Marshal. Ruby Ridge became a symbol of government overreach for many, fueling distrust and anger among militia and extremist groups.

In 1993, during President Clinton's first year in office, the Waco siege took place. This 51-day standoff between federal agents and the Branch Davidians, a religious group led by **David Koresh**, began with a botched ATF raid intended to arrest Koresh for weapons violations. It ended tragically when a fire killed 76 people, including Koresh, after the FBI launched a final assault. The Waco siege raised significant controversy and criticism over the government's handling of the situation, contributing to an escalation in anti-government sentiment among various groups.

After Waco, Clinton signed the Brady Handgun Violence Prevention Act into

law. This legislation, known as the Brady Bill, introduced a mandatory background check system for firearm purchasers, significantly changing the process of buying and selling firearms in the United States. The law was named after former White House Press Secretary **James Brady**, who was permanently disabled from an assassination attempt on President Reagan in 1981.

The response from right-wing extremists to the Brady Bill was fervent and filled with misinformation. Many falsely claimed that the legislation was a step toward the eventual confiscation of all legally owned guns in the country. This overreaction fueled a surge in gun sales, as proponents of the Second Amendment, spurred on by the National Rifle Association (NRA) and its powerful fundraising efforts, rushed to purchase firearms. This intense period marked a significant escalation in the national debate over gun control. Unfortunately, the heightened tensions and rhetoric also emboldened some domestic terrorists, leading to tragic incidents where extremists targeted innocent people, including children, further polarizing the nation on issues of gun control and public safety.

A year after the implementation of the Brady Bill, a devastating bombing at a Federal Building in Oklahoma City claimed the lives of 168 people, including

19 children. In the immediate aftermath, speculation was rampant that Islamic terrorists were responsible, leading to two days of intense anti-Muslim hysteria across the nation. However, the focus of the investigation shifted when **Timothy McVeigh** and **Terry Nichols**, both American military veterans of the Gulf War, were arrested for the attack. Influenced by the Ruby Ridge standoff, the Waco siege, and Clinton's efforts on gun control, they viewed their actions as a legitimate strike against the U.S. federal government. McVeigh infamously referred to the loss of innocent lives as "collateral damage."

At the time of the bombing, McVeigh was wearing a shirt that featured a picture of Abraham Lincoln next to the phrase "sic semper tyrannis" ('Thus always to tyrants')—the same words John Wilkes Booth proclaimed after assassinating Lincoln. This choice of attire highlighted McVeigh's profound animosity towards the government, symbolically aligning himself with historic acts of rebellion.

McVeigh was also deeply influenced by "The Turner Diaries," a novel by William Luther Pierce that is popular within white nationalist and extremist circles. The book portrays a violent overthrow of the federal government, leading to a race war and the ultimate extermination of non-whites and other targeted groups. It is presented through the diary of Earl Turner, a participant in the revolution, and is notorious for its explicit racist and anti-Semitic content. This book served as a sort of manifesto for McVeigh.

Driven by an obsession with gun rights, a perceived endorsement from the Founding Fathers, and a belief in the value of violence, McVeigh's ideologies were deeply entrenched in his actions. In an interview before his execution in

June 2001, McVeigh referred to members of the white power movement as his "brothers in arms."

In a recent interview, Clinton reflected on McVeigh's impact, stating, "McVeigh was a perfect example of a guy who thought our differences were more important than what we have in common. It doesn't matter whether he was right about anything or not. What matters is he decided he should kill people he didn't know, including little kids. But the words he used, the arguments he made, literally sound like the mainstream today. Like he won."

This observation highlights a troubling reality: the rhetoric and beliefs that motivated McVeigh's heinous act have not only persisted but have seemingly grown more mainstream in the decades following his execution. Clinton's comments serve as a stark reminder of the dangers posed by the continuation and normalization of extremist ideologies, particularly within the context of right-wing extremism.

'America First' Takes Hold

In the 1996 presidential election, Senate Minority Leader **Bob Dole** faced a turbulent primary season before securing the Republican nomination. Pat Buchanan, a recurrent contender, launched another bid for the nomination, channeling the frustrations of white workers. Buchanan painted a grim picture of America—a nation he claimed was besieged by external threats and betrayed by the elites of both parties who ignored the plight of hard-working, loyal, traditional Americans. His campaign was characterized by his own description as a populist, nationalist, "America-first" movement.

Buchanan's position on immigration was notably stringent. He criticized the federal government's inability to secure the United States borders, referring to it as an "illegal invasion" with at least a million people entering annually. His solution, dubbed the "Buchanan fence," involved a combination of a trench and a physical barrier designed to stop migration from the south. This concept, which his critics called "Fortress America," envisioned the nation as a fortress shielded by impregnable barriers against foreign people, goods, and ideas. This stance, however, was too extreme for New York City billionaire real estate and casino operator Donald Trump, who openly criticized Buchanan, labeling him an anti-Semite, a racist, and a homophobe.

Simultaneously, right-wing media outlets, including Fox News, were pressuring Dole to exploit various scandals and allegations against Clinton and the First Lady, **Hillary Clinton**. Fox News, created by Australian billionaire **Rupert Murdoch**, who also owns right-wing tabloid newspapers in the United Kingdom, was a new conservative news channel led by **Roger Ailes**, a longtime Republican operative. Murdoch and Ailes pushed their newsroom to report sensational accusations against the Clintons, ranging from concealing FBI files and involvement in the mysterious death of **Vince Foster** to alleged corrupt business dealings in Arkansas. Despite the gravity of these accusations, no criminal wrongdoing was ever established against the Clintons. Nevertheless, Fox News found a loyal audience convinced they were watching impartial news, and the network has generated billions of dollars for Murdoch and his family.

Amid the intense pressures to go negative, Dole maintained a commitment to uphold a higher ethical standard in his presidential run. Successfully fending off Buchanan for the Republican nomination, Dole chose former Congressman **Jack Kemp** as his running mate. Kemp, noted for his admiration of Abraham Lincoln and his proactive efforts to engage the African American electorate, complemented Dole's strategy of emphasizing policy differences over personal attacks.

This approach, while noble, may have limited Dole's competitive edge against the politically savvy Clinton. By focusing on a more dignified form of campaigning, Dole aimed to set a contrast not just in policy but in the tone and substance of political discourse. However, this decision underscored the complexities of competing in a political landscape that often rewarded more aggressive strategies. Clinton, for his part, managed to retain most of the Southern states he had won in the previous election, except for Georgia, as the region's shift towards the Republican Party continued to solidify. The GOP made significant inroads by aligning with cultural and social issues that resonated deeply with Southern voters, such as gun rights, religious values, and conservative views on social issues like abortion.

During Clinton's presidency, he was known for his close associations with African American musicians and entertainers, famously inviting a diverse array of artists to perform at the White House. His appearances on shows like **Arsenio Hall**'s, where he played the saxophone, were seen as outreach to the African American community. Clinton's administration actively engaged in advancing civil rights and equality, working diligently to diversify the federal government by appointing a significant number of women and minorities, and staunchly defending affirmative action against attempts to dismantle it.

Clinton was a staunch advocate for universal health care, appointing his wife, Hillary Clinton, to head the Task Force on National Health Care Reform. This initiative aimed to develop a comprehensive plan ensuring universal coverage for all Americans. Hillary Clinton's significant involvement marked one of the first instances a First Lady directly engaged in policy-making at this level.

Interestingly, the concept of universal health care also garnered support from Trump, who had recently registered as a voter with the newly formed Reform Party. In an interview with **Larry King**, Trump expressed his endorsement of universal health care, stating, "If you can't take care of your sick in the country, forget it, it's all over. I mean, it's no good. So I'm very liberal when it comes to health care. I believe in universal health care. I believe in whatever it takes to make people well and better." However, despite broader discussions and some endorsements, Clinton's proposed health plan faced intense Republican opposition and ultimately did not pass through Congress.

Clinton's tenure was not without controversies, particularly concerning LGBTQ+ rights. The 1993 "Don't Ask, Don't Tell" (DADT) policy allowed gay and lesbian individuals to serve in the military provided they did not disclose their sexual orientation. This policy led to numerous discharges and forced many service members to hide their identities. In 1996, Clinton also signed the Defense of Marriage Act (DOMA), which defined marriage federally as a union between one man and one woman and allowed states to refuse to recognize same-sex marriages, drawing sharp criticism from the LGBTQ+ community until it was overturned by the Supreme Court in 2013.

Another significant point of contention was Clinton's signing of the 1994 Crime Bill, the largest of its kind in U.S. history at that time, which aimed to tackle crime with provisions that included substantial funding for building new prisons contingent upon states enacting stricter sentencing laws. The bill introduced the "three strikes" rule, mandating life sentences for individuals convicted of three or more violent felonies, expanded the number of federal crimes eligible for the death penalty, and temporarily banned the manufacture and possession of certain assault weapons. This bill has been widely criticized for contributing to mass incarceration, disproportionately affecting Black Americans by emphasizing tougher sentencing over rehabilitation, thereby exacerbating racial disparities within the criminal justice system.

Legal scholar and attorney Michelle Alexander has highlighted that the crime bill and the ongoing 'war on drugs' have been primary causes of the explosion in the U.S. prison population, disproportionately waged in poor communities of color. She noted that people of color are no more likely to use or sell illegal drugs than whites, yet they have predominantly been the ones imprisoned. The repercussions of being labeled a felon include being denied voting rights, jury participation, and fair opportunities in employment, housing, and education, effectively relegating many to a permanent second-class status akin to the discrimination of the Jim Crow era.

In 2015, Clinton expressed regret for the crime bill's repercussions in a speech to the NAACP, admitting, "I signed a bill that made the problem worse. And I want to admit that." The following year, Hillary also apologized for her role in lobbying Congress for the bill during her presidential campaign.

Clinton's presidency, while marked by significant strides towards a more inclusive society, was also overshadowed by personal controversies, including allegations of infidelity that led to his impeachment during his second term. Despite being impeached for lying under oath about his affair with White House intern **Monica Lewinsky**, he was not convicted by the Senate and completed his presidency with relatively high approval ratings, enduring persistent Republican efforts to tarnish his reputation.

In the late 1990s, **Toni Morrison**, a celebrated author, provocatively described Clinton as the nation's "first black president" in an essay for The New Yorker. Her exact words were: "Blacker than any actual black person who could ever be elected in our children's lifetime." This bold statement sparked years of widespread debate and discussion. While some liberals and even Clinton himself embraced the title, progressive critics pointed out that his policies, notably welfare reform and the 1994 crime bill, had detrimental effects on African American families, with many experts attributing these policies to a surge in mass incarceration. Morrison later expressed regret over her statement, acknowledging that it had been widely misinterpreted.

Gored by the South

The 2000 presidential election represented a critical juncture for civil rights in America, with the candidates' stances reflecting divergent paths for the nation's future. Vice President **Al Gore**, the Democratic nominee, actively promoted a progressive civil rights agenda, advocating for expansive measures to enhance equality and protect the rights of minorities. His platform included proposals for stronger enforcement of civil rights laws, support for affirmative action, and increased efforts to combat racial profiling.

In contrast, Texas Governor **George W. Bush**, the Republican nominee, epitomized a more cautious approach that had characterized the Republican stance on civil rights since the party implemented the Southern Strategy decades earlier. While Bush spoke of compassionate conservatism and inclusivity, his policies suggested a slower pace of change.

Gore's campaign was marked by the ambitious goal of securing a third consecutive presidential victory for the Democratic Party—a rare achievement that had only been accomplished once since Franklin Roosevelt, by Bush's father in 1988. Both candidates found themselves at the center of one of the most contentious presidential elections in U.S. history. The 2000 election drew stark comparisons to the disputed 1876 election of Rutherford B. Hayes, notorious for its intense electoral disputes and the eventual compromise that decided the presidency.

On election night, the race for the presidency came down to Florida's crucial 25 electoral votes. Initially, major TV networks called Florida for Gore, projecting him as the potential winner. However, as the night progressed, the margin between the candidates dramatically tightened, leading the networks to reverse their initial call and declare Bush the president-elect. Hours later, as the race narrowed in Florida even further—with Bush leading by about 1,700 votes, a margin so slim it triggered an automatic recount because it was less than 0.5 percent—the networks retracted their declaration for Bush as the recount began. Reflecting on the confusion, NBC's **Tom Brokaw** remarked, "We don't just have egg on our face; we have an omelet."

The machine recount further reduced Bush's lead to a mere 317 votes, compelling Gore to seek a manual recount in four counties, as permitted under Florida law. During this tumultuous period, Gore initially conceded to Bush via phone, only to retract his concession as the scale of the electoral confusion became clear.

The ensuing weeks were marked by a fierce legal and political struggle over the recount process. On November 26, Florida Secretary of State **Katherine Harris** certified Bush as the winner by a margin of just 537 votes. Gore contested this certification, leading to a December 8 Florida Supreme Court decision that mandated a statewide recount of all "undervote" ballots, which were initially not counted due to issues like the infamous "hanging chad." Bush's team escalated the matter to the U.S. Supreme Court, which on December 9, halted the recount pending further hearing.

Amid the looming "safe harbor" deadline—which is set to ensure that electors are determined six days before the Electoral College meets—the Supreme Court issued a pivotal 5-4 decision in the case of *Bush v. Gore* on December 12. This decision, split along partisan lines, concluded that there was no constitutional way to rectify the recount issues by the deadline, thereby upholding Bush's certification as the election winner. The majority of justices who favored halting the recount were appointed by Republican presidents, while those dissenting were appointed by Democratic presidents. This alignment led many to perceive the decision through a partisan lens, sparking considerable controversy and debate about the role of the judiciary and its impartiality in electoral matters.

The day after the presidential election results were finalized, Gore delivered a concession speech from his ceremonial office near the White House. Despite his disappointment and criticism of the Supreme Court's ruling, Gore declared, "While I strongly disagree with the court's decision, I accept it. I accept the finality of this outcome, which will be ratified next Monday in the Electoral College. And tonight, for the sake of our unity as a people and the strength of our democracy, I offer my concession."

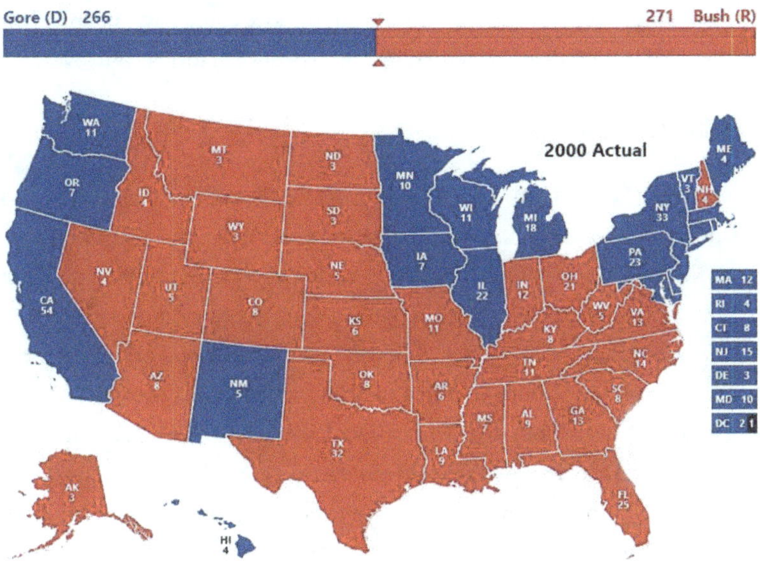

He also added a touch of humor to acknowledge the initial confusion on election night, assuring that there would be no retractions of his concession this time. "I know many of my supporters are disappointed. I am too," Gore concluded. "But our disappointment must be overcome by our love of country."

As President of the Senate, Gore was tasked with the ironic duty of ratifying Bush's controversial victory on January 6, as required by law. Despite winning the national popular vote by over half a million votes, Gore narrowly lost the presidency due to the Electoral College. This election not only underscored the profound challenges of public office but also reflected significant political shifts in the South. Gore, a Southern Democrat with deep familial ties in Tennessee, lost his home state—a personal and strategic defeat signaling the region's shift from blue to red. His reflection on needing to "spend time in Tennessee and mend some fences, literally and figuratively" underscored the critical importance of local ties and understanding regional political dynamics, emphasizing that winning Tennessee could have independently secured his presidential victory, irrespective of the Florida controversy.

Strom's Farewell

In 2002, Senate GOP leader **Trent Lott** was forced to resign his leadership position after suggesting that the nation would have been better off if Strom Thurmond had won the presidency on his segregationist Dixiecrat platform in 1948. Lott's remarks ignited significant controversy and sparked an internal debate within the GOP. The following year, Thurmond passed away at age 100, prompting South Carolina to pause in reverence. At our television station in Myrtle Beach, we interrupted regular ABC programming to cover his funeral live. I was on air for nearly three hours, discussing Thurmond's life and legacy, and the impact he had on American politics. However, during a conversation with a local university political science professor, the discussion was somewhat restrained, focusing less on his presidential campaign's racist undertones and his lifelong anti-civil rights record. Instead, we highlighted the substantial federal funding he had secured for the staunchly Republican state.

Thurmond's life exemplifies a profound series of contradictions, notably highlighted by the story of his eldest child, **Essie Mae Washington-Williams**. Thurmond, a staunch proponent of segregationist policies and a public champion of "family values," fathered a child with Carrie Butler, a 16-year-old Black maid working in his father's house when he was 22 years old. This part of his life remained hidden from the public for decades, underpinning the complex interplay between his private actions and public persona.

Washington-Williams lived under the shadow of this secrecy, unable to publicly acknowledge her heritage until Thurmond's death in 2003. For over 70 years, she was denied her true identity, reflecting a poignant narrative of denial and suppression. Her eventual public acknowledgment that Thurmond was her father marked a significant moment, not just personally but also in highlighting the broader societal hypocrisy regarding race and identity in America.

In her memoir, *Dear Senator: A Memoir by the Daughter of Strom Thurmond*, Washington-Williams sheds light on the emotional distance and formalities that marked her relationship with her father. She notes that Thurmond never verbally acknowledged her as his daughter nor did he ever address her mother by her name, underscoring the disconnect between his private life and public facade.

Washington-Williams' journey to claiming her birthright and her achievements—earning a master's degree and becoming a public school teacher—stand in stark contrast to the restrictive and oppressive ideologies Thurmond publicly supported. This dissonance between Thurmond's advocacy for certain values while simultaneously contradicting them in his personal life exemplifies the complexities and the often hypocritical nature of public figures who played roles in sustaining America's racial divides. Such contradictions are critical in understanding not only Thurmond's legacy but also the larger narrative of American history concerning race and identity.

Neoconservatives

Eight months following George W. Bush's inauguration in 2001, the terrorist organization Al Qaeda, led by **Osama bin Laden**, launched a series of attacks against the United States. The devastation in New York City, marked by the collapse of the Twin Towers, along with an attack on the Pentagon in Washington, D.C., and a hijacked jet brought down in Pennsylvania by brave passengers — believed to be targeting the White House — significantly raised Bush's approval ratings as the nation rallied together in grief and anger.

Initially, Bush's decision to target Al Qaeda in Afghanistan received widespread support. However, under the influence of neoconservatives within his administration, including Vice President **Dick Cheney**, Bush also decided to invade Iraq. Despite the absence of a direct link between Osama bin Laden and Saddam Hussein, the U.S. became entangled in a prolonged conflict. The ongoing war in Iraq gradually eroded Bush's popularity, as there was no swift resolution in sight in the Middle East.

Neoconservatives, or neocons, emerged as a political movement in the United States in the late 1960s and early 1970s. Initially, many neocons were former liberals who became disillusioned with the Democratic Party's policies on social and foreign affairs during the tumultuous 1960s. These intellectuals shifted to the right, spurred by what they saw as the failures of traditional welfare policies and an insufficiently assertive American foreign policy.

Neocons are known for advocating a strong and proactive American foreign policy aimed at promoting democracy and combating totalitarian regimes. This stance often leads to support for military intervention, as seen in Iraq and Afghanistan. On national security, they emphasize a robust defense and are willing to use military force preemptively. Economically, neocons generally support free-market principles but are not as committed to a libertarian agenda for minimal government intervention as other conservatives might be.

Culturally, neocons express concern over what they perceive as a decline in moral standards and traditional values, advocating for education that highlights the achievements of Western civilization.

Prominent figures like **Irving Kristol**, considered the "godfather" of neoconservatism, and **Norman Podhoretz** have significantly shaped the movement's philosophy. Although the influence of neocons has fluctuated, it was particularly notable during the administrations of Ronald Reagan and George W. Bush, where it had a significant impact on foreign policy decisions.

Donald Trump, best known at the time as the host of NBC's reality TV show 'The Apprentice,' emerged as a notable critic of the neoconservative movement. After leaving the Reform Party, he registered as a Democrat at the beginning of Bush's presidency. Trump began voicing his criticisms of the Iraq War relatively early, around 2004, aligning himself with many Democrats at that time. His critique intensified to the point where he even called for Bush's impeachment over the war's handling. This stance, while shared by Senators **Bernie Sanders** of Vermont and Edward Kennedy of Massachusetts, was not widely supported. Trump's vocal opposition highlighted his shifting political identity, underscored by his varied party affiliations throughout his career.

By 2004, facing tough reelection prospects, Bush's campaign committed to using culturally conservative wedge issues, particularly gay marriage, to boost voter turnout in 11 states. Although Bush's chief campaign strategist **Karl Rove** publicly denied involvement, former Republican National Committee chairman **Ken Mehlman**, who came out as gay in 2010, revealed that Rove had been working to ensure anti-gay initiatives and referenda appeared on November ballots in 2004 and 2006 to help Republicans. This strategy, detailed in the book *The Architect*, described Rove's tactic of microtargeting religious conservatives to mobilize large numbers against gay marriage and in support of Bush.

"Karl had used the gay issue for more than a decade in a very effective way," said Wayne Slater, a political journalist and author of *Bush's Brain: How Karl Rove Made George W. Bush*. "And there's something of a hypocrisy, it seems to me, because many of the people who are Republican operatives, who helped implement this exact attack on gay rights, are themselves gay."

The inclusion of a constitutional amendment on the Ohio ballot to ban gay marriage played a key role in mobilizing conservative and evangelical voters—crucial demographics for Bush's reelection. The campaign's emphasis on traditional family values and opposition to gay marriage deeply resonated with these groups, spurring them to actively participate in the election process. This approach was particularly effective in Ohio, a critical swing state essential for a victory by either party. If the Democratic nominee, Senator **John Kerry** of Massachusetts, had won Ohio, he would have secured the presidency with 272 electoral votes. However, the heightened turnout among conservative voters, driven in part by the gay marriage amendment, tipped the scales in Bush's favor in Ohio, playing a pivotal role in his 286-251 electoral victory.

This strategy demonstrated the GOP's adaptation of their traditionally Southern strategy to a Northern context, significantly influencing the outcome. The decisive electoral votes from Ohio provided Bush with the narrow margin needed for reelection. This strategic use of divisive cultural issues highlights the adaptability and enduring impact of such tactics in American electoral politics. Notably, Bush is the last Republican nominee to win the national popular vote, a distinction that has held for the last two decades.

While Bush's tenure often faced criticism for its civil rights record, including the failure to pass comprehensive immigration reform, one of his administration's significant successes was the President's Emergency Plan for AIDS Relief (PEPFAR). This initiative, which allocated billions of dollars to fight HIV/AIDS, tuberculosis, and malaria primarily in Africa, is hailed as a monumental achievement in global health. PEPFAR is credited with saving 25 million lives, providing antiretroviral treatment to 20 million people with HIV, and ensuring that 5.5 million babies born to HIV-positive mothers were HIV-free. Former President Jimmy Carter lauded Bush's humanitarian efforts, stating, "I'm filled with admiration for you and deep gratitude for the great contributions you've made to the most needy people on Earth."

However, Bush's tenure concluded with him becoming one of the most unpopular U.S. presidents, largely due to the controversies and challenges of his administration. The deeply unpopular Iraq War gradually lost public support as the justifications given in the post-9/11 atmosphere seemed increasingly tenuous. His presidency was further tarnished by the severe economic downturn of 2008, the worst since the Great Depression, characterized by major Wall Street banks failing and a contentious federal bailout. Public frustration was amplified by the perception of injustice, as only one Wall Street banker was incarcerated for their role in the crisis, leaving many Americans to struggle financially.

This period of economic turmoil and controversial decisions left a significant mark on public perceptions of Bush's presidency, shaping his legacy in the annals of American history and putting Republicans at risk in the next election.

End of Establishment GOP

In a significant turn of events in 2005, Ken Mehlman, then chairman of the Republican National Committee, delivered a groundbreaking speech to the NAACP. Mehlman openly acknowledged that the Republican Party had exploited racial dynamics in the South for electoral advantage. He issued an apology, stating, "Some Republicans gave up on winning the African-American vote, looking the other way or trying to benefit politically from racial polarization. I am here today as the Republican chairman to tell you we were wrong." This apology was a rare acknowledgment from a high-ranking party official of the GOP's strategic use of racial divisiveness and represented an effort to mend and redefine the party's relationship with African American voters. Despite this, Mehlman's message faced significant resistance within the conservative ranks, underscoring the ongoing challenges within the party regarding issues of race.

In 2008, the Republican Party nominated Senator John McCain of Arizona, who had succeeded Barry Goldwater in 1987, to pursue a third consecutive presidential term for the GOP. McCain, who had been at odds with George W. Bush, faced significant challenges from their history together. Their relationship was marked by a fierce confrontation during the 2000 GOP primaries, where Bush's strategist, Karl Rove, played a role in circulating damaging and untrue allegations about McCain prior to the South Carolina primary, effectively ending his campaign. Eight years later, as McCain entered the race, he found himself needing to distance himself from Bush's deeply unpopular presidency. This set a complex backdrop for his campaign, as he navigated the legacy of Bush while trying to connect with voters eager for change.

During the presidential campaign, McCain, a respected war hero with a distinguished military background, often exhibited significant decorum, particularly notable given the historic nature of the race against Barack

Obama, who stood on the verge of becoming the nation's first Black president. McCain's civility was prominently displayed during a town hall meeting when he corrected a woman who falsely labeled Obama as "an Arab," reflecting the conspiracy theories that questioned Obama's citizenship. McCain took the microphone and respectfully clarified, "No ma'am, he's a decent family man, citizen, that I just happen to have disagreements with on fundamental issues, and that's what this campaign is all about."

Earlier in the campaign, which I had the opportunity to cover, McCain demonstrated his respect for civil rights linked with his presidential aspirations during a Martin Luther King Jr. Day celebration in Spartanburg, South Carolina. There, he chose to read from King's poignant 1963 "Letter from a Birmingham Jail." The passage he selected reflects deeply on racial injustices and their impact on African American children:

"When you have seen vicious mobs lynch your mothers and fathers at will and drown your sisters and brothers at whim; when you have seen hate-filled policemen curse, kick and even kill your black brothers and sisters; when you see the vast majority of your twenty million Negro brothers smothering in an airtight cage of poverty in the midst of an affluent society; when you suddenly find your tongue twisted and your speech stammering as you seek to explain to your six-year-old daughter why she can't go to the public amusement park that has just been advertised on television, and see tears welling up in her eyes when she is told that Funtown is closed to colored children, and see ominous clouds of inferiority beginning to form in her little mental sky, and see her beginning to distort her personality by developing an unconscious bitterness toward white people; when you have to concoct an answer for a five-year-old son who is asking:, and at this point McCain wiped away a tear, 'Daddy, why do white people treat colored people so mean?'"

This rare emotional display suggested that had McCain not been in a race against Obama, his approach might have resonated more deeply with the

African American community. His choice to honor King's legacy on such an occasion underscored his commitment to civil dialogue and mutual respect across racial and political lines.

Alaska Governor **Sarah Palin**, when chosen as McCain's vice-presidential running mate, injected a distinctly more cutthroat dynamic into the 2008 campaign. Relatively unknown outside her home state before joining the ticket, Palin introduced a confrontational style to the Republican campaign that stood in stark contrast to McCain's typically measured approach.

One of the central points of Palin's aggressive campaign rhetoric was her frequent targeting of Obama's past association with **William Ayers**, a former member of the Weather Underground, a radical 1960s group known for its bombings. Palin's claim that Obama was "palling around with terrorists who would target their own country" represented a significant shift from McCain's decorum and was aimed at questioning Obama's patriotism. This was despite Obama being only eight years old at the time of the Weather Underground's activities, and an Associated Press analysis suggested that Palin's remarks carried a "racially tinged subtext that McCain may come to regret."

Expressing frustration with the campaign's reluctance to adopt a more aggressive stance, Palin underscored her belief in the importance of these associations to a candidate's character, stating, "To me, that does say something about character. But, you know, I guess that would be a John McCain call on whether he wants to bring that up." Her willingness to escalate attacks where McCain would not resonated with many, including Democrat Donald Trump. Palin's approach not only underscored a schism within the campaign but also highlighted a growing appetite within the party for more assertive and polarizing rhetoric, setting the stage for the evolution of political campaigns in the years to follow.

Having extensively covered McCain as a senator in Arizona and during his 2007-08 presidential campaign in South Carolina, I had the opportunity to sit down with him again for an interview in Columbus in 2012. Reviewing his campaign, I asked him when he felt he had lost the 2008 presidential race.

McCain responded, "Jim, I could tell we were in trouble. We were three points up on September 15th, then the stock market went down 300 points, and by the end of that day, we were six points down. As white, male, educated voters watched their 401Ks disappear, we fought on, but we never really recovered from that." Always gracious in both victory and defeat, McCain also quickly gave Obama credit for 'running an outstanding campaign.'

Covering Mitt

In the 2012 presidential election, former Massachusetts Governor **Mitt Romney** believed the country had grown weary of Obama's policies and was confident of victory, a narrative I delve into in my book "Covering Mitt." This book is based on extensive interviews and firsthand experiences with Romney during his 2008 and 2012 campaigns. Like his Republican predecessors Bob Dole and John McCain, Romney utilized traditional and largely straightforward campaign tactics. His campaign approach was profoundly shaped by the legacy of his father, George Romney, who as a Republican, actively supported racial equality, marching in 1963, backing the Civil Rights Act of 1964, and who was ultimately dismissed by Richard Nixon from his role as Secretary of Housing and Urban Development due to his strong commitment to enforcing open housing laws.

Mitt Romney, the first Mormon to be nominated by a major party for the U.S. presidency, faced significant challenges during his campaign, not only from conservative rivals in the Republican primaries but also from persistent skepticism about his faith—a contrast to his father George Romney's brief presidential campaign in 1968, where his Mormon faith seemingly did not emerge as an issue, partly due to the lesser influence of cultural conservatives in the GOP at the time. In regions like South Carolina, a stronghold of evangelical Christianity, influential conservative leaders made it clear that Romney would face considerable opposition from the religious right, particularly in the voter-rich upstate, which is crucial for securing a Republican victory. This religious scrutiny played a notable role in shaping the dynamics of his campaign.

This intersection of religion and presidential politics was not new. Before the 1960 election, Democratic nominee John F. Kennedy faced similar scrutiny as a Catholic. He famously reassured Protestant leaders that he would not be influenced by the Vatican. Inspired by Kennedy, I asked

Romney in 2008 if he planned a similar approach. He acknowledged the difference in theological beliefs but stressed the importance of political leadership, hinting at a future speech that would address these concerns. Nearly a year later, Romney delivered his "Faith in America" speech, echoing Kennedy's assurances. In his speech, Romney declared, "Let me assure you that no authorities of my church, or of any other church for that matter, will ever exert influence on presidential decisions." This statement was a crucial moment in his campaign, aiming to quell concerns about the role of his faith in his potential presidency.

Romney's credibility was also questioned over his changing stance on abortion. Originally pro-choice during his Senate and gubernatorial campaigns, he shifted to a pro-life position by his presidential run. When I questioned him about this during an interview, Romney tried to clarify his evolution on the issue. "What the people of Massachusetts have realized, which you can't see here, is that I was governor for four years. When the first piece of legislation that came to my desk would have ended human life in the case of an embryo, I could not sign it," he explained. He insisted that he had fulfilled his promise to the people of Massachusetts to maintain the status quo, although he was clearly irritated by the questioning.

Romney's 2012 presidential campaign faced significant hurdles after his controversial remarks at a private fundraiser became public. He described 47% of Americans as "victims" reliant on government aid and controversially stated, "it's not my job to worry about these people." These comments sparked widespread criticism and were still fresh in reporters' minds the following day, when Donald Trump, who had re-joined the Republican Party after Barack Obama's inauguration in 2009, delivered a six-minute endorsement speech for Romney at Trump's Las Vegas hotel. Known for his shifting political allegiances, Trump asserted, "Mitt's not going to allow bad things to happen to the nation we love." Romney, somewhat bemused by the endorsement, remarked, "There are things you just can't imagine happening in life. This is one of them." Adding a layer of intrigue, Trump's former lawyer, Michael Cohen, later disclosed that Trump not only contributed to SuperPACs supporting Romney but also acted as a "bundler," amassing significant contributions from undisclosed donors.

Attempting to connect with African American voters as his father had during his 1968 presidential bid, Romney visited a charter school in West

Philadelphia and declared the educational achievement gap as "the civil rights issue of our time." However, his appearance at an NAACP event was less successful, met with boos when he criticized Obama and vowed to repeal the healthcare overhaul. Ultimately, he secured only 6% of the African American vote, contributing to his decisive defeat and ensuring Obama's second term.

While Dole, McCain, and Romney adhered to more traditional and less confrontational methods, their experiences underscored the challenging balance between maintaining personal integrity and achieving electoral success. The contrast between their approaches and Trump's more aggressive style signifies a significant shift in Republican tactics, reflecting broader changes in American political culture and voter expectations.

Obama of Illinois

The 2008 presidential campaign of Barack Obama could have been scripted for a Hollywood epic, representing what might be seen as the culmination of a long-standing narrative in American history. This story traces its origins back to Abraham Lincoln, a champion for the rights of all citizens, and finds a potential finale with the election of Obama, a Black man from Illinois. Symbolically connecting himself to Lincoln, Obama announced his candidacy in Springfield, Illinois, at the Old State Capitol, where Lincoln delivered his famous "House Divided" speech. Over a century and a half after the founding of the Republican Party, Obama's presidency was viewed by many as a realization of Lincoln's vision for an inclusive America.

Obama's journey to becoming the first African American president weaves a narrative of ambition, pioneering spirit, and a transformative period in American politics. Born on August 4, 1961, in Honolulu, Hawaii, his early experiences in Hawaii and Indonesia endowed him with a broad worldview that would later shape his political ideology. His academic journey took him through Occidental College and Columbia University, culminating in his becoming the first African American president of the Harvard Law Review while at Harvard Law School.

After law school, Obama chose to immerse himself in the community of Chicago, dedicating his efforts to community organizing which profoundly influenced his political approach, focusing on grassroots activism and voter registration. His political career began in earnest with his election to the Illinois State Senate, where he was noted for his bipartisan cooperation and advocacy for ethics reform, health care, and early childhood education.

His national profile ascended dramatically after delivering a rousing keynote address at the Democratic National Convention in 2004, where he articulated a vision of unity, declaring, "There's not a liberal America and a conservative

America; there's the United States of America. There's not a Black America, and white America, and Latino America, and Asian America; there's the United States of America." He carried this momentum into his election to the U.S. Senate, where he tackled issues like nuclear nonproliferation and veterans' benefits, and maintained a consistent stance against the Iraq War. Less than three years later, he launched his historic presidential campaign, setting up a fierce contest for the Democratic nomination against New York Senator Hillary Clinton.

While the story up to this point might fit neatly into a screenplay, the reality of Obama's campaign highlighted the persistent undercurrents of racism still prevalent in America. Although Obama seldom centered his campaign on racial issues, his potential to become the first African American president inevitably brought these issues to the forefront.

While campaigning for the nomination in South Carolina, I had the opportunity to sit down with him and engage in a conversation on race. Here is a portion of the transcript from that conversation:

Heath: A white child born today, a black child, red child, brown child, an American baby born today. Do they all have an equal opportunity to achieve in America right out of the gate?

Obama: You know, my instinct is that race is still a factor. But the biggest factor is economics. If they're born to middle-class parents, they're probably going to get a pretty good education. If they're born to wealthy parents, they're going to get a very good education. And if they're born to poor parents or live in a poor district, then they're going to suffer. And, that doesn't mean that money solves all our problems. Parents have to parent. My own family wasn't wealthy, but my mother instilled a love of learning in me, even when I resisted sometimes and ended up getting an excellent education. But money does make a difference in terms of being able to hire quality teachers and retain those teachers. It makes a difference if children see that the school building is rundown while the prison is new, or the mall is new, that sends a signal to them about the value society places on education. And I do think part of where race and class intersect is that the larger society sometimes feels that black or brown children can't learn or we shouldn't expect them to learn, or it's not as important that they're doing well. And one of the things I try to emphasize is that the US workforce is going to be about half

black and brown pretty quick, and we will rise and fall as an economy, depending on how skilled our workforce is. So we all have an investment in every child.

Heath: In 2008, can Barack Hussein Obama be elected president of the United States?

Obama: Well, you know that's the question that we'll find out in the coming months. So far, we're doing pretty good. You know, I don't get a sense that I'm getting a lot of resistance because of my race or the fact that my father was from Kenya, and so I've got a foreign-sounding name. I think ultimately people are going to make a judgment based on is this a guy who can deliver on universal health care? Is this a guy who can build schools in areas like this one? Is this somebody who is going to be able to get us in an orderly fashion out of Iraq and stabilize the country and protect the country from terrorism? And if people think I'm the best guy for the job, even if I was green, I think I'd end up getting the nomination.

Heath: When you saw the copy of Time magazine asking the question, 'Is Obama black enough?' Is that a legitimate question? Or I mean, is that still relevant in a campaign in 2008?

Obama: The truth of the matter is, when I go into a barbershop on the South Side of Chicago, nobody's asking whether I am sufficiently authentically black. It speaks to, I think, some of the issues that we still have as a culture in terms of race. And one of the things that my wife and I are trying to project is that there's no one way to be African American, and we're not going to play into stereotypes about how we should behave. We're Americans. We have full claim on this country, and we want our children to feel that regardless of their skin color or their name or their background, that they have an opportunity to be part of the American community."

During our conversation, Obama emphasized his belief that both the Democratic Party and the country were ready to transition away from the Clinton era. His campaign, centered on themes of change and hope, faced significant challenges, particularly due to intense scrutiny of his background. Unfounded accusations that he was Muslim, which were partly fueled by Hillary Clinton's ambiguous comment that she took Obama at his word that he wasn't Muslim "as far as I know," compelled Obama to frequently reaffirm his Christian faith publicly.

The scrutiny escalated with the public exposure of sermons by his pastor, Reverend **Jeremiah Wright**, who used charged language such as "God damn America" and "America's chickens coming home to roost," criticizing U.S. foreign policies. These sermons attracted substantial media attention, increasing the scrutiny on Obama and necessitating a strong response amidst a tense political climate. Clinton's reaction to the controversy was pointed; she stated, "I think given all we have heard and seen, he would not have been my pastor."

In response, Obama delivered a crucial speech on race in Philadelphia in April 2008, where he not only condemned Wright's comments but also tackled broader issues of race in America. Despite his efforts, the controversy continued to overshadow his campaign, culminating in May 2008 when Obama held a press conference to unequivocally denounce Wright and sever ties, explaining that Wright's divisive comments had become a significant distraction from the campaign's objectives.

Moreover, Obama's association with **Louis Farrakhan** emerged as a contentious issue due to Farrakhan's public support for Obama. Farrakhan, known for his controversial and often divisive remarks, including anti-Semitic statements, became a focal point in the primary campaign. Obama addressed this directly during a debate, firmly stating, "I have been very clear in my denunciation of Minister Farrakhan's anti-Semitic comments. I did not solicit his support."

With only five days left until the South Carolina primary, attention from politicos and the global community was riveted on a pivotal debate, the final confrontation of the primary season. I covered this event live for our local news station, where the debate quickly escalated into an intense and personal clash between Hillary Clinton and Obama, capturing international headlines. The candidates challenged each other's integrity with unprecedented fervor, marking a significant moment in the campaign that highlighted deep divisions and the high stakes involved.

The conflict ignited early when CNN's **Suzanne Malveaux as**ked Obama to respond to Clinton's claim that he couldn't account for $50 billion in proposed new programs: "What she said wasn't true. We account for every single dollar that we propose. This, I think, is one of the things that's happened during the course of this campaign, that there's a set of assertions made by Senator Clinton, as well as her husband, that are not factually accurate," Obama retorted, to applause from the crowd.

Obama then shifted the topic to the Iraq War: "When Senator Clinton says—or President Clinton says—that I wasn't opposed to the war from the start, or says it's a fairytale that I opposed the war, that is simply not true. When Senator Clinton or President Clinton asserts that I said that the Republicans had had better economic policies since 1980, that is not the case." This marked the beginning of numerous criticisms Obama would direct at Bill Clinton, whom he believed was distorting his views.

Hillary Clinton countered with her own sharp criticism of the junior senator from Illinois: "I do think that your record and what you say does matter. And when it comes to a lot of the issues that are important in this race, it is sometimes difficult to understand what Senator Obama has said, because as soon as he is confronted on it, he says that's not what he meant."

Their debate unexpectedly delved into surreal territory when they clashed over remarks about Ronald Reagan. Clinton pressed the issue, stating, "You talked about admiring Ronald Reagan and you talked about the ideas." Obama, clearly frustrated, countered, "Hillary, I'm sorry. You just, I didn't talk about Reagan." His response grew heated as he clarified his earlier comments, explaining, "What I said was that Ronald Reagan was a transformative political figure because he was able to get Democrats to vote against their economic interests to form a majority to push through their agenda, an agenda that I objected to because while I was working on those streets watching those folks see their jobs shift overseas, you were a corporate lawyer sitting on the board at Wal-Mart!"

The crowd erupted into applause, some booed, turning the debate into a spectacle reminiscent of a wrestling match. "I just want to be clear about this," Clinton followed up. "In an editorial board with the Reno newspaper, you said two different things, because I have read the transcript. You talked about Ronald Reagan being a transformative political leader. I did not mention his name." "Your husband did," Obama interjected sharply. "Well,

I'm here. He's not!" Clinton retorted, to cheers from the audience. "Okay. Well, I can't tell who I'm running against sometimes," Obama snapped.

Then Clinton launched a personal attack, a first for her during the campaign: "I was fighting against those ideas when you were practicing law and representing your contributor, Rezko, in his slum landlord business in inner-city Chicago!" This was the first time Clinton had publicly connected Obama to **Tony Rezko**, a Chicago fundraiser indicted on federal charges of business fraud and influence peddling. Obama had done legal work for Rezko and later returned more than $40,000 in campaign contributions linked to him.

The crowd's reaction was mixed with boos, applause, and groans. Obama, clearly shaken, muttered, "no, no, no," as if struck by a physical blow. This exchange underscored the high stakes of the South Carolina primary and signaled to Democrats nationwide that the internal party battle was far from over.

That evening, anchoring the 11 p.m. news, I noted the historical significance of the moment, "You get the sense we're right on the edge of history. You have the first woman who could potentially become the president and the first African American who could do the same thing, and South Carolina is going to be critical in helping them become the nominee. The Obama campaign told me tonight an expected win here on Saturday will propel his momentum into Super Tuesday where he could finish up this fight. The Clinton team says a win here after her victory in New Hampshire would make her the inevitable nominee."

The biggest surprise of the campaign was former President Bill Clinton's decision to become the "axeman" for Hillary's campaign. Just days before the debate, he accused Obama of launching a "hit job" on him for allegedly bringing race into the campaign and blamed the media for buying into that narrative. With half of South Carolina's Democratic primary voters expected to be African American, Clinton publicly acknowledged his wife's lagging poll numbers. "They are getting votes, to be sure, because of their race or gender, and that's why people tell me that Hillary doesn't have a chance to win here." This candid admission sparked controversy, particularly among local political figures.

A week later, I was back at the anchor desk, interrupting network prime-time programming to announce that Barack Obama was poised to defeat Hillary Clinton by a comfortable margin. Ultimately, Obama secured 55 percent of the vote compared to Clinton's 27 percent. His ability to mobilize the African-American vote and engage younger voters was crucial to his resounding victory.

Bill Clinton responded to Obama's significant win in the South Carolina primary by comparing it to Jesse Jackson's victories in the 1984 and 1988 primaries. Many observers interpreted Clinton's remarks as an attempt to diminish Obama's achievement by suggesting that while Obama could attract the Black vote, his appeal might not extend to the broader electorate in a general election. This interpretation stirred considerable controversy, prompting Clinton to vehemently deny accusations of playing "the race card."

Years later, in an interview I conducted with Jesse Jackson, he expressed that he was not offended by Clinton's comparison but highlighted that his own presidential campaigns had led to rule changes that ultimately cost Hillary Clinton the nomination. "We changed the rules to proportionality, as opposed to winner-take-all," Jackson explained. "By '88, I had as many delegates as I had popular votes. In 2008, Hillary Clinton won, at the end, California, Ohio, Pennsylvania, and Texas, barely. She would have been the nominee except we had democratized democracy and opened the process up."

This proportional representation system meant that even when Hillary Clinton won large and important states like California, Ohio, Pennsylvania, and Texas, she was unable to gain a decisive lead in delegate count because the delegates were split proportionally according to the vote share. Meanwhile, Obama was able to accumulate a steady stream of delegates by performing well across a broad range of states, including smaller ones and those holding caucuses where his campaign's organizational strength and grassroots support were advantageous. This strategy allowed Obama to maintain a narrow lead and gradually build towards securing the nomination, demonstrating the significant impact of the rule changes implemented after Jackson's campaigns.

Jackson also remarked that his campaigns paved the way for both Obama and Clinton to make significant strides toward making history. "The most significant thing is we answered the question of whether a Black man or a woman could be accepted, and the answer now is yes," Jackson told me.

The rift that emerged between the Clintons and Obama during the campaign began to mend in subsequent years. This healing was markedly evident when Obama, after winning the presidency, chose Hillary Clinton as his Secretary of State, illustrating a significant reconciliation and collaboration between former rivals.

As Obama's campaign moved into the general election against Republican nominee Senator John McCain, the landscape was dramatically altered by a deepening economic crisis. The collapse of major Wall Street banks, including Lehman Brothers, sent shockwaves through the financial system and shifted public sentiment sharply. The crisis reached such a severity that both Obama and McCain temporarily suspended their campaigns to return to Washington for critical briefings with President George W. Bush, highlighting the serious economic challenges the country faced.

In response to the unfolding financial disaster, Bush signed the Troubled Asset Relief Program (TARP), which infused hundreds of millions of dollars into the private sector. This drastic measure aimed to stabilize the banking system and prevent further collapses in key industries such as the automotive sector. However, the necessity for such a significant government intervention further eroded public confidence in the then-prevailing Republican leadership, which had long championed deregulation and minimal government interference in the market.

This financial turmoil provided Obama with a unique opportunity to distinguish his economic policies from those of the McCain campaign and the outgoing Republican administration. Obama capitalized on this moment by articulating a clear vision for economic recovery and emphasizing the need for a change in governance, which resonated with voters increasingly disillusioned with the economic direction of the country. This approach helped to bolster his appeal to a broad spectrum of American voters, underlining his campaign's central message of hope and change at a time when it was most needed.

Obama's campaign was notable for its effective use of grassroots organizing and innovative social media strategies that engaged voters, particularly young people and minorities, who turned out in record numbers. Despite not winning any state traditionally considered part of the Deep South—except for Florida, which he successfully carried—Obama's ability to connect with a diverse electorate was evident. His lower polling numbers in states like Alabama, Mississippi, Louisiana, and Georgia underscored the challenges Democrats faced in these areas due to ideological differences, racial dynamics, and historical voting patterns. However, his success in Florida in both 2008 and 2012 demonstrated his campaign's broad appeal, balancing more conservative rural votes with significant support from Latino and urban populations.

After a vigorous and at times contentious campaign against McCain, Obama's message of hope and vision for change resonated widely with the American electorate, leading to his historic election as the nation's first African American president.

Progressive Progress

Barack Obama showed his admiration for Abraham Lincoln by placing Lincoln's portrait in the Oval Office. This was a symbolic gesture, highlighting the deep respect Obama had for Lincoln and his leadership qualities. Lincoln's influence on Obama was evident throughout his presidency, from his references in speeches to his emphasis on unity and reconciliation, mirroring Lincoln's approach during his time. The portrait served as a constant reminder of these values and the historical legacy that Obama aspired to emulate.

Obama's presidency was marked by significant challenges and symbolic milestones as he navigated economic, diplomatic, and social issues, bearing the historic weight of being the first Black president. His tenure saw racial incidents that sparked national conversations and highlighted deep-seated issues in America's racial dynamics.

Early in his presidency, an incident involving Harvard University professor **Henry Louis Gates Jr.**, who was mistakenly suspected of breaking into his own home, escalated into accusations of racial profiling. Obama's comment that the Cambridge police acted "stupidly" ignited a national debate on race relations. Another poignant moment occurred with the tragic shooting of **Trayvon Martin**, an unarmed Black teenager. Obama's empathetic remark, "If I had a son, he'd look like Trayvon," coupled with his reflection post-George Zimmerman's acquittal, "Trayvon Martin could have been me 35 years ago," resonated deeply across the nation.

During a joint session of Congress on healthcare, Representative **Joe Wilson**'s outburst, "You lie!" directed at Obama, was perceived by many as a disrespectful act with racial undertones, prompting Wilson to later apologize. The shooting of **Michael Brown** in Ferguson, Missouri, by a white police officer, and the choking death of **Eric Garner** in New York, were seminal events that highlighted systemic racial issues and catalyzed the Black Lives Matter movement. Obama responded by establishing the Task Force on 21st Century Policing to improve community-police relations.

In 2015, the racially motivated massacre by white supremacist **Dylann Roof** at Emanuel African Methodist Episcopal Church in Charleston underscored the pervasive impact of racial bias. Obama's eulogy for the slain Reverend **Clementa Pinckney**, which included him singing 'Amazing Grace,' was a poignant moment of mourning and reflection on the nation's ongoing struggle with racial violence.

Obama also dedicated the National Museum of African American History and Culture, emphasizing the intertwined narratives of protest and patriotism within the African American experience. Despite strides made, his presidency sometimes mirrored the nation's ongoing racial divides. Professor Melanye T. Price of Rutgers University highlighted the societal shifts during Obama's presidency, observing, "There's a way in which particularly white working-class men felt displaced during the Obama administration. And then the most important symbol in your nation, the president, no longer looks like what it looked like before. So you are losing your house, your community is changing, your job is changing, the prospects for your children are changing, and who gets to be in charge is changing. That's a lot of change."

The first law signed by Obama, the Lilly Ledbetter Fair Pay Act of 2009, aimed to bridge the gender pay gap and expanded the ability of workers to sue over pay discrimination. This legislation was named after **Lilly Ledbetter**, a former Goodyear employee who, after 19 years, discovered she had been consistently paid less than her male counterparts. Her lawsuit against Goodyear escalated to the Supreme Court, which ruled in 2007 that the statute of limitations for filing a discrimination claim began with the employer's initial discriminatory wage decision, not with each discriminatory paycheck. This ruling was widely criticized as it often took years for employees to discover pay disparities, due to opaque wage practices.

The Lilly Ledbetter Fair Pay Act addressed this issue by resetting the statute of limitations with each new discriminatory paycheck, effectively allowing the 180-day limit for filing an equal pay lawsuit to renew with every such paycheck. This act marks a significant advancement in the fight for gender equality in the workplace and has spurred additional legislative efforts to close the gender wage gap.

The Affordable Care Act (ACA), commonly known as Obamacare, enacted in March 2010, was a significant overhaul of the U.S. healthcare system aimed at increasing health insurance coverage for millions of uninsured Americans. The ACA expanded Medicaid eligibility and established health insurance marketplaces with federal subsidies to make premiums more affordable. Despite challenges and criticisms, including increased premiums and a heavier regulatory burden on businesses, the ACA significantly impacted the

American healthcare landscape by increasing insurance coverage rates and expanding access to healthcare services.

During Obama's presidency, a landmark Supreme Court decision on June 26, 2015, legalized same-sex marriage across the United States, marking a significant milestone in the history of LGBTQ+ rights in America. The case, Obergefell v. Hodges, involved **Jim Obergefell**, who sued the Ohio Department of Health director, **Richard Hodges**, to have his marriage recognized on his late partner **John Arthur**'s death certificate. Although the couple had married in Maryland, where same-sex marriage was legal, Ohio did not recognize their union at the time of Arthur's death. Obergefell's fight for recognition, which merged with related cases from Michigan, Kentucky, and Tennessee, led to a historic Supreme Court ruling that the Constitution guarantees the right to same-sex marriage. This effectively invalidated all state bans on such marriages and mandated that states recognize same-sex marriages performed elsewhere.

Obama openly supported the ruling, describing it as a victory for America and stating, "Today, we can say in no uncertain terms that we've made our union a little more perfect." His administration's endorsement of the decision reflected a significant shift in American public opinion and policy towards LGBTQ+ rights. The culmination of years of advocacy and numerous legal battles, the Supreme Court's decision extended legal same-sex marriage nationwide, affirming that same-sex couples are entitled to the same legal rights as opposite-sex couples throughout the United States. This ruling was celebrated as a transformative moment in American civil rights history and a key achievement in the fight for equality.

Tea Partiers

In early 2009, the Tea Party movement emerged as a direct result of the progressive agenda pursued by Barack Obama. Fueled by a strong opposition to the new administration's policies on economic recovery and healthcare, the movement quickly gained momentum. CNBC correspondent **Rick Santelli**'s infamous "Rant of the Year" on the floor of the Chicago Mercantile Exchange in February 2009, which criticized the government's economic policies, is often cited as a pivotal moment that helped galvanize the movement. This grassroots network advocated for fiscal responsibility, limited government, and free market principles, positioning itself as a defender of the 'average American' against perceived overreach by political and economic elites. The Tea Party's rise was marked by protests and rallies that drew significant attention and support, particularly among conservatives and libertarians who were skeptical of Obama's approach to governance.

I covered a Tea Party rally in Columbus, Ohio, before the 2010 midterm election, attended by thousands. Many attendees wore anti-Obama shirts, including one that declared 'Obama sucks' and

another depicting the president as the Joker from the Batman movies. "When you enact policies that go against the American taxpayer, you're a socialist," Tea Party supporter Paul Haft told me. "The reason he's the Joker? If you saw the movie, what did the guy want? He just wanted to watch the world burn."

Another protester wore a shirt proclaiming, 'Impeach Obama, Hussein Obama. He is ruining our country. He is sending it down the tubes.' In response to these sentiments, Democratic State Representative David Leland noted that having America's first Black president created fear among some people. "They have a president of the United States who looks different than all the presidents they have on their dollar bills. I mean, things are different," he explained.

During another protest in Columbus against healthcare reform, demonstrators berated and mocked a pro-reform advocate who had Parkinson's disease. "Got Parkinson's? I do and you might. Thanks for your help," read his sign. The responses from the Tea Party protesters were shockingly callous and cruel. "If you're looking for a handout, you're in the wrong part of town. Nothing for free. You have to work for everything you get," one protester chided, bending over to confront the seated older man. Another dropped a dollar in front of him mockingly, saying, "Start a pot, I'll pay for you. I'll decide when to give you money." Amid some muttering about "Communism," another voice yelled, "No more handouts!"

In May 2010, at a private White House dinner, Obama suggested that racial dynamics were likely a significant factor in the growing Tea Party movement. He noted that many middle-class and working-class whites felt the government was overlooking them while aiding others such as bankers, automakers, and those who defaulted on their mortgages. A guest at the dinner suggested that when Tea Party activists said they wanted to 'take back' their country, their real motivation was anxiety and anger over having a Black president, a notion Obama acknowledged as a 'subterranean agenda' rooted in racial bias. He expressed regret that there was little he could do to change these undercurrents, aiming instead to be an effective and empathetic president for all Americans, which he believed would advance racial progress more than anything else.

Nationwide surveys found that Tea Party supporters were predominantly older white men. A Gallup poll revealed that 62 percent of Tea Partiers identified as conservative Republicans. The Tea Party dichotomy of the 'freeloader' versus the 'hardworking taxpayer' carried racial undertones that distinguished it from a simple reiteration of the longstanding American creed. Racial resentment stoked Tea Party fears about generational societal change and fueled the movement's strong opposition to Obama. A New York Times poll revealed that 52% of Tea Party followers believed too much attention was given to the problems facing Black people, compared to 28% of the general American populace. Other polls showed a stark contrast in perceptions of Black Americans: only 35% of Tea Party advocates viewed Blacks as hardworking, compared to 55% of opponents; 45% considered Blacks intelligent, versus 59% of opponents; and 41% found Blacks trustworthy, against 57% of opponents. Another poll highlighted a significant divide in perceptions of racism: 62% of whites identifying as Tea Party members, 56% of white Republicans, and 53% of white independents believed that discrimination against whites had become as significant a problem as discrimination against Blacks and other minorities, a view shared by only 30% of white Democrats.

Particularly strong in the Southern states, the Tea Party's racial undertones were pronounced. Denny Stouffer, vice president of the Hagerstown Tea Party encapsulated this sentiment by criticizing Obama's policies: "He just has socialist ideas. He thinks you and I should give all of our money to the state and then they—the powers that be—are gonna best decide how we're gonna live." This resentment was further analyzed by Alan Abramowitz, a professor of political science at Emory University, who noted, "It goes beyond just the economic issues. It's a reaction against the trends the Tea Party dislikes. And that includes growing racial and ethnic diversity. It's not old-fashioned racism exactly. It's not like they want to bring back segregation. But there's no question that there's an element of hostility there." The movement was characterized by its anti-establishment rhetoric, vividly symbolized by Gadsden flags at rallies and a deep discontent with traditional Republican leadership, perceived as too moderate. This sentiment of challenging the status quo later resonated strongly with Donald Trump's 2016 and 2024 campaigns, where he embraced similar themes of anti-Washington sentiment and populist communication, bypassing traditional media to speak directly to the electorate.

These issues culminated in a broader cultural and demographic anxiety, exacerbated by Obama being the first African American president, illustrating the complex chapter of Obama's presidency in America's ongoing racial narrative. The NAACP's condemnation of racist elements within the Tea Party, demanding that they 'expel racists from the ranks,' highlighted the need for the movement to distance itself from these factions to gain broader societal acceptance.

The movement's impact peaked during the 2010 midterm elections when it played a significant role in helping the Republican Party reclaim a majority in the House of Representatives. This victory underscored the Tea Party's influence and its ability to mobilize voters around its agenda.

Thorn In His Side

Donald Trump rejoined the Republican Party following Obama's election and quickly emerged as a leading figure in the "birther" movement. This baseless conspiracy theory argued that Obama was not born in the United States, thereby making him ineligible to be President. As a vocal advocate of this claim, Trump repeatedly and falsely alleged that Obama's birth certificate was a forgery, suggesting it wrongly listed his birthplace as Hawaii instead of Kenya. His frequent media appearances to promote these claims significantly boosted his visibility in certain political circles.

Trump's speculation about Obama's birth certificate played into deeply rooted racial prejudices and xenophobia. In interviews, Trump suggested there could be something on the birth certificate that Obama "doesn't like," hinting that it might be either nonexistent or falsified. His remarks in a notable interview with Fox News host **Bill O'Reilly**, where he even floated a conspiracy theory that the certificate might list Obama's religion as Muslim, intensified the controversy. This relentless questioning of Obama's legitimacy as President is often viewed as an act of "othering"—portraying him as different, foreign, and not truly American. Such tactics are seen as attempts to appeal to racial biases, framing Obama's identity in a way that resonated with certain prejudicial views and historical racial anxieties.

The controversy reached its peak when, in April 2011, Obama released his long-form birth certificate from Hawaii, confirming he was born in Honolulu on August 4, 1961. The subsequent evening, at the White House Correspondents' Dinner, Obama humorously targeted Trump, who was present in the audience, poking fun at the birther controversy and Trump's role in it.

Obama humorously addressed the crowd, saying, "Donald Trump is here tonight! Now, I know that he's taken some flak lately, but no one is happier, no one is prouder to put this birth certificate matter to rest than the Donald." The audience erupted in laughter and applause as Obama continued, "And that's because he can finally get back to focusing on the issues that matter—like, did we fake the moon landing? What really happened in Roswell? And where are Biggie and Tupac?" The laughter and applause grew as Obama critiqued Trump's credentials, "But all kidding aside, obviously, we all know about your credentials and breadth of experience. For example—just recently, in an episode of Celebrity Apprentice—at the steakhouse, the men's cooking team did not impress the judges from Omaha Steaks. And there was a lot of blame to go around. But you, Mr. Trump, recognized that the real problem was a lack of leadership. And so ultimately, you didn't blame Lil' Jon or Meatloaf. You fired Gary Busey." Obama quipped, "And these are the kind of decisions that would keep me up at night." The crowd roared with laughter as Trump remained stoic.

Roger Stone, a longtime friend of Trump, reflected on the significance of the event, which took place amidst Washington, D.C.'s political and media elites. He remarked, "I think that is the night he resolves to run for president. He seemed motivated by it, almost as if thinking, 'Maybe I'll just run. Maybe I'll show them all.'"

Despite this public mockery, Trump continued to express skepticism and did not fully retract his statements about Obama for several years. It wasn't until September 2016, during his own presidential campaign, that Trump publicly acknowledged that Obama was born in the United States. In a brief statement at his new hotel in Washington D.C., Trump declared, "President Barack Obama was born in the United States, period."

This episode highlights how personal motivations and public humiliations can sometimes propel individuals toward significant political decisions. Trump's disdain for Obama only intensified, further fueling his ambition and setting the stage for his eventual presidential campaign.

Age of Trumpism

After Mitt Romney's defeat in the 2012 presidential election, the Republican National Committee released the "Growth and Opportunity Project" report, often called the "autopsy report." This analysis highlighted the GOP's urgent need to adapt to America's evolving demographics, predicting that whites would become a minority by the 2040s. It emphasized the importance of attracting Latino, Asian American, and African American voters to remain competitive and cautioned that failing to broaden the party's appeal could increasingly tilt future elections in favor of the Democrats.

Contrary to the report's recommendations, Donald Trump's 2016 presidential campaign adopted a markedly different approach. Trump made several disparaging remarks about Mexican immigrants and famously promised to build a border wall, insisting that Mexico would pay for it. He retweeted white supremacists and hesitated to disavow former Ku Klux Klan leader **David Duke**. His ongoing promotion of the birther conspiracy against former President Obama also played a significant role in reinforcing the burgeoning white nationalist movement that supported his candidacy. This marked a stark departure from earlier Republican leaders like Ronald Reagan, who insisted that the Republican Party should not be a house for bigots.

Trump's history with racial controversies dates back decades. In the 1970s, he and his father were sued by the Justice Department for refusing to rent to African Americans. Later, in 1989, Trump took out full-page ads in New York newspapers condemning five Black and Hispanic teenagers accused of raping a jogger in Central Park. Though the "Central Park Five" were later exonerated by DNA evidence, and another man confessed to the crime, Trump has never apologized for his actions, further complicating his public stance on racial issues.

Despite his controversial background and actions, Trump's staunch rejection of "political correctness" struck a powerful chord at his rallies, particularly among evangelical conservatives. This demographic has largely overlooked his varied and contentious past, including multiple bankruptcies, extramarital affairs, and avoidance of military draft due to claims of bone spurs, as well as his tendency to harshly criticize anyone who disagrees with him. This reveals a complex dynamic within his supporter base, where his political stance and promises significantly outweigh concerns about his personal conduct.

Andra Gillespie, an associate professor of political science at Emory University, has remarked on Trump's controversial image, stating, "Trump is perceived by many in the United States as racist. That's bad advertising and negates the praise he wants for his policies that affect black communities. People can't separate the behavior from the messenger." This perception underscores the challenges Trump's image posed for the broader GOP strategy, which has struggled between a need for greater inclusivity and the divisive tactics employed during his campaign.

The 2016 Republican primary was indeed a turning point in American politics, marking a significant shift in the Republican Party's dynamics.

Trump's rise was not just a rejection of individual establishment candidates like **Jeb Bush**, **John Kasich**, **Ted Cruz**, and **Marco Rubio**, but also a broader repudiation of the traditional party leadership and its policies. His appeal lay in his outsider status and his ability to channel the grievances of a significant portion of the party's base, who felt alienated by the political mainstream.

Trump's 2016 campaign effectively leveraged widespread dissatisfaction with traditional political leadership by positioning him as an alternative to the perceived inadequacies of both Republican and Democratic administrations. His blunt and often controversial rhetoric resonated with voters who were frustrated with conventional political discourse, particularly on topics such as trade, immigration, and foreign policy. This approach became particularly pronounced following a mass shooting in San Bernardino, California, in December 2015, where the attackers, a couple inspired by extremist ideologies, heightened national and international concerns about domestic terrorism and its connection to global terrorist networks. In response, Trump made the contentious proposal to completely ban Muslims from entering the United States. While establishment figures labeled this stance as extreme, it resonated strongly with the Republican grassroots.

By the time party leaders acknowledged his viability as a candidate, Trump had already secured a significant delegate lead and built a substantial base of support. In response, Mitt Romney, who had received Trump's endorsement for president in 2012, issued a stark warning about Trump's candidacy. Romney criticized, "Here's what I know. Donald Trump is a phony, a fraud. His promises are as worthless as a degree from Trump University. He's playing the American public for suckers: He gets a free ride to the White House and all we get is a lousy hat." This critique was punctuated by a nod to the proliferation of red "Make America Great Again" (MAGA) hats, symbolizing Trump's campaign.

This situation presented the Republican Party with a stark choice: adapt to the new political landscape shaped by Trump's ideology or risk political obsolescence. Most of the party chose to align with Trump, reflecting a strategic, albeit uneasy, embrace of his populist approach. This alignment has had lasting implications on the party's policies and its approach to both national and international issues.

In contrast to her opponent, former Secretary of State Hillary Clinton, the first woman nominated by a major party for president, addressed the issue of systemic racism more directly than any of her modern predecessors, including Barack Obama. In her historic acceptance speech, she emphasized the urgent need to bridge the nation's deep divides. Specifically, Clinton called for greater understanding and empathy towards young Black and Latino individuals who suffer the consequences of systemic racism and often feel marginalized. Her plea was heartfelt and clear: "Let's put ourselves in the shoes of young Black and Latino men and women who face the effects of systemic racism and are made to feel like their lives are disposable."

Trump's approach to discussing race provoked controversy during a campaign rally when he pointed out a Black man in the crowd and exclaimed, "Oh, look at my African-American over here. Look at him." The man, **Gregory Cheadle**, who initially supported Trump in 2016, later distanced himself from the Republican Party, criticizing Black Republican conservatives as "ventriloquists' dolls—puppets employed by powerful white people to mouth political platitudes that hurt Black people."

Trump also faced criticism for requesting that a federal judge overseeing a lawsuit against Trump University recuse himself due to his Mexican heritage. Trump argued that the judge's bias stemmed from his own campaign promise, which became a central and controversial pledge: to build a wall along the U.S.-Mexico border. Despite facing accusations of racism, Trump has consistently rebutted these claims, asserting that he is "the least racist person that you have ever met."

This campaign promise to build a massive border wall, and Trump's insistence that Mexico would pay for it, were met with fervent support at his rallies, where supporters often chanted "build the wall." Having started my journalism career in Yuma and extensively covered border issues, I firmly believe that no wall is large enough to be insurmountable—it can always be climbed over, cut through, or tunneled under. Interestingly, one of the most practical proposals I've heard for stabilizing the border came from an interview I conducted with former Vice President **Dan Quayle**. He suggested that the focus should be on economic investment, stating, "One of the things I have urged throughout my years in politics is to concentrate on economic development south of the border. Because if you have good jobs and a good life, you'll have a tendency to stay in your neighborhood." This perspective underscores the importance of addressing the root causes of migration, such as economic disparity, rather than solely relying on physical barriers.

During the campaign, Trump and the media heavily focused on Clinton's use of a private email server while she was Secretary of State. Trump capitalized on this issue to intensify attacks on Clinton, suggesting that her election could lead to an "unprecedented constitutional crisis." He speculated that the United States "could very well have a sitting president under felony indictment and ultimately a criminal trial," which he claimed would "grind government to a halt." Trump's rhetoric escalated as he vowed to have Clinton prosecuted if he were elected, a promise that resonated with his supporters, who often chanted "lock her up" at his rallies.

Trump encountered the most significant scandal of his campaign weeks before the election. A 2005 recording from an "Access Hollywood" interview surfaced, revealing Trump discussing how his celebrity status allowed him to behave inappropriately towards women, including using phrases like "grab them by the pussy." This revelation caused widespread outrage and led to calls from the then-chairman of the Republican National Committee for Trump to withdraw from the race. Concurrently, Trump's attorney, **Michael Cohen**, was involved in arranging payments to suppress allegations from adult film actress **Stormy Daniels** and Playboy centerfold **Karen McDougal** about their affairs with Trump. These efforts included collaboration with **David Pecker,** the CEO of the tabloid newspaper National Enquirer, to suppress damaging stories. These actions later resulted in significant legal repercussions for Trump. In 2024, he was indicted and convicted on 34 counts of business fraud related to these dealings, marking him as the first major party nominee in U.S. history to seek reelection as a convicted felon.

As controversies intensified, the loyalty among Trump's supporters seemed to only strengthen. In 2016, he famously remarked to reporters, "I could stand in the middle of Fifth Avenue and shoot somebody, and I wouldn't lose any voters." Over time, this statement seemed to hold increasingly true, highlighting the unwavering support from his base despite numerous political storms.

Despite these controversies and often divisive rhetoric, Trump secured 41% of the female vote on election day, a slight decline from Mitt Romney's 44% in 2012. In contrast, Hillary Clinton garnered 41% of the male vote, down from Barack Obama's 45% in the previous election. This widening gender gap ultimately played to Trump's advantage. He also captured a significant 58% of the white vote, compared to Clinton's 37%. A notable decline in Black voter turnout, which fell by eight points from 2012, significantly impacted Clinton's chances of winning the presidency. Moreover, despite Trump's controversial statements and policies on immigration, only 65% of Latino voters supported Clinton, while 29% voted for Trump. For context, Obama had secured 71% of the Hispanic vote in 2012, while Romney received 27%.

Despite winning the popular vote by nearly 3 million, Clinton lost the Electoral College due to narrow margins in critical states like Michigan, Pennsylvania, and Wisconsin. In Michigan, where 14 percent of the population is Black, Trump's margin of victory was just 10,704 votes out of nearly 4.8 million cast. Similarly, in Pennsylvania, where more than a tenth of the population is Black, Trump won by 44,000 votes out of 6.2 million. In Wisconsin, Clinton lost by a mere 22,748 votes. Notably, places like Madison, with a significant college-aged and African American population, saw a notable drop in voter turnout. If Clinton had secured these three states, she would have won the presidency.

Despite having led in all major polls, including in the internal polls of the Trump campaign, Clinton delivered a concession speech the morning after the election. She urged Americans to give Trump a chance to lead, emphasizing the importance of the democratic process and national unity. "We owe him an open mind and the chance to lead," she stated. "Our constitutional democracy enshrines the peaceful transfer of power. We don't just respect that. We cherish it."

Return of Nationalism

During his inaugural speech on January 20, 2017, Donald Trump adopted a Jacksonian populist tone, emphasizing nationalism and addressing the concerns of the "forgotten men and women." A memorable line from his address that encapsulates his message and commitment to immediate change was, "This American carnage stops right here and stops right now." This bold declaration aimed to address what he depicted as pervasive decline and decay throughout America, blaming these conditions on the failures of past political leaders. With this rhetoric, Trump promised a swift and decisive end to these issues, resonating with his supporters' desire for a radical shift in governance. Following the speech, former President George W. Bush leaned over to Hillary

Clinton, who had lost the recent election to Trump, and whispered, "That was some weird shit."

The transition from Obama to Trump in 2017 offered a deep dive into the intricacies of the American electorate, illuminating issues of race, identity, and cultural divisions. Obama's presidency marked a significant milestone in racial relations and civil rights progress, but Trump's rise to power underscored stark divisions within the electorate concerning these issues, signaling a notable backlash against the cultural and demographic shifts associated with Obama's tenure.

Trump's campaign successfully mobilized segments of the white electorate, particularly in rural and suburban areas, who felt marginalized by economic and cultural transformations. His message, which resonated with voters disillusioned by globalization and the political establishment, contrasted sharply with the diverse coalition that had supported Obama. Trump's rhetoric on immigration, law enforcement, and nationalism appealed to voters concerned about identity and cultural preservation, marking a departure from Obama's emphasis on unity and bridging divides. Some analysts argue that Trump's election was partly a reaction to the racial progress symbolized by Obama's presidency, suggesting that racial tensions and cultural anxieties played a significant role in shaping the election's outcome.

Trump's presidency was marked by several controversial moments. The Charlottesville rally, officially known as the "Unite the Right" rally, took place in Charlottesville, Virginia, on August 11-12, 2017. It was organized by various far-right groups, including white supremacists, neo-Nazis, and other extremist factions, ostensibly to protest the removal of a statue of Confederate General Robert E. Lee from a local park.

The rally began with a torch-lit march across the University of Virginia campus, where participants chanted racist and anti-Semitic slogans, such as

"You will not replace us" and "Jews will not replace us." The next day saw a larger gathering in downtown Charlottesville, which quickly descended into chaos as violent clashes erupted between the rally participants and counter-protesters who had assembled to oppose the hate groups.

The situation escalated dramatically when a white supremacist drove his car into a crowd of counter-protesters, killing 32-year-old **Heather Heyer** and injuring many others. This act of domestic terrorism underscored the dangerous and violent nature of the rally.

The Charlottesville rally was widely condemned by politicians, civil rights organizations, and citizens across the country. However, it also drew criticism for the controversial remarks by Trump, who suggested that there was blame on "both sides," a statement that was widely interpreted as equivocating between the actions of white supremacists and those protesting against them.

The "Unite the Right" rally in Charlottesville brought the resurgence of white nationalist and extremist ideologies in the United States into sharp focus, sparking a nationwide discussion on racism, historical memory, and

Confederate monuments in public spaces. The event centered around statues of Confederate figures Robert E. Lee and **Stonewall Jackson**, which were prominently displayed during the rally and subsequently removed several years later. The Southern Poverty Law Center has noted that many of the 2,000 Confederate war memorials still standing were not erected immediately post-Civil War but during the era of Jim Crow.

In 2016, San Francisco 49ers quarterback **Colin Kaepernick** began kneeling during the national anthem as a protest against systemic racism and police brutality, particularly towards African Americans. He initially sat during preseason games, but after consulting with **Nate Boyer**, a former NFL player and U.S. military veteran, he opted to kneel as a gesture of respect for military personnel while continuing his protest. This act was intended to highlight social injustices and spur dialogue and change.

However, Kaepernick's protest became highly controversial, especially after Trump's vocal criticism. Upon becoming president, Trump repeatedly denounced the kneeling at rallies and through social media, arguing that it disrespected the flag and the country. He urged NFL owners to fire players who participated in such protests. This stance by Trump not only deepened the national divide over the issues of patriotism and racial equality but also amplified the conversation around free speech and the role of athletes in social activism.

Trump frequently clashed with the Black Lives Matter (BLM) movement, which encompasses a range of activities including peaceful demonstrations, rallies, and marches. While many protests were peaceful, some escalated into riots involving property damage and confrontations with law enforcement. These more violent incidents often erupted in response to the deaths of Black individuals at the hands of police, highlighting broader systemic issues of racism and injustice in the United States.

Significant BLM protests, and sometimes riots, were spurred by several prominent cases. The death of **Freddie Gray** in 2015, who suffered spinal injuries while in police custody in Baltimore, Maryland, led to major protests and riots in the city. The 2016 deaths of **Philando Castile** in Minnesota and **Alton Sterling** in Louisiana, both at the hands of police officers, also ignited nationwide protests. The death of **George Floyd** in 2020, after a Minneapolis police officer kneeled on his neck for over nine minutes, triggered some of the largest protests in U.S. history, with demonstrations spreading worldwide. Some of these protests turned violent, resulting in property damage and clashes with police.

A particularly contentious incident occurred in Kenosha, Wisconsin, on August 25, 2020, during protests following the police shooting of **Jacob Blake**, a Black man. **Kyle Rittenhouse**, a 17-year-old armed with an AR-15-style rifle from Illinois, shot and killed two protesters and injured a third. Claiming he wanted to protect businesses from looting and vandalism, Rittenhouse's actions ignited a heated debate over vigilante behavior versus defending property and self-defense rights.

In the aftermath, Trump did not explicitly condemn Rittenhouse's actions. Instead, he suggested that Rittenhouse acted in self-defense, claiming that the teenager was "trying to get away" and might have been "probably been killed" had he not fired his weapon. This stance drew criticism from those who believed Trump should have unequivocally condemned the violence.

Rittenhouse's case quickly became a flashpoint in the national debate over gun rights, self-defense, and the Black Lives Matter movement. Many on the political right rallied around Rittenhouse, viewing him as a symbol of Second Amendment rights and self-defense. He received substantial financial support for his legal defense from conservative groups and individuals.

After being acquitted of all charges in November 2021, Rittenhouse's status as a figure celebrated by the right was solidified. He made numerous appearances on conservative media and at events, often receiving standing ovations and hero's welcomes. His case remains a deeply polarizing issue, reflecting the profound divisions in American society over issues of race, justice, and gun control.

During the Trump era, the term "woke" became a significant point of debate. Originally emerging in the early 20th century within African American communities, "woke" refers to a heightened awareness of social injustices and systemic racism, stemming from the phrase "stay woke," which means to remain aware and alert to the realities of racial and social inequalities. Over time, "woke" evolved to encompass a broader awareness of various social justice issues, including gender equality, LGBTQ+ rights, and economic disparity.

However, in recent years, the term has been heavily politicized, particularly by some Republicans, who have framed "woke" as synonymous with excessive political correctness or radical left-wing ideology. They argue that "wokeness" undermines traditional values, stifles free speech, and promotes divisive identity politics. High-profile figures such as Trump, Tucker Carlson, Joe Rogan and other conservative leaders have used the term pejoratively in speeches and social media, characterizing concerns about civil rights and social justice as part of a broader "woke" agenda. This rhetorical strategy has turned what were initially calls for greater awareness and equality into points of contention.

By politicizing "woke," those on the political right have managed to mobilize support by portraying these issues as threats to personal freedoms and societal cohesion, effectively making concern for civil rights appear as a negative or extreme stance. This shift has not only influenced public perception but also impacted policy debates, where measures to address inequality are often met with accusations of promoting a "woke" agenda, thereby complicating efforts to address these deep-rooted issues.

Pandemic Presidency

For the first three years of his presidency, Donald Trump oversaw a robust U.S. economy, characterized by low inflation and interest rates, low unemployment, and a strong stock market. However, his administration faced a significant challenge with the onset of the COVID-19 pandemic in early 2020.

Before the Trump administration, significant efforts were made to enhance the United States' readiness for pandemics. Under President George W. Bush, the U.S. government launched a comprehensive strategy to prepare for pandemic influenza, which included large-scale stockpiling of antivirals and developing plans for widespread vaccine distribution. President Barack Obama furthered these efforts following the 2009 H1N1 pandemic, which led to the establishment of the Global Health Security Agenda in 2014 aimed at increasing international capacity to prevent, detect, and respond to biological threats.

However, some of these initiatives were scaled back during the Trump era. In 2018, the National Security Council's global health security unit was disbanded, and the Centers for Disease Control and Prevention (CDC) saw reductions in their global health programs. Critics argue these actions weakened the U.S. and global readiness for a pandemic like COVID-19.

As COVID-19 began to spread, President Trump initially downplayed the severity of the virus, comparing it to the flu and suggesting it would disappear with warmer weather. Despite early warnings from health experts and intelligence briefings, he reassured the public that the situation was under control. Trump stated in February 2020, "By April, you know, in theory, when it gets a little warmer, it miraculously goes away." This optimistic assertion contrasted with the growing concern among public health officials.

At the end of January 2020, Trump implemented travel restrictions on China, which he frequently cited as evidence of his proactive stance. Nonetheless, the administration was slow to enhance testing and preparedness for the pandemic. Throughout the crisis, Trump frequently clashed with public health experts, including Dr. **Anthony Fauci**, and endorsed unproven treatments like hydroxychloroquine. In a widely criticized press briefing in April 2020, Trump suggested researchers should investigate the injection of disinfectants as a potential treatment for COVID-19, a comment that was met with alarm and confusion by medical professionals.

A notable success of his administration was the initiation of Operation Warp Speed, which significantly accelerated the development, manufacturing, and distribution of COVID-19 vaccines. This initiative led to the rapid approval and distribution of vaccines starting in December 2020. Trump actively promoted these vaccines, stating, "We have delivered a safe and effective vaccine in just nine months – this is one of the greatest scientific accomplishments in history."

However, Trump's overall handling of the pandemic was often seen as inconsistent and fraught with mixed messages, undermining public trust and exacerbating political polarization. His public events and rallies frequently ignored public health guidelines, complicating efforts to manage the pandemic effectively.

The pandemic significantly impacted the 2020 presidential election. In his reelection battle with former Vice President Joe Biden, Trump lost key states like Georgia largely due to a significant increase in Black voter turnout. Trump also failed to retain the "blue wall" states of Pennsylvania, Michigan, and Wisconsin, where he had defeated Hillary Clinton four years earlier.

Biden secured 92% of the Black vote, with notable increases among Black men, reflecting a strong alignment of African American voters with the Democratic Party and a clear rejection of Trump's policies and rhetoric. The election saw record turnout, partly driven by public concerns about the pandemic.

Biden won the election with 306 electoral votes and the popular vote by a margin of 7 million. Despite this clear victory, Trump refused to admit defeat. Republican election officials in states like Georgia confirmed Biden's win, and numerous court challenges, including those dismissed by judges appointed by Trump, failed to prove any wrongdoing. **Christopher Krebs**, Trump's appointee as director of the Cyber Security and Infrastructure Security Agency, declared the 2020 election "the most secure in American history." Additionally, Fox News settled a nearly billion-dollar lawsuit with Dominion Voting Machines, a company Trump and his allies accused of election fraud.

Despite these clear indicators, Trump continued to promote election-related conspiracies. This was a significant departure from the precedent set by Al Gore in 2000, who conceded after a close election for the good of the country.

On January 6, 2021, a large group of Trump supporters gathered in Washington, D.C., for a rally. During his speech at the rally, Trump reiterated his unproven claims of widespread voter fraud in the election. He encouraged the crowd to march to the Capitol, saying, "We will walk down Pennsylvania Avenue, and I'll be there with you." This statement implied he would join his supporters in their march, although he did not actually participate in the march himself.

The objective of many in the crowd was to disrupt the certification of the Electoral College results, a process overseen by Vice President **Mike Pence**. Trump and his allies had pressured Pence to reject the certified results from certain states, hoping this would either delay the certification or lead to a scenario where the House of Representatives would decide the outcome of the election, potentially favoring Trump due to the structure of the voting process in such a case.

As the crowd reached the Capitol, they breached security barriers and forcibly entered the building. This unprecedented event resulted in significant damage to the Capitol, including broken windows, vandalized offices, and stolen property. Lawmakers were evacuated, and the certification process was temporarily halted. The rioters chanted threats against several officials, including Pence and Speaker of the House **Nancy Pelosi**. There were confrontations with Capitol Police, leading to injuries and the deaths of five people related to the events of that day, including Capitol Police Officer Brian Sicknick.

As of now, over 1,200 people have been charged for their roles in the attack, and over 900 have pleaded guilty to various offenses ranging from trespassing to assaulting law enforcement officers. The Department of Justice has undertaken an extensive investigation, resulting in numerous convictions and ongoing prosecutions. January 6, 2021, marked the first time in American history that a sitting president actively attempted to disrupt the peaceful transfer of power.

When Trump left office, the U.S. economy was grappling with the severe impacts of the COVID-19 pandemic. The unemployment rate, which had peaked at an alarming 14.8% in April 2020—the highest level since the Great Depression—had fallen to 6.3% by January 2021. However, this rate was still significantly higher than the pre-pandemic level of 3.5% recorded in February 2020.

The economy suffered a sharp contraction in 2020, with the Gross Domestic Product (GDP) declining by an annualized rate of 3.5% over the year, marking the worst economic performance since World War II. The pandemic forced many businesses, especially small ones, to close due to lockdowns and reduced consumer spending. Industries such as hospitality, travel, and retail experienced severe disruptions, leading to widespread job losses.

In response to the economic crisis, the federal government under Trump's administration implemented several stimulus measures to mitigate the impact, despite concerns about potential inflation risks. Notable among these was the CARES Act, which provided direct financial assistance to individuals, expanded unemployment benefits, and supported businesses through initiatives like the Paycheck Protection Program (PPP).

The federal budget deficit surged to record levels as a result of the stimulus spending, with the national debt exceeding $27 trillion by January 2021. The fiscal response to the pandemic significantly increased the debt-to-GDP ratio, highlighting the economic strain. The economic fallout from the pandemic also exacerbated existing inequalities, with lower-income workers, particularly in the service industries, disproportionately affected by job losses and economic instability. In contrast, higher-income individuals, especially those who could work remotely, faced fewer economic disruptions.

While there were signs of economic recovery as vaccines began to be distributed and economic activity resumed, the overall economic outlook remained fraught with uncertainty. The path to recovery was heavily dependent on the effective control of the pandemic and the continuation of government support measures.

As Biden moved into the White House, he faced significant challenges, including high unemployment, business closures, increased public debt, and exacerbated economic inequality. Despite losing the election and leaving behind a difficult economic situation exacerbated by the pandemic, Trump made it clear, like Grover Cleveland before him, he intended to stage a political comeback in 2024.

From Lincoln to Jackson

The narrative on how the South transitioned from Democratic to Republican dominance culminated symbolically when Donald Trump chose to install a portrait of Andrew Jackson in the Oval Office just five days after his inauguration. This act marked a significant shift in presidential symbolism. While Democrat Barack Obama had chosen to display a portrait of Abraham Lincoln, the first Republican president, in recognition of Lincoln's focus on civil rights, Trump opted for Andrew Jackson, the first Democratic president. This decision signaled a pivot towards Jackson's brand of populist nationalism and reflected the evolving values of the Republican Party over the past century.

"Like Andrew Jackson's populism," Trump adviser **Steve Bannon** told the *Hollywood Reporter*, "we're going to build an entirely new political movement. It's everything related to jobs. The conservatives are going to go crazy. I'm the guy pushing a trillion-dollar infrastructure plan. With negative interest rates throughout the world, it's the greatest opportunity to rebuild everything. Shipyards, ironworks, get them all jacked up. We're just going to throw it up against the wall and see if it sticks. It will be as exciting as the 1930s, greater than the Reagan revolution — conservatives, plus populists, in an economic nationalist movement."

The decision to favor Jackson over Lincoln represents a stark pivot from ideals of equality and justice to a more divisive and aggressive nationalism. This change aligns with a broader populist surge within the party, characterized by a rejection of political elitism and a push for American sovereignty. It marks a profound ideological shift from a party once known for championing abolition and unity to one now advocating for strong state rights and minimal federal oversight.

"And for those who oppose this form of populism," Bannon asserts, "darkness is good. Dick Cheney. Darth Vader. Satan. That's power. It only helps us when they get it wrong. When they're blind to who we are and what we're doing."

This transition goes beyond changes in political leadership; it mirrors the evolving social and cultural fabric of the South. Factors such as cultural conservatism, deeply embedded in the region's strong evangelical presence, and complex racial dynamics have significantly contributed to this political realignment. Although overt racism has declined, its historical echoes continue to influence the political climate, intertwined with pressing issues like economic policies and social concerns.

The Republican Party's alignment with Southern values has deeply resonated with voters who are skeptical of federal oversight and prioritize states' rights. This ideological shift is evident in the party's stance on issues such as immigration, economic policies, and social conservatism, including white Christian nationalism, abortion, and LGBTQ+ rights.

Trump's choice to hang Jackson's portrait was not just a decorative decision but a potent symbol of this ideological shift, effectively encapsulating the South's transition to a red stronghold. It underscores a return to grassroots conservatism, emphasizing a battle against perceived federal overreach and a longing for past governance that favored state autonomy.

The transformation of the South encapsulates both political change and social evolution, influenced by significant legal and social reforms over the last century. Initially a Democratic stronghold that supported segregationist policies, the region has transitioned to Republican dominance. Although this new dominance formally opposes racial segregation, it often challenges modern civil rights legislation and has adopted an increasingly conservative cultural stance. This ongoing evolution is driven by a complex mixture of historical legacies, demographic shifts, and new political realities.

In 1838, amid escalating mob violence, Abraham Lincoln addressed the Young Men's Lyceum in Springfield, Illinois, expressing his concerns about the rise of Jacksonian politics. He warned of the dangers posed by ambitious politicians who might operate outside the law and the threat of mob violence undermining republican government. Lincoln eloquently stated, "At what point then is the approach of danger to be expected? I answer, if it ever reach us, it must spring up amongst us. It cannot come from abroad. If destruction be our lot, we must ourselves be its author and finisher. As a nation of freemen, we must live through all time, or die by suicide."

Christian McWhirter, a Lincoln Historian at the Abraham Lincoln Presidential Library and Museum, elaborated on Lincoln's views, noting, "Lincoln believed America's young democratic institutions were fragile and advised his audience that their political concerns could only be properly addressed through the law. Although mob action may seem expedient, it ultimately damages the rule of law, and with it the Constitution, and with that democracy itself."

One might wonder what Lincoln would think of the events at the U.S. Capitol on January 6, 2021, an attempt to halt Vice President Mike Pence from fulfilling the constitutional requirement to count and confirm electoral votes, or even the proliferation of conspiracy theories, some promoted by Trump and his top aides like Bannon, that foster anti-government mistruths and stoke fear.

While the possibility of the major parties switching places again seems unlikely, the portrait of Andrew Jackson in Trump's Oval Office not only reflects the ideological pivot within the Republican Party but also symbolizes the broader transformation of the South. This region, historically crucial in American politics, now represents the dramatic shifts that continue to define the nation's democratic journey.

Blue to Red Timeline

Here's a timeline illustrating the shift in political alignment from blue (Democratic) to red (Republican) in the Southern United States:

1. **Andrew Jackson (Democrat, President 1829-1837)**: The first Democratic president, who supported slavery, thereby helping to solidify the Democratic Party's pro-slavery stance, particularly in the South.

2. **Abraham Lincoln (Republican, President 1861-1865)**: The first Republican president, who opposed slavery, signed the Emancipation Proclamation, led the nation through the Civil War, and advocated for granting African Americans the right to vote.

3. **Post-Civil War and Reconstruction (1865-1877)**: Lincoln's immediate successor, Andrew Johnson (Democrat), and later Ulysses S. Grant (Republican), faced challenges enforcing strong federal actions in the South, eventually leading to the end of Reconstruction under Rutherford B. Hayes (Republican) through the Compromise of 1877.

4. **Republican Indifference (1877-1933)**: From Hayes to Herbert Hoover, Republican presidents generally did little to advance civil rights, focusing on other national issues.

5. **Enforcement of Jim Crow Laws by Southern Democrats (Late 19th Century to Mid-20th Century)**: Southern Democrats played a central role in the establishment and enforcement of Jim Crow laws across the South. These laws enforced racial segregation and disenfranchised African Americans, reinforcing a system of racial inequality.

6. **Franklin D. Roosevelt (Democrat, President 1933-1945)**: Influenced by his wife Eleanor, FDR slowly pushed initial civil rights support marking a shift towards more inclusive policies.

7. **Harry S. Truman (Democrat, President 1945-1953)**: Advanced civil rights further by supporting the inclusion of civil rights in the 1948 Democratic Party platform. This led to a split where Southern Democrats, led by Strom Thurmond of South Carolina, formed the Dixiecrat Party on a segregationist platform.

8. **Civil Rights Era (1960s)**: John F. Kennedy (Democrat) proposed significant civil rights legislation, which was passed following his assassination by his successor, Lyndon B. Johnson (Democrat), who signed the Civil Rights Act of 1964 and the Voting Rights Act of 1965. This legislation and subsequent rights expansions alienated many Southern Democrats.

9. **Party Realignment (Mid to Late 1960s)**: Strom Thurmond switched to the Republican Party, symbolizing the shift of many Southern Democrats, especially as Richard Nixon implemented the Southern Strategy to attract disaffected white voters in the South.

10. **Ronald Reagan (Republican, President 1981-1989)**: Consolidated the Southern shift to the Republican Party, appealing to conservative values and states' rights, which resonated with many former Southern Democrats.

11. **Barack Obama (Democrat, President 2009-2017)**: His election as the first African American president marked a significant historical milestone, one that Lincoln would have found reaffirmed his belief that we are, at heart, one nation and one people.

12. **Donald Trump (Republican, President 2017-2021)**: Symbolically replaced the portrait of Lincoln in the Oval Office with Andrew Jackson, illustrating the symbolic completion of the Blue to Red transition.

Blue to Red Key Moments

Timeline Of Key Moments in How the South Turned Red

- **1776** - Thomas Jefferson agrees to remove anti-slavery language from the Declaration of Independence under pressure from delegates from slaveholding states.
- **1793** - The Fugitive Slave Act of 1793 is enacted, allowing for the capture and return of runaway slaves within the territory of the United States.
- **1820** - The Missouri Compromise is enacted, admitting Missouri as a slave state and Maine as a free state, maintaining the balance between slave and free states in the Union.
- **1828** - Andrew Jackson becomes the first Democrat to be elected President of the United States.
- **1830** - The Indian Removal Act is signed by President Andrew Jackson, leading to the Trail of Tears, the forced relocation of Native American tribes from their ancestral homelands.
- **1841** - Former President John Quincy Adams successfully argues the Amistad case before the U.S. Supreme Court, securing the freedom of 53 Africans who had been captured and transported illegally.
- **1849** - Harriet Tubman escapes from slavery and subsequently becomes one of the most famous conductors on the Underground Railroad, helping other slaves reach freedom in the North.
- **1850** - The Compromise of 1850 includes several laws, strengthening the Fugitive Slave Act and addressing the status of territories acquired during the Mexican-American War.
- **1850** - The Fugitive Slave Act of 1850 is passed, intensifying the requirements for capturing and returning runaway slaves and imposing severe penalties for those who aid them.
- **1854** - The Kansas-Nebraska Act is passed, allowing the territories of Kansas and Nebraska to decide the issue of slavery by popular sovereignty, effectively repealing the Missouri Compromise and leading to increased tensions in the pre-Civil War era.

- **1854** - The Republican Party is founded, largely in response to the Kansas-Nebraska Act, with a platform that opposes the expansion of slavery into new territories.
- **1857** - The Dred Scott decision by the U.S. Supreme Court declares that African Americans, whether free or slaves, cannot be American citizens and therefore have no standing to sue in federal court.
- **1860** - Abraham Lincoln is elected as the first Republican President of the United States.
- **1861** - The American Civil War begins, largely driven by the divide over slavery and states' rights.
- **1863** - President Abraham Lincoln issues the Emancipation Proclamation, declaring all slaves in Confederate-held territory to be forever free.
- **1865** - The Civil War ends. President Lincoln publicly supports voting rights for blacks just before his assassination by John Wilkes Booth, a Southern sympathizer.
- **1865** - The 13th Amendment is ratified, abolishing slavery throughout the United States.
- **1868** - The 14th Amendment is ratified, granting citizenship to all persons born or naturalized in the United States and ensuring equal protection under the law.
- **1870** - The 15th Amendment is ratified, granting African American men the right to vote.
- **1877** - The Compromise of 1877 is agreed upon, effectively ending Reconstruction in the South. This compromise results in the withdrawal of federal troops from the South and the end of efforts to protect the civil rights of African Americans.
- **1896** - The Supreme Court decision in Plessy v. Ferguson upholds the constitutionality of racial segregation under the doctrine of "separate but equal," marking the beginning of the Jim Crow era of racial segregation.
- **1920** - The 19th Amendment is ratified, granting women the right to vote in the United States.
- **1948** - President Harry Truman signs Executive Order 9981, desegregating the armed forces.

- **1948** - President Truman signs Executive Order 9980, ensuring fair employment practices in the civil service.
- **1955** - Rosa Parks refuses to give up her seat on a Montgomery, Alabama bus, sparking the Montgomery Bus Boycott.
- **1957** - President Dwight D. Eisenhower signs the Civil Rights Act of 1957, primarily a voting rights bill, which is the first civil rights legislation since Reconstruction.
- **1960** - Four black college students stage a sit-in at a Woolworth's lunch counter in Greensboro, North Carolina, challenging racial segregation.
- **1960** - President Eisenhower signs the Civil Rights Act of 1960, which introduced penalties for anyone who obstructed someone's attempt to register to vote or actually vote.
- **1961** - Freedom Rides begin, with integrated groups traveling through the South to challenge segregation in interstate bus terminals.
- **1963** - Martin Luther King Jr. delivers his "I Have a Dream" speech during the March on Washington for Jobs and Freedom.
- **1963** - President John F. Kennedy calls for comprehensive civil rights legislation in June, leading to the Civil Rights Act of 1964.
- **1963** - President Kennedy is assassinated in Dallas, Texas.
- **1964** - President Lyndon B. Johnson signs the Civil Rights Act of 1964, prohibiting discrimination based on race, color, religion, sex, or national origin.
- **1965** - The Voting Rights Act of 1965 is signed into law by President Johnson, eliminating various devices used to prevent African Americans from voting.
- **1965** - The Selma to Montgomery marches highlight the fight for voting rights, leading to the passage of the Voting Rights Act.
- **1968** - President Johnson signs the Civil Rights Act of 1968, also known as the Fair Housing Act, providing equal housing opportunity regardless of race, religion, or national origin.
- **1968** - Martin Luther King Jr. is assassinated in Memphis, Tennessee.
- **1968** - Robert Kennedy is assassinated in Los Angeles, California.
- **1968** - Democratic National Convention in Chicago is marked by violent clashes between police and protesters.

- **1970** - President Richard Nixon signs the extension of the Voting Rights Act.
- **1970** - President Richard Nixon establishes the Environmental Protection Agency (EPA).
- **1972** - Watergate scandal begins with the break-in at the Democratic National Committee headquarters.
- **1974** - President Richard Nixon resigns in the wake of the Watergate scandal.
- **1986** - President Ronald Reagan signs the Immigration Reform and Control Act, known as the amnesty bill, granting legal status to certain undocumented immigrants.
- **1990** - President George H.W. Bush signs the Americans with Disabilities Act, a major civil rights law prohibiting discrimination based on disability.
- **2009** - President Barack Obama signs the Lilly Ledbetter Fair Pay Act to combat pay discrimination.
- **2010** - President Obama signs the Don't Ask, Don't Tell Repeal Act of **2010**, allowing gays, lesbians, and bisexuals to openly serve in the U.S. military.
- **2017** - President Donald Trump hangs a portrait of Andrew Jackson, the first Democratic president known for his controversial policies including the Indian Removal Act, in the Oval Office.

Blue to Red Map Comparisons

1860 Election Results

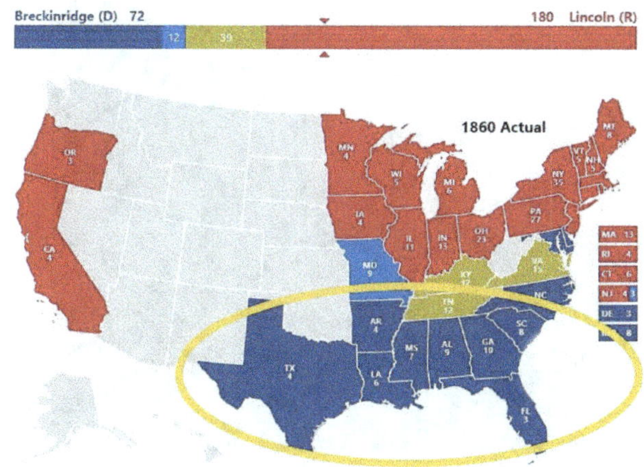

2016 Election Results

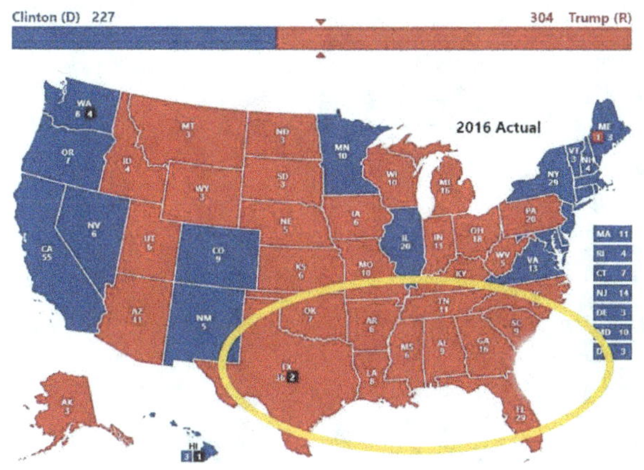

Contrasts

President Obama holds Arianna Holmes, 3, in front of a Lincoln portrait in his Oval Office.

President Trump smiles in front of a Jackson portrait in his Oval Office.

About the Author

Jim Heath is a distinguished television news anchor, correspondent, author, and political analyst whose significant contributions have shaped American journalism and political coverage over the last two decades. His career trajectory has taken him from the sunlit avenues of Arizona to the historic landscapes of South Carolina, and  onto the politically charged environment of Ohio, where his commitment to uncovering the truth and dedication to storytelling have truly flourished.

Jim launched his broadcasting career as the main nightly anchor at KYMA in Yuma, Arizona, where he extensively covered border-related stories. He then moved to Myrtle Beach, South Carolina, to serve as the main anchor and political reporter at WPDE, covering the presidential campaigns of 2004 and 2008 with deep analytical insight. His next role brought him to WBNS in Columbus, Ohio, where he excelled as the chief political correspondent and moderator of "Capitol Square." During the 2012 election, Jim's coverage was pivotal, providing live reports from both political conventions and from Washington, D.C. during President Barack Obama's second inauguration.

Beyond his role at the news desk, Jim has also distinguished himself as a skilled documentarian, producing six comprehensive documentaries on presidential elections. These documentaries, accessible on the Jim Heath Channel on YouTube, offer insightful reflections on pivotal moments in American political history.

As an accomplished author, Jim wrote *Front Row Seat at the Circus: One Journalist's Journey through Two Presidential Elections*, giving readers an intimate view of his experiences during the 2008 and 2012 presidential races. His book *Covering Mitt* provides a close look at Mitt Romney's presidential campaigns, highlighting Jim's interactions with key political figures. Additionally, his analytical book *How the South Turned Red: From a Democratic Past to a Republican Present*, explores the complex evolution of American political parties from the era of Lincoln to today.

Expanding into children's literature, Jim authored *Mylo the Panda*, aimed at countering the negativity prevalent in American discourse and tailored specifically for young readers. His commitment to fostering positive societal change is further exemplified in *Taking Care of Mom*, a deeply personal narrative that has been praised for its insightful exploration of caregiving.

Before stepping into the media spotlight, Jim served as a congressional press secretary and chief of staff to a state Corporation Commissioner, experiences that provided him with invaluable insights into the intricacies of political machinery. This background, coupled with his years in precinct politics, has informed his incisive analysis and reporting.

Jim's career has been marked by numerous accolades, including the Walter Cronkite Award for Excellence in Television Political Journalism and two Emmy Awards for his political reporting. His contributions to journalism have also been recognized by the Associated Press and the Ohio Society of Professional Journalists, reinforcing his status as a respected figure in the field.

"We are not enemies, but friends. We must not be enemies. Though passion may have strained, it must not break our bonds of affection. The mystic chords of memory, stretching from every battlefield and patriot grave to every living heart and hearthstone all over this broad land, will yet swell the chorus of the Union, when again touched, as surely they will be, by the better angels of our nature."

— President Abraham Lincoln, First Inaugural Address, March 4, 1861